THIS BOOK BELONGS TO

....

....

READER'S DIGEST

Story of the
Bible World

READER'S DIGEST
Pictorial Map of the
HOLY LAND

ZAREPHATH

Cedars of Lebanon

DAMASCUS

Rebekah at the well

TYRE

DAN

Abraham enters Canaan

ACCHO

Noah's Ark on Mt. Ararat

Sea of Galilee

Kishon R.

Gideon defeats the Midianites

Yarmuk R.

Mediterranean Sea

DOR

Joseph sold by his brothers

The fall of Babylon

DOTHAN

SAMARIA

Jacob wrestles with the Angel

SHECHEM

PENUEL

Jonah and the whale

Jezebel's death

Elijah in the fiery chariot

Jabbok R.

SHILOH

JOPPA

Return of the Ark of the Covenant

Daniel in the lions' den

River Jordan

JERICHO

JERUSALEM

Jericho falls as the trumpets blow

Moses beholds the Promised Land

Esther saves her people

BETH-SHEMESH

Elah R.

Salt Sea

ASHKELON

Samson destroys the Philistine temple

HEBRON

Solomon's Temple

Arnon R.

BEER-SHEBA

David slays Goliath

GOMORRAH
SODOM

Ruth follows Naomi

The sacrifice of Isaac

Aaron's rod turns into a snake

Robert d. Lee

Lot escapes from Sodom

ITALY
GREECE
ASIA MINOR
SYRIA
Mediterranean Sea
HOLY LAND
LIBYA
EGYPT
Red Sea

Moses breaks the tablets

N
W   E
S

The Queen of Sheba visits Solomon

READER'S DIGEST

Story of the Bible World

IN MAP, WORD AND PICTURE

By Nelson Beecher Keyes

The Reader's Digest Association
Pleasantville, New York

Acknowledgments

During the past five decades, our knowledge of the Bible ages has tremendously increased. This wealth of information, gathered by historians, archaeologists and other scholars, permits a retelling of the Bible story with an accuracy not possible in earlier times.

This book endeavors to assemble in one flowing pageant of history the most recent research, modern map making and photography, in such a way as to transmit a feeling of the vitality and strength of that incomparable age.

Nelson Beecher Keyes has written the text with the vigor and immediacy which distinguish his style. He has not been permitted to live to see this book in print. It represents the culmination and fulfillment of his creative effort, and the publishers wish to dedicate it to his memory.

The editing and revision of this edition are the work of Manuel Komroff, in consultation with Dr. Dewey M. Beegle and other Bible authorities.

The editors wish to express their appreciation for a final reading of the book to Rabbi Theodore Friedman, Congregation Beth El of the Oranges and Maplewood, New Jersey (for the Old Testament period); Reverend Louis F. Hartman, Executive Secretary, Catholic Bible Association, Washington, D.C.; and Dr. Ralph W. Sockman, Christ Church Methodist, New York City.

Contents

Introduction

The Bible unfolds the story of a long period, a time from the Creation to the dawn of Christianity. These were the centuries that molded our Western civilization. They witnessed the rise of such mighty nations as Egypt, Assyria, Babylonia, Greece, Persia, Macedonia and Rome. They witnessed the origin of our religion, our art, our laws, our languages, medicine, astronomy and mathematics. Though many of us are familiar with the Bible, we have not read the flow of the biblical story, nor related it to the land where it occurred. Why did the Egyptians who had once honored Joseph and his people later put them into bondage? Who were the "Peoples of the Sea" and how did they clash with Samson and Saul? Where was Solomon's Temple? What do we know of Jerusalem in the days of Jesus? What was the difference between the Syrians and the Assyrians? How was Babylonia overthrown?

The pivotal point of all this great history is the little land of Palestine, the Holy Land. Although small in area, it has played a large and important role in the affairs of humanity. It can be compared to a small stage at the center of a huge arena embracing all the world.

How extensive is this land, so small in size but large in deeds? The most northerly of its towns in Bible times was Dan, which stood at the foot of mighty Mount Hermon. At the southern extremity was a sort of oasis about a series of wells, called Beer-sheba, where the central highlands drop down to a wilderness steppe known as the "south country," or Negeb. The distance "from Dan to Beer-sheba" is only one hundred fifty miles, yet three thousand years ago a camel caravan might well have consumed five days traveling this distance, while herdsmen burdened with flocks, like the patriarch Abraham, would have needed half a month for even a fairly hurried crossing. In width, this "land of promise" varied considerably. In the north it was but thirty miles from the shore of the Mediterranean to the long, deep trench known as the Jordan Valley. In the south this distance increased to about eighty miles. Palestine also took in some of the hill country to the east of the Jordan, and so embraced in all something like 11,000 square miles of plains, mountains and valleys, an area close in size to Belgium.

The Mediterranean, which has been called "the sea in the midst of nations," forms Palestine's western border. Its beaches stretch mile after mile with hardly an interruption and with few promontories. As a consequence, during biblical times there were only two port cities and not a single good harbor along its entire length. One of these port cities was Joppa, where Peter raised Tabitha from the dead, and from which at an earlier time Jonah, trying to escape from God, set sail on his eventful journey. The other port city was Caesarea, the official residence of the Roman procurators, built by Herod the Great. It was the city where Paul was imprisoned before being sent to Rome.

The level land, or coastal plain, bordering the Mediterranean along the entire length of the Holy Land served an important purpose, even in the north where it was very narrow, for it was heavily planted and cultivated. In the north, on the Plain of Phoenicia, were located the cities of Tyre and Sidon. Ships from these pagan cities sailed far across the sea, and it was the king of Tyre who sent his friend King Solomon workmen and cedars of Lebanon for building the first great Temple.

Below the headland known as Mount Carmel, the coastal plain broadens out into the Plain of Sharon — an extremely fertile and beautiful district covered in the spring with scarlet anemones, known in the Bible as the "lily of the valleys," and white narcissus called the "rose of Sharon" in the Song of Solomon. Across this idyllic land dotted with orchards, gardens and flocks of gentle sheep moved camel caravans traveling the great route from Babylonia and Assyria to distant Egypt.

South of Sharon the coastal lands broaden out still more into what was then known as the Plain of Philistia. There, in a belt twelve to twenty-five miles wide, was the great grain-raising section dominated in Old Testament times by a federation of five cities including the renowned city of Gaza. This was the land of the Philistines, those hard-working and hard-fighting people who had originally come from Crete and who were constantly making war on the Israelites.

East of this Philistine coastal plain lies the Shephelah or "low country," a series of chalky hills, 600 to 700 feet above sea level, separated by broad pleasant valleys. In a generally thirsty country the Shephelah valleys are fairly well watered, and their red soil formerly supported fine grainfields along with orchards, olive groves and vineyards. It was there that the scouts sent out by Moses gathered pomegranates, figs and grapes as proof of the richness of the land. Of much interest, too, are the Shephelah's broad valleys, some of which came into prominence in the Bible. Its most northerly valley, Ajalon, was the site of the battle between Joshua and the five kings at which the sun and moon stood still. Just south of this lies the Vale of Sorek, where Samson was born and where, in a moment of great anger, he let loose three hundred foxes with flaming torches tied to their tails, thus destroying the ripening harvest. Still farther south is the dry Vale of Elah where David slew Goliath. This section is also dotted with caves and caverns, some of which are seemingly endless. David made the one known as Adullam famous as a hideaway for himself and his outlaw band, while centuries later thousands of Jews sought refuge in these hidden lairs following their last revolt against their Roman masters.

Inland and to the east of the coastal plain and hill country already described, there is a mountain range which stretches from Syria through the whole length of Palestine and into the Sinai Peninsula. It has been lowered through countless ages by slow weathering and occasional earthquakes, and it forms what is known today as the "central highlands" of Palestine. Its northern section — primarily a plateau — formed Galilee, which, according to the Bible, was one of the garden spots of the Holy Land. There Jesus lived as a child in the little town of Nazareth, and there as a man He first preached the Gospel of the Kingdom of Heaven in such towns as Capernaum, and performed miracles, such as turning water into wine at the wedding feast at Cana. In this northern section of the Holy Land also lies the Plain of Jezreel, or Esdraelon, as it was called in Greek. It was there that Gideon triumphed over the Midianites and there that Saul and Jonathan were overthrown and killed by the Philistines.

South of the Plain of Jezreel is a rugged hilly section of the central highlands called Samaria, after the beautiful capital of the short-lived northern Kingdom of Israel. Here lived Ahab and his evil queen, Jezebel, and here invading Syrian and Assyrian armies terrorized the people. Here, long before, Abraham camped with his flocks close to ancient Shechem. Here Jesus spoke to the Samaritan woman at the well, and in this land echoed the voices of such steadfast prophets as Elijah and Hosea.

The lower fifty-mile stretch of the central highlands, which was at one time assigned to the tribe of Judah, became known as Judaea. It is a dry, hilly, even mountainous country; tiny Bethlehem, where Jesus was born, stands 3540 feet above the shore of the Dead Sea fourteen miles to the east. But in spite of its arid ruggedness many of the most dramatic events of the Bible story took place there, and its past rings with the sound of such names as Jerusalem, David, Solomon, the queen of Sheba, Jeremiah, Sennacherib, Sargon II, Bethany, the Holy Temple, Lazarus, Jericho, Hebron, Pontius Pilate, the Maccabees, Peter and Paul and Titus.

There is a huge scar on the face of the earth in this corner of Asia, very like the deep wound of an immense cutlass. It is the Great Rift which forms the Jordan Valley, the Dead Sea, and the depression of the Arabah which runs south toward the Gulf of Aqaba. The historic River Jordan, which drains the upper reaches of this mighty rift, rises just above its north end. From northern springs on the shoulders of towering, snow-capped Mount Hermon, the possible scene of the Transfiguration, its waters plunge within a few miles to tiny Lake Huleh, which is only 230 feet above sea level. In another twelve short miles the Jordan drops over 900 feet to the Sea of Galilee, 696 feet below sea level. It was on the banks of this picturesque lake that Jesus found several of His Apostles and it was there that He stilled the tempest. Close to this lake, on the slopes of the Horns of Hattin, He delivered the undying Sermon on the Mount. It was also there that He appeared for the last time to His Apostles before ascending into heaven.

It is but sixty-five miles in a direct line from the point where the Jordan leaves the Sea of Galilee to where it empties into the Dead Sea, whose waters are so salty a human body will not sink in them. Yet the stream twists and turns some two hundred miles in this short space, dropping an average of three feet per mile to the Dead Sea, which is 1292 feet below sea level, the lowest known point on the earth's surface. It was this river that the Children of Israel under the leadership of Joshua crossed to enter the Promised Land. In its waters Jesus was baptized by John the Baptist.

Beyond the rocky walls which form the eastern edge of the Jordan Valley there is a long strip of hill country, the easternmost territory of the Holy Land. It manages to extract the last moisture from the clouds rolling in from the Mediterranean, so that it has long been a rich and fertile land. The northern portion furnishes good pastures and became noted for its "bulls of Bashan." Farther south there were woods, orchards and farms in a section which gave origin to the once popular phrase "balm of Gilead." Here at a place called Penuel, Jacob wrestled with the Angel of the Lord. Below it and east of the Dead Sea rose Mount Nebo, from whose heights Moses saw the land of Canaan. Farther south lay the land of Moab, where Naomi's husband and two sons died and from which she and her faithful daughter-in-law, Ruth, made the long journey back to Bethlehem. There, too, in a section now inundated by the waters of the Dead Sea, once stood the wicked cities of Sodom and Gomorrah.

Certainly, the Bible story and the history of the Holy Land are closely linked. And while much of its history has receded into the long dim past, we are able to bring it to life once more by placing it in its original setting, that small geographical stage which is Palestine. It is the blending of legend, history and geography, and the drama of modern discoveries, which make up the story of the Bible lands that unfolds in the following pages.

1. The Sons of Noah

Where Adam and Eve first trod this earth and suffered the punishment of their sin, we do not know. Neither do we know where they made their home after being driven from Paradise. While the Bible tells us about their two sons, and how Cain, in his jealousy, murdered his brother, Abel, it is vague about the land of Nod in which Cain dwelt. Nor does the Bible reveal very much about the ten patriarchs between Adam and Noah; it gives us their names and ages, but does not tell us in which land they lived. However, from the description of Eden found in Genesis 2:10-14, it is generally believed that the cradle of mankind was Mesopotamia, that land which lies in the valleys of the Tigris and Euphrates rivers.

This could very well have been. Archaeologists, searching for evidence of ancient man, have in recent years dug up some remarkable finds in this small and remote part of the world at the southeast end of the Fertile Crescent, that huge semicircle of inhabited and cultivated land which reaches from Egypt through Palestine and Syria to the Persian Gulf. Working there, in the Tigris-Euphrates Valley, they not only uncovered some of the earliest known houses and farm buildings but, well beneath the present valley floor, they found another indication that history as we know it may have begun in this area. This last discovery has to do with Noah and the Flood, that dreadful time when God in His wrath poured rain and destruction upon the earth for forty days and forty nights.

It is recorded in the Bible that, in accordance with God's wishes, Noah built an ark and, load-ing it with provisions and one or more pairs of all beasts and fowl and other living creatures, rode out upon the mounting flood together with his wife and his sons and their wives. It is also recorded that after the great devastation, during which the earth was washed clean of its gross wickedness, the ark came to rest upon a mountain, and that Noah and his family and the creatures aboard were all that remained alive upon the earth.

In this way did Noah's three sons, Shem, Ham and Japheth, and their wives become the parents of all who followed the cleansing flood. It was by means of the family of Noah, he who was chosen by the Lord, that the earth was repeopled and the family of nations established (Genesis 9:19).

Where did this occur? On the seventeenth day of Tishri, the seventh month, Noah and his craft came to rest on the mountains of Ararat (Genesis 8:4) in what we know today as eastern Turkey. It is very likely they sought the area in which they had formerly lived, where the flood had overtaken them. Where is there any evidence of a flood such as that described in Genesis? Quite remarkable indications have been uncovered near Ur of the Chaldees, the city in lower Mesopotamia where the great patriarch Abraham appears to have been born.

While archaeologists were investigating this ancient place in 1928-29, a test pit was sunk outside the city. In it a heavy stratum of clay, seven to nine feet deep, was encountered. It was at first thought to be the former bed of the Euphrates. Fortunately digging continued, and beneath this heavy deposit of waterborne silt

Head of Nimrod, excavated at Calah on the Tigris River. According to Hebrews, the mighty Nimrod, son of Cush and great-grandson of Noah, colonized the Babylonian cities (Genesis 10:10).

were uncovered the remains of a very early civilization, with bricks, hand-painted pottery, stone tools and other objects.

This had been no mere river flood, but something far, far greater which had brought a whole way of life to a complete stop and, as other diggings, notably at Kish near Babylon, seemed to prove, had ravaged a very great area. Had this section been Noah's former home and did he return to it again? Life did start anew here, and it can well be that it was from this centrally located valley that his descendants spread out over the earth. And spread out they did — into Asia, Africa and Europe.

At Ur on the Euphrates River, a great flood deposited nine feet of silt.

The Flood

The story in Genesis and discoveries of silt deposits place the stirring event of the Deluge in the Tigris-Euphrates Valley.

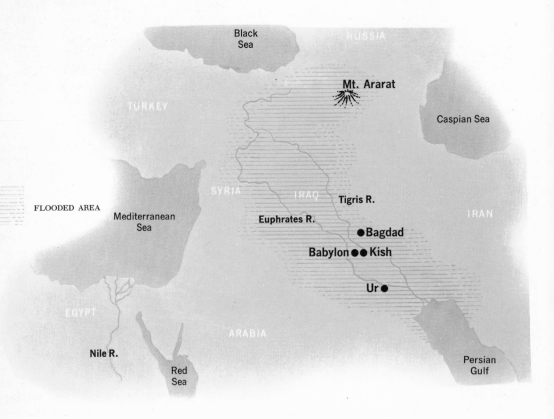

The Euphrates, the "great river" of the Bible, is traditionally known as one of the four rivers of Eden, and with the Tigris supported the most ancient civilizations.

THE TENTH CHAPTER of Genesis is indeed a unique document. It is maintained that no compilation just like it has ever been found in the literature of any other ancient people. The fundamental spirit of it is still being tested in our own land and throughout the world today. It seeks to show that the nations sprang from a common ancestry, and that all men are brothers, with a human unity like unto the Unity of God.

There is a religious purpose in it, a serious attempt to show that mankind has a common origin and that, despite our being separate peoples and races, we are one in the sight of our Creator. The belief in, and practice of, this moral truth raises Western civilization high above heathenism and offers the promise of universal peace.

Apart from its religious and moral values, the tenth chapter of Genesis is proving to be a most dependable table of nations, peoples and places of ancient time. The names given are those of the descendants of Noah's sons, the eldest of whom was Shem, followed by Ham, with Japheth as the youngest. The descendants of Ham and Japheth receive far less attention in the Bible than those of Shem, among whom was the great patriarch Abram, or Abraham.

Japheth's sons are named in Genesis 10:2 and their names prove to be those of Indo-European peoples inhabiting western Asia and parts of Europe in early Old Testament times. The name of the son Gomer undoubtedly designates the Cimmerian people — the *Kimmerioi* of Homer, a gloomy tribe which lived in or near the Crimean peninsula. Magog's name is that of a people whose land has never been clearly identified. There can be little doubt that Madai means the Medes, who lived in the hill country between the Caspian Sea

Nations Founded by the
Sons of Noah

(According to Genesis 10)

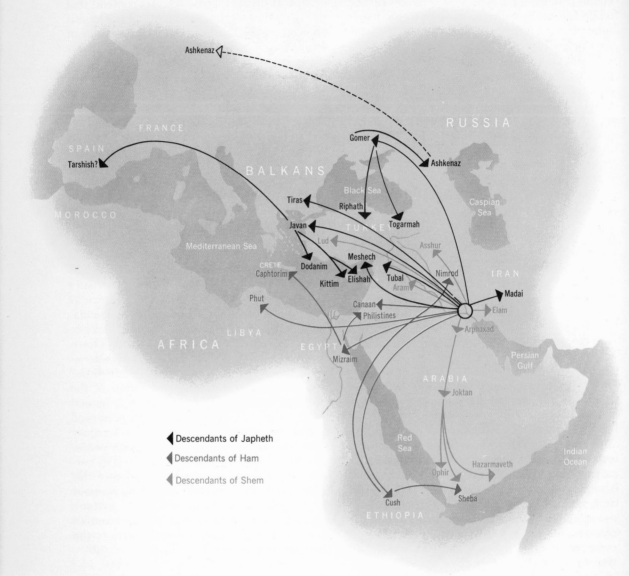

Ashkenaz

RUSSIA

Gomer

Ashkenaz

FRANCE

SPAIN

Tarshish?

BALKANS

Black Sea

Caspian Sea

MOROCCO

Tiras

Riphath

Togarmah

Javan

TURKEY

Lud

Asshur

Mediterranean Sea

CRETE

Caphtorim

Dodanim

Meshech

Kittim   Elishah

Tubal

Nimrod

IRAN

Aram

Madai

Phut

Canaan

Philistines

Elam

Arphaxad

AFRICA

LIBYA

EGYPT

Mizraim

Persian Gulf

ARABIA

Joktan

Descendants of Japheth

Descendants of Ham

Descendants of Shem

Red Sea

Indian Ocean

Hazarmaveth

Ophir

Cush

Sheba

ETHIOPIA

and the Persian Gulf. From Javan comes the term Ionian, meaning the Greeks and especially that branch inhabiting the Aegean islands and western Asia Minor. Tubal and Meshech perhaps peopled parts of Asia Minor, while Tiras very likely became the Thracians.

The descendants of Gomer's eldest son, Ashkenaz (Ashchenaz), seem to have been the Scythians, who, according to Jeremiah 51:27,

lived in the vicinity of Mount Ararat. The tribe may have pushed on into Europe; in later Jewish literature the name Ashkenaz denoted the German peoples. Riphath and Togarmah, sons of Gomer, were peoples of Asia Minor.

Javan's four children were Elishah and Kittim, whose descendants lived on the island of Cyprus; Tarshish, whose people lived in Spain; and Dodanim, whose descendants probably inhabited Rhodes and neighboring islands in the Aegean Sea.

Ham's son Cush gave his name to what we know today as Ethiopia, while Mizraim is a common name for Egypt. Phut signifies Libya, while Canaan gave his name first to the maritime plains of Palestine and then to all the land west of the River Jordan.

The sons of Cush, as listed in Genesis 10:7, peopled the southwestern part of the Arabian peninsula bordering on the Red Sea and the Indian Ocean. Outstanding among his descendants were the people of Sheba, whose famous queen at a later time made a well-known visit to Solomon. Nimrod, in Genesis 10:8-10, also deserves mention, for this mighty one was a founder of the Babylonian civilization.

Now we come to the tribes of the Holy Land itself. Mizraim seems to have sired or fostered not only the Egyptians but also the Philistine peoples. Canaan and his sons populated not only the land which came to bear his name but surrounding areas as well. The name of his firstborn, Sidon (Zidon), stood for the whole Phoenician coast; Heth refers to the Hittites, who built a remarkable civilization in Asia Minor; the Jebusites, until dispossessed by David, held the site which later became Jerusalem; the Amorites settled east of the Jordan, the Hamathites to the north of Canaan. The other names in Genesis 10:16-18 designate local Canaanite tribes. These various nations descended from Ham were politically subject to Egypt at the time this ancient list was drawn up.

The names of Shem's immediate descendants can be quite readily connected to certain eastern Semitic groups. Elam is unquestionably the Elamites immediately north of the Persian Gulf. Asshur (Assur) is surely the Assyrians, and Arphaxad is generally conceded to be the Chaldeans. Lud is the Lydians of Asia Minor, and Aram the Aramaean peoples of Syria and Mesopotamia, more generally known as the Syrians.

The forebears of Abraham — the Habiru, or Hebrew, from whom God's Chosen People descended — lived in Mesopotamia for some generations, so it would seem from Genesis 10:24-25. Arphaxad, the grandson of Noah, typifies the inhabitants of the area about Ur. His grandson was Eber, from whose name some scholars believe the term Hebrew was derived. Abraham was of the sixth generation, or era, following Eber — a generation which seems surely to have had Ur as its place of birth (Genesis 11:27-28).

Eber had two sons, Joktan and Peleg, in whose days, as Genesis 10:25 explains, the earth was divided. Some scholars contend that this division was the one described in Genesis 11, wherein the Lord showed the supremacy of His power over that of man by causing a diversity of languages, so that the work on the Tower of Babel had to stop and the nations joined together in this labor were scattered once more over all the earth.

The Bible does not describe this second relocation of peoples. But the name Peleg is believed to be derived from the Assyrian *palgu*, which means "canal." Some scholars, therefore, believe that Peleg the son of Eber may have had a prominent part in introducing the system of irrigating canals so important to life along the Tigris and Euphrates rivers. Another clue was added in the 1930s when French archaeologists uncovered a lost kingdom centered at Mari on the upper Euphrates. In the wealth of records recovered, the names of Abraham's forefathers listed in Genesis 11:16-28 appear as those of cities in northwestern Mesopotamia.

The thirteen sons of Peleg's brother, Joktan, seem to have lived in another land. Down through the ages this biblical character — whose name means "he will be made little" — has been looked upon as the father of the southern Arabs. One of his sons was named Hazarmaveth, which name has been preserved in that of modern Hadramaut, the territory along the southern coast of the Arabian peninsula. Another of his sons was Ophir, who perhaps gave his name to another section of this land, which in Solomon's time was famous for its gold, sandalwood and ivory. Joktan's remaining sons also appear to have settled somewhere in this great desert country to the southeast of the Holy Land.

THERE would be other dispersions of peoples during Bible times, as one member of this family of nations fought against another. Many of these clashes between brother nations will be related in the following pages. But now we must follow in the footsteps of one of the grandest individuals not only of the Bible but of all time, the man Abraham, whom the Lord called to do His bidding and who served His sublime purposes so well that he came to be known as the friend of God.

From the walled city of Ur on the banks of the Euphrates Abraham's father, his family and servants set out on their long journey to Haran four thousand years ago.

2. Abraham and His Children

In the past, it was generally felt that Abraham stemmed directly from a nomadic people who lived a pastoral life, far removed from large cities and concentrations of population. Still, if he was born in Ur of the Chaldees, as the Bible indicates, he grew up in one of the largest, most progressive and important metropolises of the ancient world. Ur was a thriving commercial and political center long before and after the days of Abraham.

Scholars have long believed that Ur was much closer in those days to the open water of the Persian Gulf. Modern research indicates, however, that the ancient coastline was much the same as that of today. The city stood on the bank of the Euphrates River, high upon an artificial plateau, within huge walls, teeming with a quarter million or more residents. It lay on an island formed by the river and a huge feeder canal which supplied water through smaller canals to an irrigated area stretching away as far as the eye could see. This planted area included grainfields, gardens and date-palm groves, for there were many mouths to be fed in the closely crowded city at its center. Farms, hamlets and villages were scattered through this agricultural land.

Behind its protective city wall, Ur was a huge and intricate maze of narrow streets, most of them not more than six to eight feet wide. Along these streets a front of houses — windowless for the most part — ranged on both sides without a break. They were mainly brick cubes, two stories high, with flat roofs, built around a central patio onto which the rooms opened for air and light. On the first floor were public rooms, sometimes used for weaving, metalwork and other crafts. Sleeping rooms were on the second floor while much of the family life was lived on the roof, sheltered by awnings.

Terah, father of Abraham, was presumably of the middle or merchant class, and his must have been a pleasant home in the city, containing ten to twenty spacious rooms. His son probably went to a private school where he learned to read, write and figure; beyond this schooling, he would also have been taught a trade.

Abraham must have attained his majority in a city which was one of the most highly civilized and enterprising centers of that time. Why, then, did his father pull up stakes and move some six hundred miles to Haran, a place far north in the Euphrates Valley? The answer is not clear, but the archaeologist Sir Leonard Woolley, who found many interesting things in Ur, thinks he may have uncovered a sound reason in the family chapels attached to almost all but the poorest homes. In them a "family god" was being worshiped, evidently a new custom in Abraham's day. The fact that this family god came to mean more to the people of Ur than did the worship of the moon god — which centered at the huge temple tower, or ziggurat, that dominated the city — may have prompted Terah and his family to move to Haran, another center of the moon-god cult. The move could, of course, have been merely a matter of business, or perhaps it had something to do with the death of one of the sons; but, whatever the reason, move they did.

In what period did this dramatic episode occur? The Patriarchal Age of the Bible corresponds to the Middle Bronze Age of 2000-1500 B.C., but exactly when Abraham lived is as yet uncertain. Modern Bible scholars place the migration from Ur to Haran in the twentieth or nineteenth century before Christ. Thus the traditional date of 1926 B.C. found in some editions of the Bible may not be far wrong.

In the northwestern part of Mesopotamia there is a prairie area called Padan-aram, or the Plain of Aram. Close to its center lay Haran, where important caravan trails met. It was far removed from Ur in distance, size and importance, yet it was not, as was formerly thought, a trail village well beyond the limits of civilization. At the time when the patriarchs called it home, it must have been a flourishing city, and its frequent mention in cuneiform tablets of the nineteenth and eighteenth centuries B.C. is clear evidence that it was an important junction and trading point.

The ziggurat of Ur, the huge temple tower for worship of the moon god, was constructed at the beginning of the Patriarchal Age of the Bible, before 2000 B.C. At right: The ziggurat of Ur as it stands today.

THE BIBLICAL WORLD
AT THE TIME OF THE PATRIARCHS
2000 to 1600 B.C.

Copyright by C. S. HAMMOND & CO., N.Y.

Scale of Miles

0   50   100   200   300

Capitals .... ✦

Caspian Sea

ELBURZ MTS.

Tepe Siyalk

I n d o - I r a n i a n s
(Aryans)

ZAGROS MTS.

Kassites

After Hammurabi's reign the highlander Kassites conquered Babylonia.

Susa

ELAM

Persian Gulf

According to some scholars the ancient coastline of the Gulf extended as far as Ur.

After 1500 B.C. the Hurrians established the powerful Kingdom of Mitanni in Padan-aram & Assyria.

Hurrians (Horites) before 1700 B.C.

Mt. Ararat

Lake Van

Lake Urmia

Hurrians 1700-1600 B.C.

Mt. Nisir

Tepe Gawra
Nineveh
Calah
Ashur
Mlefaat
Arbela
Jarmo
Nuzi

A S S Y R I A

Eshnunna

OLD BABYLONIAN
(under Hammurabi c. 1700 B.C.)

BABYLONIA c. 1700 B.C.

A k k a d

Babylon
Sippar
Kish
Nippur
Issin
Shuruppak
Adab
Umma
Lagash
Umma
Larsa
Kazallu
Erech
Ur
Eridu

S u m e r

Diala R.

Tigris R.

Euphrates River

KINGDOM OF MARI
(conquered by Hammurabi c. 1700 B.C.)

Raided by Hittites c. 1600 B.C.

Mari

Tadmor (Palmyra)

Habor River
Balikh R.

Haran
PADAN-ARAM

A m o r i t e s

ROUTE OF THE PATRIARCHS

D E S E R T

Carchemish
Khalab
Alalakh
Hamath
Qatna
Ugarit
Arvad

Orontes

Byblos
Sidon
Damascus

ROUTE OF ABRAHAM

The Egyptians controlled Canaan at this time.

Hazor

Lake Merom
Sea of Galilee
Jordan

C A N A A N

Shechem
Jebus (Jerusalem)
Bethel
Dothan
Gerar
Beer-sheba

Lake Mareotis (Salt Sea) (Dead Sea)

About 2000 B.C. the Indo-European Hittites invaded Asia Minor and conquered the aboriginal Khattians.

Excavations at Beycesultan suggest that southwestern Asia Minor, at this time, was inhabited by peoples related to the Greeks.

OLD HITTITE KINGDOM
(after 1700 B.C.)

Khattushash (Bogazköy)
Kushshar (Alisar Huyuk)
Kanish

Halys River
Lake Tuz

G A S G A S

ANTI-TAURUS

KIZZUWADNA

TAURUS MTS.

A R Z A W A

ASSUWA

KITTIM (CYPRUS)

Beycesultan

Hermus R.

Meander R.

Sangarius R.

Troy (Minoan)

MINOAN DOMINIONS (c. 1600 B.C.)

CAPHTOR (CRETE)

The Great Sea (Mediterranean Sea)

Aegean Sea

Black Sea

Cyrus River

Araxes River
Aras River

Lake Sevan

The Amorites, Semitic nomads from the desert, invaded the Fertile Crescent c. 2000 B.C. They later founded the kingdoms of Mari & Babylonia.

The Hyksos, Semitic people from the East, conquered Egypt about 1700 B.C.

EGYPTIAN KINGDOM 2000-1788 B.C.
(12th Dynasty 2000-1788 B.C.)

SINAI PENINSULA

Royal Egyptian x copper mines

Mt. Sinai

Tanis

On
Memphis
Lisht
Xois
Labyrinth
Beni Hasan

Lake Moeris

Pyramids

L I B Y A N   D E S E R T

Haran lay on the bank of the Balikh River, about sixty miles north of its juncture with the Euphrates. About sixty miles to the east of Haran was famous Tell Halâf — Gozan of the Bible — from which have been dug some of the earliest indications of man's rise above the primitive life and of his transition from stone to metal tools. Here too the first evidence of a wheeled vehicle was found.

About two hundred fifty miles from Haran, down the Balikh and the Euphrates, was the long-forgotten city of Mari, which was uncovered beginning in 1933. In it was perhaps the largest castle of the ancient world, containing more than two hundred rooms. But of far greater importance were the twenty thousand tablets removed from the palace archives. It will take many years to translate all of them, but those already deciphered have added materially to the knowledge of this whole section, ruled in the time of Abraham by peace-loving kings of Mari.

Not only Haran is mentioned in these tablets, but frequently another place, called Nakhur.

This is none other than Nahor, the home of Rebekah, who became the wife of Abraham's son Isaac. This country in the Plain of Aram is most closely identified with the forebears of the Hebrew people.

We know little about the life of Terah and his family in Haran. The first details concerning Abraham are given us in the Bible as God spoke to him saying he should leave his father's house and go into a land which He would show him. He promised, "I will make of thee a great nation and I will bless thee."

So Abraham obeyed the Lord and started out for Canaan, that portion of the Fertile Crescent which acts as a land bridge linking Asia and Africa, which men have crossed since the beginning of time in search of land, trade or conquest, and which therefore has served as a thoroughfare and battlefield. How did Abraham journey? By the most direct route, moving south along the banks of the Balikh, he would have forded the Euphrates and then crossed the Syrian desert seeking biblical Tadmor, better known by its Roman name, Palmyra.

Gold bull's head on a lyre and a queen's necklace of gold set with carnelians, excavated from the royal cemetery of Ur

This pillar of salt among the pinnacles at the mountain of Sodom is traditionally known as "Lot's Wife."

This huge oasis for many centuries supported a splendid city which was long ruled by merchant princes.

From there Abraham would have moved on another hundred fifty miles to fair Damascus, which, if it was spring when he arrived, would have been most colorful with its great groves of apricot and almond trees in bloom. The city is probably the oldest continuously inhabited place of any size in the world. Few cities stand in so beautiful a spot, with snow-capped Mount Hermon to the west and the desert stretching off in other directions. The town itself is ringed with trees and other green growth springing from irrigated soil made rich and lush by the waters of the Abana (modern Barada) River.

How long did Abraham stay in this city, which to the Arabs is paradise upon earth? Long enough at least to acquire a most able bond servant, Eliezer, who became his steward and prospective heir (Genesis 15:2).

Below Damascus, Abraham had a choice of three routes. One skirted the base of Mount Hermon, forded the Jordan near its source, and descended its west bank to the point where it emptied into the Sea of Galilee, then known as the Sea of Chinnereth. A more direct, and probably the most traveled, route would have led directly southwest, crossed the Jordan

about six miles above its mouth, and there joined the first. The third route started down the very ancient road later known as the King's Highway, and then veered to the south shore of Galilee, crossing the Jordan where that river leaves the lake. Keeping along the west bank for a short distance, the route then swung up into the throat of the Plain of Jezreel to the powerful fortress city of Beth-shan.

Which of the routes Abraham took is not certain, for they were all in active use four thousand years ago. We do know that his first recorded campsite was in the broad valley before ancient Shechem — a town that lay well up on the highlands some twenty-five miles southwest of Beth-shan, guarded by the twin mountains Ebal and Gerizim, towering some three thousand feet above sea level.

Abraham's own household, composed of his childless wife, Sarah (Sarai), and his bond servants or slaves, must even then have made up a substantial group. Presumably there were several hundred in all, and many flocks and herds. Yet Abraham's household and livestock did not comprise all of the large band of humans and creatures which made its leisurely way down through northern Canaan seeking pasture in the central highlands. His nephew Lot had his own household and his own flocks and herds and herdsmen, probably inherited from his father. Together these two large bands must have seemed a dire threat to the Canaanites, whose land was subject to frequent invasion by nomads who stole in from the desert, robbed and pillaged, and quickly disappeared again into the wilderness. Abraham and Lot must have been looked upon with real foreboding as they pitched their black goat-hair tents on the broad valley floor before Shechem.

The people about Bethel, twenty miles to the south along the highland trail, might have been equally apprehensive when this horde moved on down into that area, even though Abraham's peaceful ways had no doubt been frequently commented upon along the caravan routes. The city of Bethel was walled, but it was not a stronghold; the neighboring place known as Ai, there is now reason to believe, had recently been reduced to a heap of ruins owing to an attack by nomads. Also there was a drought; water was scarce and the pastures were already overgrazed. The Bethelites must have been relieved when their uninvited guests moved down the route to the south.

Because of drought, the grazing areas of Canaan could not support the combined flocks and herds of Abraham and Lot; and so, like many nomads of that age, Abraham and his nephew had to seek refuge in the land watered by the mighty Nile. What was their course? Most likely they continued down the highland route through the plateau country later to be called Judaea. If so, they would have passed stout little Jebus, a walled city which would grow in size and importance and later be known as Jerusalem. Moving south, past small villages and camps, they would have descended from the higher country to a trail junction at the wells of Beer-sheba.

Here began a two-hundred-mile thrust across the desolate Wilderness of Shur. It must have been slow, worrisome going, with hungry beasts contesting for the lean grazing. So it was perhaps with strongly mixed emotions that Abraham and Lot arrived at one of the stout forts that made up the Princes' Wall by which the border of Egypt was protected. Beyond lay good pastures, but would they be permitted to pass through to them?

Pass they did, however, and Abraham seems to have been a sufficiently important personage so that the Egyptian pharaoh sought to make an alliance with him. This caused that unhappy incident between them. Having been told that Sarah, who was very beautiful, was Abraham's sister, the pharaoh took her into his palace. That very night, the pharaoh learned that Sarah was really Abraham's wife. Angered by this deception, the mighty king banished Abraham and all his people from the land of Egypt. But before this happened, the husband and wife must have had ample opportunity to see many of the wonders of that remarkable land.

Here an outstanding civilization had been in the making for many, many centuries. As Abraham made his way to and from the pharaoh's palace in Memphis, he would have seen the pyramids, the temples and priestly college at On, or Heliopolis, fine cities and other notable features of this country that rivaled the distant land in which he had been born. But while his progeny, in later days, would live in this lush land of Egypt for several generations, Abraham was soon turned back across the border.

Grazing their flocks and herds, Abraham and his nephew Lot now began to work their way back north across the Wilderness of Shur. Before long they again found themselves in the drought-stricken highlands of Canaan where once more they were hard pressed for pasturage, and so they decided to part.

From the high hills at Bethel, about twenty miles south of Shechem, they surveyed the country. Lot, given his choice, decided in favor of the torrid, lush, but excessively wicked area in the lower Jordan Valley around the cities of Sodom and Gomorrah. There he and his household soon came to grief, captured by four kings who came down from Mesopotamia to collect tribute from five other kings, who ruled this region. It is perhaps in commemoration of these nine kings that the King's Highway was named (see map on page 32). While the Jordan Valley has long seemed to be virtually uninhabitable except just below the Sea of Galilee and in the oasis surrounding Jericho, it now yields evidence of once having been fairly well populated. It must have been a wealthy district four thousand years ago to have attracted those marauding kings from far to the east.

Abraham, learning what had befallen his nephew Lot, armed his bondsmen and set out in pursuit. He rescued Lot, driving away the four kings; in so doing he made his position in southern Canaan most secure. Lot later came to ruin and his wife was turned into a pillar of salt when God rained fire and brimstone upon the evil cities of Sodom and Gomorrah. As for Abraham, he and his people grew and prospered there among strangers so far away from their homeland.

It was there that God appeared again to Abraham, as He had long before in Haran, and repeated His promise that Abraham would become the father of many nations and that he and his seed would inherit the land of Canaan forever. There Hagar, Sarah's handmaiden, bore him a son called Ishmael who was destined to be the forefather of the Arabian people. There the aged Sarah, who had long been barren, bore Abraham his beloved son Isaac in fulfillment of God's promise. And there also in Canaan the Angel of the Lord stayed Abraham's hand when Abraham, in his deep love for God, offered Isaac as a sacrifice.

In spite of all the blessings which came to him in Canaan, Abraham considered that land a heathen place. He buried Sarah there in the Cave of Machpelah near Hebron; but in later years, rather than ally his descendants with the people of Canaan, he sent his steward far to the north to his former homeland in the Plain of

Aram, there to choose a wife for his son Isaac from among the daughters of his kindred still inhabiting that area.

Abraham's steward first beheld the fair Rebekah at the well outside of the city of Nahor, where she had the grace to draw water for him and his camels. On meeting her parents and learning that they were related to his master, Abraham, he arranged for her marriage to Isaac and took her back with him to Canaan.

Isaac and Rebekah loved each other, and even after Abraham's death they continued to live in Canaan, the Promised Land, spending their lives mostly in the "south country" along the edge of the wilderness stretching inland from the Philistine towns on the coastal plains, around the wells at Beer-sheba, and in the higher valleys about Hebron.

Their twin sons were surely not an unmixed blessing. Isaac loved his willful, lusty elder son, Esau, who insisted upon uniting with the local people; he married their daughters and became the father of the Edomites, who in generations to come were to make much trouble for the Chosen People — descendants of the wily, artful younger son, Jacob.

Jacob was jealous of his twin brother, Esau, who had been born only a moment before him, and he coveted the elder's inheritance. One day, seeing Esau faint from hunger, he bought Esau's birthright for some bread and a pot of lentils. The misused Esau threatened to kill his brother, and so Rebekah advised Jacob, her favorite, to flee to her old home in Padan-aram and live with her brother Laban. It was during this flight that Jacob dreamed of the ladder reaching to heaven and heard the voice of the Lord saying that he, Jacob, and his seed, progeny of Abraham and of Isaac, would inherit the land of Canaan.

Jacob served a stern apprenticeship as shepherd and herdsman to Laban in Padan-aram. He wished to marry Laban's younger daughter, Rachel, and, while Laban agreed to this, he tricked Jacob first into marrying his elder daughter, Leah. Jacob had to serve Laban seven years for Leah and seven more for Rachel. Finally, having won his desire, he fled from Laban secretly and, with his two wives and his flocks and herds, headed back toward his home in Canaan. This marks the distinct break between the developing Hebrew people and the Aramaean land and peoples.

Jacob, as he set out for his home in Canaan,

The land of Jacob and Joseph: a plain in the central highlands

no doubt at the start followed the route taken by his grandfather years before. But below Damascus he seems to have kept east of the Jordan, perhaps seeking better pasturage in the hills of Bashan and Gilead. There, on the bank of the twisting, brawling Jabbok River, he wrestled with the Angel of the Lord and received the name by which he and his people were henceforth to be known — Israel. On the following day he made peace with his brother, Esau.

Jacob probably forded the Jordan at the mouth of the Jabbok, where a trail from the east pressed up the steep grade out of the deep valley to Shechem and then continued on to the coast. In the plain to the east of Shechem, he set up his tents in this land of promise, near or at the very spot where his grandfather Abraham had camped nearly two centuries before.

For the next thirty-odd years Jacob and his growing family pitched their tents and fed their flocks at many familiar points in the central highlands of Canaan and in the lower "south country." He had married several wives, not an unusual arrangement in a time when many children died in infancy and those who grew to a working age could add materially to the parents' wealth.

His most beloved wife was the lovely Rachel, and her elder son, Joseph, had become his favorite. The boy's half brothers were much older than he, and his boyish imprudence, together with the father's partiality, made him much hated by his ten grown brethren.

Jacob's tents were pitched near Hebron the year that Joseph was seventeen and the ten inflicted their vengeance upon him. He seems to have been a sort of messenger between his now elderly father in the main camp and the sons seeking better outlying pastures, sometimes at quite a distance. It was on one of these missions that young Joseph, clad in his coat of many colors, hurried north to Shechem. Not finding his brothers and their cattle there, he continued another twenty miles to Dothan, and it was at that place that they laid hands upon him with the intention of killing him. However, they spared his life but sold him into what might have been a living death — slavery.

The Ishmaelites who bought him were traders who had forded the Jordan and were heading for the main route into Egypt that ran through the seacoast plains. The transaction they had just completed was perhaps not unusual in those times, particularly in this rather lawless, thinly populated land.

The scene of the Bible story now shifts from Canaan to Egypt, following the unfortunate Joseph into the land where he will unwittingly be preparing a home for the people who will one day possess Canaan — the Children of Israel — his own descendants and those of his brothers.

WHAT WAS the situation in the narrow land along the Nile when Joseph arrived there?

Presumably he came into Egypt in the period between the Middle and New Kingdoms, during the days of the Hyksos. The Jewish historian Josephus, writing in about 80 A.D. and quoting an ancient Egyptian priest and historian named Manetho, explains how it happened that the land of the pharaohs fell under the control of the Hyksos, the "Shepherd Kings," as he called them. "There was a king of ours whose name was Timaus, in whose reign it came to pass, I know not why, that God was displeased with us. And there came unexpectedly men of ignoble birth, out of the East, who were bold enough to invade our country and conquer it by force without a battle. And when they had our rulers under their power, they burned down our cities, and demolished the temples of the gods and treated the people most barbarously. . . . At length they made one of their number king, whose name was Salatis. He lived at Memphis and made both Upper and Lower Egypt pay tribute, and left garrisons at all strategic places."

For the first time in its already long history, Egypt was in the hands of foreign conquerors; the Hyksos continued to hold the land for a century or more, and it could well be that they were ruling at the time Joseph arrived there. Since the Hyksos were a Semitic people, the rulers and their more important officers were of the same background as this able young man. In other words, like Joseph, they belonged to peoples or nations of western Asia whose languages had a common root, peoples who had supposedly descended from Noah's son

One of the sphinxes with non-Egyptian faces at Avaris, inscribed with names of Hyksos kings, from the time of Jacob and Joseph. Later Egyptian pharaohs inscribed their own names on these sphinxes.

Shem — Hebrews, Syrians, Assyrians, Arabs, Phoenicians and others.

Little is known about the Hyksos. For thirteen centuries, from about the year 3000 B.C., no nation had been more careful about preserving a record of its history than Egypt. However, there are no records of the period during which the Hyksos sat upon the Egyptian throne. When control was again returned to Egyptian hands after the Hyksos had been driven out, what records those "barbarians" may have left seem to have been destroyed. Although Joseph had become prime minister, and would certainly have been known in succeeding reigns, a passage in Exodus (1:8) states that a new pharaoh came to power who had no knowledge of him. Apparently Joseph served during that unhappy period which every native Egyptian forever after was supposed completely to forget.

We are entirely dependent upon the Bible for the story of the long Israelite sojourn in the country along the Nile. From it we learn that Joseph rose to a position of great prestige under one of the Hyksos pharaohs. He came into Egypt as a slave and became prime minister through his ability to interpret the pharaoh's mysterious dreams. He predicted a famine and saved the nation by setting aside the grain of seven fat years to be used during the seven lean years. Joseph also brought his people down into Egypt and settled them in the rich delta area known in the Bible as Goshen. Although, as told in the Bible, herdsmen as a class were repugnant and an abomination to the native Egyptians (Genesis 46:34), Joseph apparently reached an understanding with the foreign Semitic Hyksos in power.

From the Bible we also learn certain things about Egyptian history. The elevated Joseph rode in the "second chariot" (Genesis 41:43), a fact which agrees with historical and archaeological finds. Before the days of the Hyksos, there were no chariots in Egypt. We know that the wheel was in use in Babylonia, at the other end of the Fertile Crescent, fully fifteen hundred years before it was adopted in Egypt, and that four-wheeled carts were in use in Ur when Abraham lived there as a youth; so we may assume that the Hyksos from the East were first to introduce into the land of the pharaohs wheeled vehicles and horses to pull them.

Another historical fact about Egypt revealed in the Bible is that extensive confiscation of property took place during the Hyksos regime. In Genesis 47:20-26 we learn that, when the great famine was upon the land during Joseph's time, the Egyptians were forced to sell all their fields to the pharaoh in exchange for grain to eat. From that time on they worked as tenant farmers and it became the law that they had to give the pharaoh one fifth of all they raised.

While the Hyksos were warlike and brought about evil changes in Egyptian life, culture and customs, they also made many contributions. They were competent smiths and metalworkers and expert potters, and they were skilled in masonry and the building of fortifications.

During the early years of the Hyksos occupation, the Egyptians seem to have accepted their conquerors without resistance. The house of Israel flourished. That last of the patriarchs, Jacob, finished his years in peace in the delta country of Egypt. On his deathbed he exacted a promise from his beloved son Joseph that Joseph would take his remains back to the Promised Land and place them in the sepulcher at Machpelah beside those of his grandparents Abraham and Sarah; his parents, Isaac and Rebekah; and his first wife, Leah. And so, when the body had been embalmed and forty days of mourning were past, Joseph set out dutifully upon his somber journey at the head of a great funeral procession, accompanied by the pharaoh's chariots and horsemen. This cortege was made up of all the elders of the pharaoh's house and the elders of the land of Egypt as well as those of the houses of Joseph and his father and all his brothers (Genesis 50:7-9).

Egypt had long had important interests in the country through which they passed. There were copper and turquoise mines in the Sinai Peninsula, and important commercial relations with the far larger Arabian peninsula beyond. From Memphis a busy route skirted the north end of the Gulf of Suez and ran across the Wilderness of Paran to the upper end of the Gulf of Aqaba. There, at a town known as Ezion-geber, began the famous King's Highway leading north toward Damascus. Jacob's funeral procession probably traveled this way.

About two hundred miles to the north, after the King's Highway had traversed Edom and Moab, it intersected at the town of Heshbon an east-west trail which plunged down into the valley of the Jordan. After fording the river at Jericho, this trail climbed steeply to the tight-walled little city of Jebus on the heights.

In Egypt, the Israelites may have witnessed the worship of Apis, the sacred bull, though Aaron's golden calf probably did not derive from it.

There it met the highland route that not only Jacob but Isaac and Abraham before him had traveled and known so intimately. Not far south of Jebus were Hebron and the Cave of Machpelah that held the "parents" of the Hebrew race. Here Jacob-Israel was laid to rest.

Why had Joseph chosen this roundabout way of going to Hebron instead of traveling directly from Memphis across the Wilderness of Shur or along the Mediterranean coastal route? Was the route he chose better traveled and therefore safer? We do not know. This much is certain: the Palestinian land bridge was well supplied with trade routes and highways even four thousand years ago.

After the burial, Joseph and his brethren returned to Egypt, where he gained further honors and enjoyed a long and useful life. And the Children of Israel — Joseph's family and the families of his eleven brothers, which constituted the Twelve Tribes — settled permanently in Egypt at that time, making it their home for the next twelve or fourteen generations, or until the time of Moses.

Not for many years after the time of Joseph did that day of reckoning come in Egypt when the foreign Hyksos were driven from the land.

Finally the native Egyptian princes began to revolt. One of the first was the Theban prince Sekenenre, but he came to a violent end; his mummy shows five major skull wounds, any of which might have been fatal. His elder son, Kamose, was more successful, while the younger one, Ahmose, put the Hyksos to rout.

To accomplish this, the hard-hitting Prince Ahmose raised and trained a sizable army. Not content with having driven the Hyksos and their supporters over the border, he harried them all up and down the length of Canaan, sacking the cities in which they hid and carrying home much booty. The recollection of the years of humiliation under the Hyksos fostered a militant and aggressive attitude among the Egyptians. In the years that followed, Egypt became a power to reckon with.

Ahmose I, an able soldier, also became a competent ruler and the founder of the Eighteenth Dynasty in the year 1580 B.C. Under this dynasty, Egypt's power extended over ever increasing areas. Before the death of Ahmose I's great-great-grandson Thutmose III, this new Egypt was mistress of an immense area running north from the Fourth Cataract of the Nile to the upper shore of the faraway Euphrates.

Reared in the royal palace of Rameses II, Moses witnessed the harsh forced labor of the Israelites in the rebuilding of the pharaoh's military-supply cities of Pithom and Raamses.

3. The Exodus

It is unfortunate that much misunderstanding and confusion have resulted because of Bible chronology. Today we are very aware of time; its accurate computation and recording seem both natural and necessary to us. We insist on exact dates of all occurrences and we want them to be arranged in proper sequence.

However, during Bible times and the centuries that followed, there was a lack of interest and precision in this matter. As a result biblical dates and episodes vary greatly; sometimes they conflict. It was not, in fact, until the year 1701 that Bibles were first published which attempted to establish an accurate chronology. They were printed in English, the work having been done nearly a half century before by Archbishop Ussher of Armagh. While his efforts were careful, they were based upon the limited knowledge of that time; and although they have served very well for two and a half centuries, his dating has since proved inaccurate in many instances.

One of Archbishop Ussher's findings which is subject to serious question is the time of the Exodus. Students have long doubted the year 1491 B.C. set by Ussher. It was not until archaeologists had uncovered in the Nile delta the ancient cities of Pithom and Raamses, mentioned in the first chapter of the Book of Exodus, that a more accurate date could be computed. Competent authorities today set the withdrawal at *about* the year 1290 B.C., during the reign of the pharaoh Rameses II, or approximately two hundred years later than Ussher's computation.

The fact that Egypt became a warlike nation and conquered all the lands north to the Euphrates following the expulsion of the Hyksos has already been pointed out. For the better control of her border and the buffer state of Canaan, the capital was moved from Thebes down the Nile into the eastern delta country. This happened while Rameses II, "This Beloved of Amun," occupied the throne. He appears to have been every inch a king and, while perhaps a greater builder than a warrior, he did tend zealously to his country's safety.

Rameses rebuilt or strengthened the Princes' Wall of forts stretching from the shores of the Mediterranean to Lake Timsah. And then, for their better maintenance as well as for the use of his soldiers in Canaan, he rebuilt and enlarged the cities of Pithom and Raamses, making them into supply cities. For this he used forced labor, recruited largely, it would seem, from among the Israelites living in that section of the delta known as Goshen.

The first of these cities, Pithom, is the mound Tell er-Reṭâba in the Wâdī Ṭumilât, and in ancient times it seems to have been called Pitum, or "house of the god Atum (Aton)." The second city, Raamses, mentioned in Exodus, is almost certainly Tanis, the delta residence of the Rameside pharaohs. It was formerly thought to be Tell el-Maskhûṭa, about eight miles east of Pithom, but this mound is now considered to be biblical Succoth, the first campsite of the Exodus (Exodus 12:37). Excavation at these sites leaves little doubt that they were built by Rameses II; to him falls the dubious honor of being the pharaoh of the Exodus.

Opposed to this powerful pharaoh was one of the greatest leaders and lawgivers of all time — Moses. Although he was born into the bondage his people had been destined to suffer, fate made him a foster son of the pharaoh's daughter, so that he was reared in the royal palace. But his loyalty to his own people was unshakable. He would often go out and, filled with sorrow, watch as they labored for their Egyptian masters. One day, seeing an Egyptian beating a Hebrew, he killed him and hid his body in the sand.

When the pharaoh heard of this, Moses was forced to flee. In what direction did he go? He fled to the south and east, thus missing the border patrol, and headed toward the land of Midian, which lay along the shores of the Gulf of Aqaba, the eastern arm of the Red Sea. There, among descendants of father Abraham, he lived the life of a shepherd and was trained for his future task of leading the Israelites during their years of wandering through the neighboring wilderness.

It was at the foot of a rugged, colorful but forbidding mountain in this wilderness that God called Moses to his herculean task. There the Angel of the Lord appeared to him as a flame of fire in the midst of a bush and announced that He had chosen him to lead the Children of Israel out of their bondage in Egypt (Exodus 3:2-10). The traditional spot in the shadow of Mount Sinai has been marked, first by a church and then by a monastery, during the past fourteen centuries.

Following the Lord's command, Moses now returned to Egypt, where he was joined by his elder brother, Aaron. Together they pleaded with the pharaoh to let their people go, but the pharaoh refused, and so God, to prove their divine purpose, manifested Himself in many miraculous ways.

He caused Aaron's rod to turn into a serpent when it was cast upon the ground. When that failed to move the pharaoh He visited Egypt with ten plagues: He turned all the waters of Egypt into blood, sent frogs and insects, afflicted the Egyptians and their beasts with diseases; each curse was more terrible than the one before. It was not until the Angel of the Lord, passing over the homes of the Hebrews, struck dead the firstborn of every Egyptian family and of every beast in the field that Moses finally won permission from the unwilling pharaoh to lead his countrymen from Egypt where they had been enslaved.

It was the spring of the year and the Twelve Tribes of Israel hurriedly assembled at the royal city of Tanis, or Raamses, forming in numbers the greatest migration in all history (Exodus 12:37). Their objective was the Promised Land. What would be their route? The shortest would be by way of the Mediterranean coastal highway; but this was a route of invasion and war and was heavily fortified. Therefore, as implied in Bible text, the Israelites considered it too risky an avenue of exit.

So they headed for Succoth, thirty-two miles to the southeast, where they made their first camp. Though only a short distance to travel, it probably took them two or three days, burdened as they were with household possessions, many small children, and flocks and herds that needed to graze along the way. They then went on to Etham on the edge of the wilderness. Now the pharaoh's heart had changed, so the Israelites, perhaps as a deceptive measure to confuse the pursuing Egyptians, backtracked to Baal-zephon near "the Reed Sea."

The exact spot where the waters parted and the crossing of the sea was made may never be positively established. There are a number of possible places. The Hebrew name for the body of water which the Israelites crossed in leaving Egypt means "the Sea of Reeds" or "the Reed Sea." This would seem to refer to the region of marshland and shallow water through which the Suez Canal was later cut. The Greek version of the Old Testament (the Septuagint), translated several centuries before Christ, was apparently the first to confuse this body of water with the Red Sea, some miles to the south. Hence the Greek New Testament also speaks of the Israelites crossing "the Red Sea."

With the pharaoh's army destroyed by the closing in of the waters of "the Reed Sea," the Israelites were now safe, and they went forward with joy into the Sinai Peninsula. Miriam, the sister of Moses and Aaron, took a timbrel in her hand and all the women followed after her, dancing and singing (Exodus 15:20-21). They set off along the route leading to the copper and turquoise mines near the tip of this harsh spearpoint of land.

In recent times this whole area has not been able to support more than about seven thousand underfed wanderers. What a wilderness it must have seemed in those ancient days to almost a hundred times that many people, completely inexperienced in the rigors of this arid steppe! As in Bible times, there still are long waterless stretches, with infrequent brackish wells, any one of which may have been Marah. One tempting oasis of palm trees and clear, good water still exists, which is probably biblical Elim.

During the spring and fall migrating quail traveling between Africa and Central Europe drop down to feed in this part of the Sinai

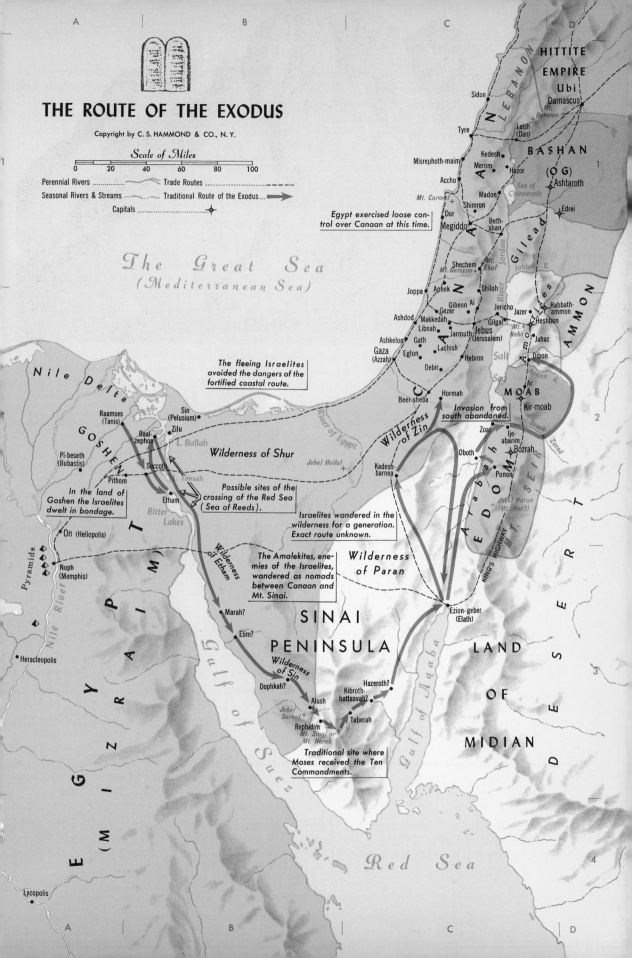

THE ROUTE OF THE EXODUS

Copyright by C. S. HAMMOND & CO., N. Y.

Scale of Miles

0   20   40   60   80   100

Perennial Rivers ....
Seasonal Rivers & Streams ....
Capitals ....◆
Trade Routes ....
Traditional Route of the Exodus ...➤

Egypt exercised loose control over Canaan at this time.

The Great Sea
(Mediterranean Sea)

The fleeing Israelites avoided the dangers of the fortified coastal route.

In the land of Goshen the Israelites dwelt in bondage.

Possible sites of the crossing of the Red Sea (Sea of Reeds).

Israelites wandered in the wilderness for a generation. Exact route unknown.

Invasion from south abandoned.

The Amalekites, enemies of the Israelites, wandered as nomads between Canaan and Mt. Sinai.

Traditional site where Moses received the Ten Commandments.

HITTITE EMPIRE
Ubi
Damascus
Mt. Hermon
BASHAN (OG)
Ashtaroth
Edrei
Laish (Dan)
LEBANON
Sidon
Tyre
Kedesh
Misrephoth-maim
Merom
Hazor
Accho
Madon
Shimron
Mt. Carmel
Dor
Megiddo
Beth-shan
Gilead
Jabbok R.
River Jordan
Ammon
Rabbath-ammon
Heshbon
Shechem
Mt. Gerizim
Mt. Ebal
Shiloh
Jazer
Aphek
Joppa
CANAAN
Gibeon Ai
Gezer
Jericho
Gilgal
Jebus (Jerusalem)
Mt. Nebo
Jahaz
Ashdod
Makkedah
Libnah
Jarmuth
Lachish
Gath
Hebron
Debir
Eglon
Ashkelon
Gaza (Azzah)
Salt Sea
Dibon
Arnon R.
MOAB
Kir-moab
Ar
Zered Brook
Beer-sheba
Hormah
Wilderness of Zin
Zoar
Ije-abarim
Bozrah
Oboth
Punon
EDOM
Kadesh-barnea
Jebel Harun (Mt. Hor?)
MT. SEIR
Arabah
KING'S HIGHWAY

Nile Delta
Raamses (Tanis)
GOSHEN
Baal-zephon
Zilu
Sin (Pelusium)
L. Ballah
Pi-beseth (Bubastis)
Pithom
Succoth
Wilderness of Shur
River of Egypt
L. Timsah
Etham
Bitter Lakes
On (Heliopolis)
Jebel Hellal
E G Y P T   (MIZRAIM)
Noph (Memphis)
Pyramids
Wilderness of Etham
Nile River
Heracleopolis
Marah?
Elim?
SINAI PENINSULA
Wilderness of Paran
Wilderness of Sin
Dophkah?
Alush
Jebel Serbal
Rephidim
Mt. Sinai or Mt. Horeb
Taberah
Kibroth-hattaavah?
Hazeroth?
Ezion-geber (Elath)
LAND OF MIDIAN
Gulf of Suez
Gulf of Aqaba
DESERT
Lycopolis
Red Sea

Mount Sinai (Râs eṣ-Ṣafṣâf), where Moses received the Ten Commandments. The traditional Arab site, Jebel Mûsā, is directly behind.

Peninsula and are pounced upon by hungry Bedouin wanderers just as they were pounced upon so long ago by the hungry Children of Israel. And if you journey near this area you will probably be offered honey-sweet manna, drippings from tamarisk trees whose bark is attacked by a minute insect found only in Sinai (Exodus 16:4-35).

Three months after escaping from Egypt the Israelites arrived at the foot of Mount Sinai, where, some time before, Moses had beheld the burning bush and received God's command. Here they camped and, during the months that followed, Moses on several occasions climbed the slopes of Mount Sinai to commune with God. It was there that God revealed to Moses the tenets of the faith which the Children of Israel were to follow forevermore, and there that He gave Moses the Ten Commandments inscribed on two tablets of stone.

However, when Moses descended from the mountain with the Ten Commandments, he found that the people were worshiping a golden calf which they had fashioned from their jewelry under the direction of Aaron. In his anger that they had abandoned God in this fashion, Moses shattered the tablets. Then, upbraiding the people for their sin, he cast the golden calf into a fire, burned it and ground it into powder.

After this the Children of Israel repented and God forgave them. His Commandments were inscribed upon two new tablets of stone and, remembering His vow to their forefathers, Abraham, Isaac and Jacob, He said that He would lead them into the Promised Land, a land flowing with milk and honey.

When spring came the Israelites broke camp, formed into a great procession and started on their trek to far-off Canaan. Their priests led the way carrying the sacred Ark of the Covenant — a chest built of acacia wood overlaid with gold and containing Aaron's rod, some manna from heaven and the tablets inscribed with the Ten Commandments. The Twelve Tribes with all their belongings and flocks and herds followed. And the spirit of the Lord hovered above the Ark of the Covenant as a cloud by day and a pillar of fire by night.

During the weeks that followed, the Children of Israel moved to the north, paralleling the shore of the Gulf of Aqaba. To locate all their campsites listed in the 33rd chapter of the Book of Numbers would be impossible and largely fruitless. Some of their stopping places, however, do have special significance.

One of them, the little town of Ezion-geber, at the head of the gulf, came to prominence in Solomon's time, for he had a copper smelter and navy yard there. It is known today as Elath and is most important as a southern seaport of modern Israel.

Swinging to the northwest, the Israelites headed for the "south country" of Canaan, where Moses hoped to enter the land of promise. They apparently found sufficient water and pasture in the vicinity of Kadesh-barnea, in the Wilderness of Zin, to set up a permanent camp while a reconnaissance party sought information on which the strategy of invasion might be planned.

The scouts, who included a man named Joshua, went only as far as Hebron. There ten out of the twelve scouts became so frightened that they lost spirit and quickly returned to headquarters, telling of the richness of the land and bearing an enormous cluster of grapes and some pomegranates and figs as proof. Yet they babbled their fear of the Canaanites in words that sounded like silly caravan gossip.

Moses was shocked and angered when the Israelites, camping at Kadesh-barnea, were intimidated by the report of the scouts and hesitated to enter Canaan. In order to strengthen their spirit and await the rise of a new and more courageous generation, he led them back into the wilderness south of the Salt (Dead) Sea. There they wandered many years, searching for water and grazing their flocks and herds upon the sparse grass. When at long last, after almost thirty-nine years of stern discipline and the weeding out of the fearful, he felt that the Children of Israel were ready, he made new plans for entering the Promised Land.

DURING those long years, Moses and the other leaders of the Israelites certainly must have been aware of conditions in both Egypt and Canaan, where changes were taking place. The land along the Nile had again grown less warlike, but had succeeded in bleeding white the city-states in Canaan. That land bridge had been measurably weakened and the time for the Israelites to strike was at hand. For reasons not too clear, Moses seems to have felt that it would be more promising to attack from the east than from the south, which faced toward Egypt.

As the Israelites swung over toward the land of Edom, they suffered the loss of their first High Priest, Aaron, the brother of Moses. A grave was found for him on Mount Hor. Its location is not definitely known; the traditional

spot is marked by a tomb on an eminence now called Jebel Harun.

For a time the Israelites were once again at Ezion-geber, the plan being to move up along the King's Highway, which ran directly north from that port, through the lands of Edom, Moab, Sihon the Amorite, Ammon, Gilead and Bashan, toward Damascus. Many people in those days lived along this active trade route, and it was only natural that they would resist the passage of so great a horde through their lands. The past years had been fairly free of hostilities; but now there occurred a decided change. Active resistance to the Israelites began with the refusal by the Edomites of right of passage through their country.

So an attempt to bypass Edom had to be made, and a route was chosen through the Arabah, the great depression leading north to the lower end of the Salt Sea. One campsite mentioned in this valley, Punon, is the copper town which the local Arabs today call Feinân. Pressing on to the Brook Zered, which empties into the great Salt Sea near its southern extremity, the Israelites then swung east up its dry valley, which formed the boundary of Moab. And since they had been forbidden right-of-way through that land too, they bypassed it by a swing out over the desert along its eastern edge.

Coming to the Arnon River, which marked the southern border of the Amorite kingdom, they turned west. Sihon, the Amorite king,

The land of Moab, through which the Israelites dared not pass on their way to the Promised Land

CANAAN BEFORE THE CONQUEST

Copyright by C. S. HAMMOND & CO., N. Y.

Scale of Miles

0 5 10   20   30   40

Perennial Rivers
Seasonal Rivers & Streams
Capitals ....

Phoenicians from the cities of Sidon and Tyre traded throughout the Mediterranean.

HITTITE EMPIRE
Ubi

Damascus

Sidon

Zarephath

Tyre
Kanah

Misrephoth-maim
Achzib

Accho
Achshaph

Laish (Dan)

Kedesh

Hazor
Merom

Chinnereth
Madon

Sea of Chinnereth (Galilee)

BASHAN (KINGDOM OF OG)

Karnaim
Ashtaroth

Yarmuk R.

Edrei

Shimron
Jokneam
Dor
Megiddo
Taanach
Ibleam
Dothan
Sochoh

Mt. Carmel
Mt. Tabor

Ham
Beth-shan
Pella
Jabesh-gilead
Mahanaim

Ramoth-gilead

The 13th- and 12th-century kingdoms of Bashan, Ammon, Moab and Edom displaced the Rephaim, Zuzim, Emim and Horites respectively.

The Great Sea
(Mediterranean Sea)

Plain of Sharon

Tirzah?
Shechem
Jacob's Well
Mt. Ebal
Mt. Gerizim

Succoth
Penuel (Peniel)

Jabbok

KING'S HIGHWAY

Joppa
Aphek
Tappuah
Ono
Lod

Adam

Jazer

Rabbath-ammon

AMMON

Canaan at this time was an Egyptian province organized on a city-state system. The local kings were only required to pay tribute and to furnish labor for Egyptian royal projects.

Bethel
Ai
Beeroth
Gibeon
Jericho
Gilgal

Gezer
Ekron
Chephirah
Kirjath-jearim

Heshbon

KINGDOM OF SIHON

Plains of Moab

Mt. Nebo (Pisgah)

Ashdod
Beth-shemesh
Jebus (Jerusalem)
Jarmuth
Adullam
Bethlehem

Medeba

Ashkelon
Libnah
Gath
Lachish
Mamre
Hebron (Kirjath-arba)
En-gedi

Jahaz

Shephelah

Gaza (Azzah)
Eglon
Kirjath-sepher (Debir)
Gerar

Kiriathaim

Dibon
Aroer

Salt Sea (Dead Sea)

Arnon R.

Raphia
Sharuhen
Beer-sheba
Arad
Hormah

Ar?

Kir-moab (Kir-haresheth)

MOAB

Rehoboth

Ascent of Akrabbim

Hazezon-tamar?

Zoar

The destroyed cities of Sodom and Gomorrah are believed to be beneath the shallow waters of the Dead Sea which now cover the Vale of Siddim (shaded portion).

Wilderness of Zin

Brook Zered

Bozrah

Oboth

EDOM

Kadesh-barnea (En-mishpat)

Punon

River of Egypt

Besor

Gerar

Arabah

Mt. Seir

offered the third refusal, and the Israelites had their baptism of blood and, with the Lord's help, were victorious (Numbers 21:24-26).

It might be well for us at this point, while the Children of Israel are preparing to strike for their new home in the Promised Land, to revisit Canaan to learn some very interesting things about its history and its ancient life.

THE YEARS between the two World Wars, and the postwar years until the upsurge of Arab nationalism, provided a most fortunate period for archaeologists working in Palestine. Comparatively stable conditions and easily acquired permits to dig made possible the uncovering of a more detailed picture of human evolution, especially in prehistoric times, than in any other area in the world.

The caves with which the Holy Land abounds began to be searched in the early 1920s, and the floors and terraces in front of many of them proved to be happy hunting grounds. The skeletons of their inhabitants, the stone tools these people made and used, the bones of the animals they either consumed as food or fought against, even the ashes of their fires have been subjected to the closest scrutiny. The result is that we now have a pretty good idea of what life was like in that land

bridge between Asia and Africa during that long span of time when glaciers had much of the northern hemisphere in their icy grasp, before man took up agriculture and began to live in houses and behind protecting city walls.

Arrowheads and spearpoints reveal the countless ages during which these very early men and women subsisted through hunting. There were also fishhooks; some of their tiniest flints were probably fish "points," similar to those used by certain of the North American Indians. But the impression is that fish was not important as an item of diet.

Toward the latter part of this prehistoric period, sickles began to appear. They were skillfully made from deer ribs and other long and, preferably, curved bones. Slotted on the concave side, they were inset with a series of short, sharp flints to form a blade. With these sickles prehistoric men probably reaped wild grain. Later, as they moved slowly from hunting into agriculture and learned to till and seed the earth and domesticate animals, they undoubtedly used these same sickles to reap grain which they had grown.

From archaeological diggings we also know that over the centuries the climate of this land bridge varied widely. In ages when certain animal bones predominate, such as those of

Palestine in Profile

EAST-WEST SECTION

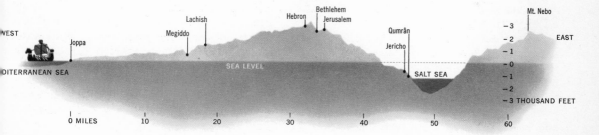

NORTH-SOUTH SECTION

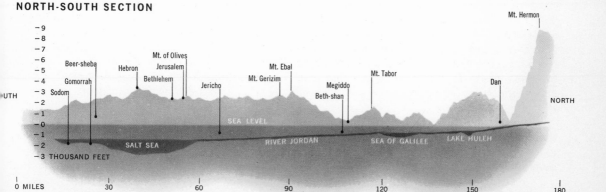

Walls of Jericho constructed of unbaked brick dating from sixteenth and fifteenth centuries B.C., already decaying when the Hebrews assaulted them c. 1250 B.C.

ligious forms and observances, attempted civil government and extended trade.

Stone tools gave way to those of copper. These later gave place to bronze and, after the Israelite conquest of this land bridge following the Exodus, to more effective iron. Garments made of woven goods replaced those of animal hide, and permanent homes replaced shelters of a more temporary sort, even though the fringe of the population in Palestine has continued to live in tents and caves down into modern times.

Progress was also made in the production of pottery; improvement in kind, form, size, decoration, and particularly in baking gave it wider use and greater permanence. Of the various artifacts which have come down through the ages, pottery has proved to be the most frequent and most useful means of locating man in the scale of time and progress. And since life came to be concentrated in cities, their ancient sites, called tells, have proved to be rewarding spots for archaeologists seeking to learn about man as he moved more rapidly toward the beginning of written history.

Fortunately Palestine has some very early city sites, and the most ancient of those that have been investigated is one whose name is widely known — Jericho. However, its fame has to do principally with its recorded destruction, rather than with its long and highly interesting period of occupancy.

Early Canaanite city builders usually sought a knoll or hill convenient to a spring and to a clay pit or limestone outcropping. With water from the spring, they molded bricks of the clay and made mud mortar with which to lay them. They used the same kind of mortar to build walls of stone broken from the limestone ledge. Jericho was just such a site, lying about nine miles northwest of the place where the River Jordan empties into the Dead Sea. Very primitive men had lived on this site during the Stone Age and were among the earliest groups that organized for city life. Their first efforts were pitiably crude in many respects, but in time those who followed them did make progress, although the city was destroyed a number of times during its long life, perhaps by earthquakes, which are sometimes severe in this trenchlike valley. The modern city of Jericho is, therefore, quite distinct from the city which bore that name in early Bible times.

Archaeological diggings have shown that

the gazelle, it is safe to believe that the rainfall was light and the area quite dry. But by contrast there were periods when not only the elephant but the rhinoceros, hippopotamus and crocodile were numerous. In such times the rivers and marshes must have contained plentiful water throughout the year.

At long last, when man did begin to gather his grain and bray it into coarse flour with a crude mortar and pestle, and to tame animals, he also began to move out of his caves, into tents or other types of shelter, and finally into permanent houses. As he learned husbandry and could obtain greater sustenance from it than from hunting, his numbers began to increase. Then, where he had once had to protect only his hunting rights against others of his kind, he now had to protect his fields, creatures and home. Life grew more complicated, as many bits of evidence tend to show: pins made of bone appeared, clearly indicating that man had begun to cover his nakedness with some sort of garments.

Actually, beginning perhaps nine or ten thousand years ago, man began to take some giant steps. He grouped his houses into communities — building cities — and developed reeach time ancient Jericho was destroyed it was rebuilt upon its ruins. Its knoll or hill grew higher and higher with each level, and when the city was finally abandoned its site formed a great mound, or tell, from which all surface indications were eventually obliterated by time and weather. In fact, nature's work was so complete that the Jericho tell was long thought to be merely an eighty-foot-high pile of worthless refuse, and simply not worthy of investigation. Even some of those who first delved into it came to this conclusion and nearly ruined it for systematic examination. But when it began to be properly opened up in 1929, it yielded one of the most complete and valuable records of life in early Canaan yet uncovered.

Some of Jericho's layers of occupancy just above bedrock reach back as far as nine or ten thousand years. In its lowest strata was found ample evidence of the long apprenticeship man served in the school of experience while learning to bake lasting pottery. There, too, were found the remains of some of his earliest shrines and of figurines used in his rituals. These were perhaps not too unlike the images which Rachel, centuries later, took from her father's house and hid in the saddle of her camel when her husband, Jacob, hurriedly left Padan-aram with all his family, camels and flocks (Genesis 31:19, 34).

Well over five thousand years ago Jericho began to increase in size and importance, for the walls were expanded to enclose as much as four acres. Influences also began to appear which are thought to have been Babylonian, evidence of interchange with that land nearly a thousand miles away. The houses and grain silos grew larger and more numerous, and for a period of five hundred years or more Jericho seems to have enjoyed peace and a measure of prosperity and progress.

Then, about 2500 B.C., the city was completely destroyed, but by what means is uncertain, although fire was an accompaniment. Some believe its destruction was the result of a violent earthquake, while others believe it was due to war. However, this much is certain: the city was begun anew and, while the walls and houses were more soundly built, the latter were much smaller and more crowded. Evidently the population had increased. This may have come about because those who formerly had lived outside the walls had experienced the ravages of an invading army and now demanded the protection of the thick, double ramparts.

While Jericho was gaining in size and importance other major cities also were growing up in other sections of Canaan. Notable among them was Beth-shan, in the Plain of Jezreel west of the Jordan. Its eighteen distinct periods reach far back to primitive conditions in the times of the painted-pottery people. It was a strategic military center, dominating that whole area long before history was written, for it controlled both east-west and north-south caravan routes that ran close by.

Another important ancient city standing beside a trade thoroughfare was Megiddo, in the vale through which flowed the main traffic between Mesopotamia and Egypt. While probably not quite as old as Jericho, Megiddo, like Beth-shan, became an organized community as early as 3500 B.C. It was to achieve its

Canaanite scarabs from Tell Beit Mirsim, 1780-1580 B.C., centuries before the Israelite conquest

greatest development during the Golden Age of Solomon.

These three were major cities, in size, strength, population and general importance. Among others was Taanach, fortified with huge walls built of so-called cyclopean masonry, or giant stones filled in between with smaller rocks. It seems to have been the headquarters of a famous oracle of the goddess Astarte. Still another was Bethel, a much larger but not nearly so strategically located city as Jebus (Jerusalem), a few miles to the south. A third was Beth-shemesh, west of Jebus. It was a rich city, as its fine pottery, jewelry and weapons testify, and was the site of a conflict in ancient times between two cultures — between East and West — the same conflict that still plagues this area today.

One of the largest of the ancient cities of Canaan whose ruins have been studied must go nameless, for nothing unearthed there indicates what it was called long ago, and it presumably missed mention in Bible text. It is the Tell el-'Ajjûl, or "mound of the little calf," one of three city sites in the long wadi which empties into the ocean just below modern Gaza. Despite the fact that it cannot be identified, it was a thriving place in ancient times — perhaps the former site of Gaza — and covered about thirty acres. This was really a large city,

three times the size of David's Jerusalem and at least twice that of Megiddo.

While most native Canaanites made their homes in protected communities by the seventeenth or sixteenth century before the beginning of Christian times, not all the people lived within city walls. Some of these places were relatively small, little more than fortified settlements; the king and his officers and courtiers lived within the walls, while the common people lived in squalor in wattle huts built outside the parapets. Other places quite frankly were fortresses, not only for protection of pioneer areas, but in many instances for the collection of tolls from passing caravans. Such was Gerar, near which Abraham once lived in the "south country" between Gaza and Beer-sheba (Genesis 20:1). It evidently controlled a well-traveled route, and the men and animals that waited beneath its walls while the toll was collected must have been legion, for the trench worn by their feet over the years is a deep one.

When the Canaanites were hunters they lived on meat, but as they took up agriculture they became primarily vegetarians. In the storage bins at Jericho have been found remnants of their cereal crops, a few grains each of millet and barley, a few pealike lentils, together with the residue of grapes. There were stone winepresses, too, scattered through the hill coun-

Egyptian wall painting from the time of Abraham showing a caravan of Semitic people

A figurine of Astarte, goddess of fertility, ninth century B.C., *whose worship tempted the Israelites in Canaan for centuries*

try. Surely there was familiarity with figs, dates, olives and a variety of other fruits which man first had gathered wild and then slowly brought under cultivation.

Flax seems to have become a staple crop, as in Egypt, and was used for clothing, as was the wool of sheep. Certainly shearing must have been a far easier task after hard bronze knives, which could be ground to a reasonably keen edge, came into rather general use. Goat's hair was also much used for making cloth, and later camel's hair. However, the camel was not common in Canaan until toward the time of the Exodus of the Israelites from Egypt. Although clothing from this period has not been found in Canaan, we know from tomb paintings in Egypt how people in early Canaan dressed. There, in the crypt at Beni Hasan, is the now world-famous sketch of a Semitic family of about the time of the patriarchs, which gives a fair impression of clothing as well as arms, gear and pack-bearing animals in the second millennium before the Christian era.

Life was certainly not humdrum. Man had his lighter moments. He wrestled for sport in Egypt, he ran races there, and almost certainly did so in Canaan too. He had time for music, even from very early days, for deep down in the tell at Jericho were found bone flutes on which he could play a tune. That he danced is very probable, expressing rhythm not only with his feet but also with his hands, as he clapped them together.

Ancient man in Canaan also found time for expression in various art forms. In the Middle Bronze period his efforts were still rather crude; he leaned heavily upon Egypt for ideas, and many of his attempts were rather sketchy copies of the exquisite productions from that ancient civilization to the south. As a craftsman, he was far less dexterous and skilled than the Syrians and Phoenicians to the north. He was a husbandman, a grain grower, the tender of small herds and flocks, and not much of an artisan. Toward the end of the Bronze Age he became familiar with writing — not with just one single system, but with four, and perhaps five, separate systems. They were the wedge-shaped cuneiform writing used in Mesopotamia; the pictorial Egyptian hieroglyphs; a modified cuneiform alphabet perfected in Ugarit far to the north; a rather transient syllabic script used for a time in Byblos in Phoenicia, the city from which comes our word *Bible;* and also a linear alphabet (one which is written, rather than drawn, or impressed) from which, via Hebrew, come our own Greek and Roman characters.

Archaeological evidence proves that Canaan was a fairly civilized land by the year 1300 B.C. when it came under the control of Egypt. The Hyksos had passed through Canaan en route to the conquest of Egypt, and had sought refuge in the cities on that land bridge when at last they had been routed out of the land along the Nile. To avoid another such invasion the Theban princes who had returned to the Egyptian throne felt need of a buffer state; and that is precisely what they made of Canaan.

It was not an unkind fate. Before the Egyptian occupation Canaan had often been ravaged, but after it came under the Egyptian yoke some degree of protection from attack seems to have been given the many little city-states that dotted the country. They were not leveled and rebuilt with such great frequency. In another way, as the remains of its ancient centers of population indicate, Canaan did pay for this overlordship. Prosperity slowly waned, and by the time the Israelites came into the Promised Land much of the area's former vitality was spent.

4. The Founding of Israel

After the years of wandering in the wilderness, Moses had led his people north beyond Edom, circled east to avoid battle with the Moabites, but finally had struck a blow at King Sihon of the Amorites. The armed seizure of a homeland had begun here well to the east of the Jordan. Quickly following up this first success, the Israelites pushed north and were soon masters of Gilead and Bashan, the whole area on the east side of the deep Jordan Valley and the Sea of Chinnereth (Galilee). It was a well-watered, fertile and satisfying land, with woods and good pastures.

This swift conquest brought terror to the people of Moab and Midian, lands to the south. Balak, the Moabite king, fearing the Israelites might now turn against him, decided to use magic and trickery. Joining with the Midianites, he hired the arch diviner Balaam to curse the Children of Israel. But King Balak failed; the Lord intervened and changed Balaam's curses into blessings (Numbers 22-24).

So, too, did the women of Moab and Midian fail in their attempts to encourage idolatry among the people of Israel. The only result was that the Midianites were slaughtered in great numbers, while the Moabites, whom God refused Moses the right to attack — they were descendants of Lot, Abraham's nephew — were excluded from the congregation of Israel to the tenth generation.

The country east of the Jordan was now secure and open to settlement. Arrangements for dividing and settling this land were completed between Moses and the tribes of Reuben and Gad and the half tribe of Manasseh. (The original tribe of Joseph had become two half tribes under his sons Ephraim and Manasseh.) The future of the rest of the Twelve Tribes lay in the lands west of the Jordan.

And what of Moses, old by now in years and experience, but still young in spirit and ability? Since God had denied him the right, as He had Aaron, to enter the Promised Land, his task was virtually ended. One duty still remained. It was essential he give an account of his great stewardship and review the laws ordained by God for His people's guidance. So, calling the leaders and the people together at the base of Mount Nebo (Pisgah), he addressed them in three great orations which make up the major part of the Book of Deuteronomy, the Greek name of which means the Second Law.

Having completed his instruction, this grand old man added his farewell song and his parting benediction. Then, turning up the slope of the mountain, which lies about ten miles east of the mouth of the Jordan, he made his way to the summit. From its top there is a breath-taking view of the land of Israel, and his eyes feasted upon the scene as he communed with the Lord, whom he had served so well. And his heart, like his life, now being full, he died there on the heights of Pisgah. So that his remains would be safe from heathen hands, he was secretly buried close by in a sheltered valley.

Not far to the north of Mount Nebo lay the trail which dropped down from Heshbon, the former capital of the Amorites, to the ford of the Jordan, about six miles east of Jericho. The trail then climbed up to Jebus (Jerusalem) and pushed on west through the city of Gezer to Joppa on the Mediterranean. The Israelites' camp was presumably near this highway in the flatlands known as the Plains of Moab. As had been their custom ever since the day God gave them the tenets of their faith at Mount Sinai, the Twelve Tribes camped in the formation of a great square. There were three tribes on each side, and in the center rested the sacred Ark of the Covenant, housed in a beautiful tent called the Tabernacle.

The valley of the River Jordan

With Moses dead, Israel acquired a new leader, Joshua, a prince of the tribe of Ephraim, a brave soldier and a clever strategist. He and Caleb, prince of the tribe of Judah, had been the only two of the twelve scouts sent into Canaan thirty-nine years before who had favored making an attack at that time. Now the moment to strike was at hand. The Lord had but to speak to Joshua's heart and

he would lead the way. Instructions were thus given the people to be in readiness for the march. Scouts were dispatched to Jericho to gather information; and, pending their return, Joshua bided his time.

The report of these scouts, not only in regard to this first large city but also with respect to the fear engendered throughout the land, was so favorable (Joshua [Josue] 2) that Joshua

THE CONQUEST OF CANAAN

Copyright by C.S.HAMMOND & CO., N.Y.

Scale of Miles

0 5 10   20   30   40

Perennial Rivers ⌇⌇⌇⌇   Seasonal Rivers & Streams ⌇⌇⌇

Route to the Promised Land ....

Israelite Campaigns ....

Israelite Expansion & Settlement ....

Capitals ....

The Great Sea
(Mediterranean Sea)

HITTITE EMPIRE
Ubi

Joshua defeated the allied kings of northern Canaan at the battle by the Waters of Merom.

Joshua occupied the hill country of central Canaan without recorded resistance.

The Gibeonites, fearing destruction, made a cunning peace treaty with the Israelites.

After the fall of Jericho, Joshua conquered the fortress cities of the league of Amorite kings.

Before he died, Moses led the Israelites to victory east of the Jordan.

BASHAN
(KINGDOM OF OG)

Damascus

Sidon
Zarephath
Tyre
Kanah
Laish (Dan)
Kedesh
Misrephoth-maim
Achzib
Accho
Hazor
Merom
Achshaph
Chinnereth
Madon
Karnaim
Ashtaroth
Shimron
Jokneam
Dor
Megiddo
Mt. Tabor
Taanach
Ibleam
Dothan
Sochoh
Beth-shan
Pella
Jabesh-gilead
Mahanaim
Edrei
Ramoth-gilead
Tirzah?
Shechem
Mt. Gerizim
Succoth
Penuel
Ham
Aphek
Ono
Tappuah
Adam
Joppa
Lod
Beth-horon
Bethel
Beeroth
Gezer
Gibeon
Chephirah
Ekron
Kirjath-jearim
Ai
Jericho
Gilgal
Jazer
Rabbath-ammon
Makkedah
Azekah
Libnah
Jarmuth
Jebus
(Jerusalem)
Bethlehem
Plains of Moab
Mt. Nebo
(Pisgah)
Heshbon
Ashdod
Gath
Adullam
Ashkelon
Beth-zur
Mamre
Hebron
Medeba
Jahaz
Gaza
Eglon
Lachish
Debir
En-gedi
Kiriathaim
Kir-moab
(Kir-hareseth)
Dibon
Aroer
Gerar
Arad
Ar?
Raphia
Sharuhen
Beer-sheba
Hormah
MOAB
Rehoboth
Zoar
Bozrah
Ascent of Akrabbim
Kadesh-barnea
Oboth
EDOM
Punon

The Great Sea (Mediterranean Sea)

Plain of Sharon
MT. CARMEL
Kishon R.
Canaanites
Sea of Chinnereth (Galilee)
Yarmuk R.
Jordan River
Gileadites
Jabbok R.
Hittites
Ajalon
Jebusites
KINGDOM OF SIHON
AMMON
Salt Sea (Dead Sea)
Arnon R.
Hittites
Canaanites
Amalekites
Kenites
Wilderness of Zin
Brook Zered
MT. SEIR
Arabah
River of Egypt
Gerar
Besor
Sidonians (Phoenicians)
MOUNT LEBANON
Leontes R.
MT. HERMON

The shofar, or ram's horn, ceremonial instrument of the kind blown before the walls of Jericho

acted immediately. The camp was struck; the tribes formed into their accustomed marching order (Numbers 2:34) and, following the priests who carried the sacred Ark of the Covenant, they started forth. At this place the trail drops rapidly to the floor of the Jordan Valley, so the east bank of the river must have been reached easily before nightfall. There camp was pitched again; the people rested while Joshua prepared to ford the stream and to set up a base camp beyond it from which the attack on Jericho would be launched.

These preparations appear to have consumed three days. On the afternoon of the third the officers passed through the camp giving instructions for the morrow. The crossing of the Jordan, like the crossing of "the Red Sea," would be a memorable day in Israel's history — and here it was upon them. The following morning they would enter the Promised Land!

It was early April, for the Passover season was at hand, when the Israelites paused on the eastern bank of the Jordan. What year was it? There is still disagreement as to the time of the destruction of the older city of Jericho and the beginning of its long abandonment; a date not far from 1250 B.C. is probable.

There was, of course, the River Jordan to ford. The stream, swollen with melting snow water as it is each spring, was overflowing its banks. In spite of this a crossing was made — though the miracle of the dry riverbed (Joshua [Josue] 3:14-17) may well have been the result of a landslide upstream, touched off by an earthquake. There are on record a number of phenomena of this kind resulting from earth temblors and bringing about a temporary damming of the stream, one of them as late as 1927.

Once across the Jordan the Israelites established a permanent camp at Gilgal. This place seems to have been halfway between the river and Jericho, their first military objective, and all the old people, women and children remained there in safety while the fighting men went out to conquer the land.

Before the campaign started, solemn religious observances were held at this base camp, which was consecrated as holy ground and remained a sacred center until at least the early years of the kingdom. Troops from the tribes of Reuben and Gad and the half tribe of Manasseh assembled there, too, for they had agreed to aid with the conquest of the remainder of the land (Joshua [Josue] 4:12).

Jericho, as the well-known Bible account relates, fell quickly, utterly and also miraculously, even though another temblor may have hurled its double walls to the earth. The manner in which their remains are scattered indicates that an earthquake may have been the means the Lord selected to aid His Chosen People. It also could have touched off the fire that consumed this oldest city of Canaan.

What now lay ahead? Able strategist that he was, it hardly seems probable that Joshua merely meant to smash his way into and through Canaan. His fighting men had gained valuable experience in the encounters east of the Jordan, but still they could not hope to sweep all before them. So scouts such as those that had visited Jericho were sent to gather data on which to base the campaign. There were the opinions of sharp-eyed caravan men to be sought and weighed. The land, its cities, mountains, valleys and people had to be studied.

The first move beyond Jericho may have been by way of the trail used by Lot, centuries before, when he parted from Abraham and sought a home in the fertile area around Sodom and Gomorrah. The Israelites were now moving in the opposite direction, climbing up the steep path toward Bethel and Ai, thirteen miles west of Jericho and 3200 feet higher.

According to the Bible, there was first a defeat and then a victory at Ai. However, the sites of both Ai and Bethel have been very carefully unearthed and we know that Ai was destroyed much earlier than Joshua's time, about 2200 or even 2400 B.C., and never rebuilt. Its very name, ha-'Ai, means "the Ruin." On the other hand, archaeological evidence tells us that Bethel — about a mile and a half away — was reduced to burned rubble about the time of the Israelite invasion. Its overthrow very likely provided their first foothold in the central highlands.

The Canaanites now knew they were in for trouble. The tactics of the crafty Gibeonites; whose cities stood close to Bethel, clearly indicate as much. Knowing that they were next in line of attack, they sent emissaries to the Israelites. These men, dressed in rags and pretending that they were exhausted from the "very long journey" from their "far country," tricked the leaders of Israel into swearing a solemn oath that they would live in peace with them and act as their protectors (Joshua [Josue] 9).

As shepherds and nomads, the Israelites would have been most interested in those sections of Canaan — the highland areas — which were best adapted to the pasturing of flocks. Two tribes and part of a third had already decided to settle in the grazing lands to the east of Jordan, but about three quarters of the people still had to find homes.

Joshua turned his attention next to the confederacy of the five Amorite kings who made war against his ally, the city of Gibeon. Israelite forces had returned to the base camp at Gilgal, but, receiving an urgent plea from Gibeon, they made a forced march to that city, present-day el-Jib, about five miles north of Jerusalem. There, and in the Vale of Ajalon to the west, the sun stood still and the moon stayed — long enough for a decisive battle to be won by the Israelites with heavenly aid. The five enemy kings were hung on five trees. Joshua and his men then took the city of Makkedah, where the five kings had hidden, and went on to take Libnah (Joshua [Josue] 10).

The next encounter, as they moved southwest through low rolling hills known as the Shephelah, was at the ancient, wealthy city of Lachish. This place seems to have fallen to Joshua and his forces about the year 1230 B.C., according to archaeological remains dug up on the city site at Tell ed-Duweir.

After they had taken Eglon and Hebron, Debir was the next objective, and there are two separate accounts of its fall (Joshua [Josue] 10:38-39 and 15:15-17, and Judges 1:11-13). Now known as Tell Beit Mirsim, or "the mound of the house of the fast camel driver," it has yielded a wealth of evidence concerning the life of olden times and the dating of its capture a number of years before 1200 B.C.

Other places in this same section, such as Beth-zur, also give evidence of having changed hands at the close of the Late Bronze Age, and so indicate that some important Canaanite towns did fall to these invaders. Israel also gained a footing in the southern highlands, although that campaign may not have been the whirlwind affair the Bible intimates.

A second and somewhat larger league of Canaanite kings then sought to stop the inroads of the Israelites. They assembled their forces in the upper Jordan Valley under the command of King Jabin. There, by the Waters of Merom, a battle took place in which the Israelites were eminently successful.

Joshua then went on to take the capital of this northern confederacy, a city called Hazor which lay hard by. When a careful archaeologist, writing about its recent excavation, speaks of it as a big city, he is far from exaggerating. Its built-up area of some two hundred acres made it by far the largest center of population in the Canaan of its day, and ten, twenty or more times as large as any other fortified place.

While the list of Joshua's conquests is impressive, it is frankly admitted in the Bible that all of Canaan was not immediately subdued. Yet so many cities now had been conquered that the remaining tribes could divide the land west of the Jordan among them. Territory also had to be provided for the half tribe of Manasseh, which had left Gilead and Bashan. With this accomplished it was then safe to remove the women, children, old people, and herds and flocks from Gilgal, and the camp was abandoned.

The areas assigned to the tribes by the drawing of lots, ranging from north to south, were roughly as follows: Asher received a coastal strip of rich green plains, about twelve miles wide, stretching from the Leontes River above Tyre to the upper edge of the Plain of Sharon below Mount Carmel. The tribe of Naphtali was given an adjoining piece of land, hilly but fertile, running south from the Leontes to Mount Tabor and east to the upper Jordan River and the Sea of Chinnereth. Below these two was the small tract which fell to Zebulun, and east of it was the area, about equal in size, which became the land of the tribe of Issachar.

To the south of this lay a large, very irregular-shaped block stretching from the

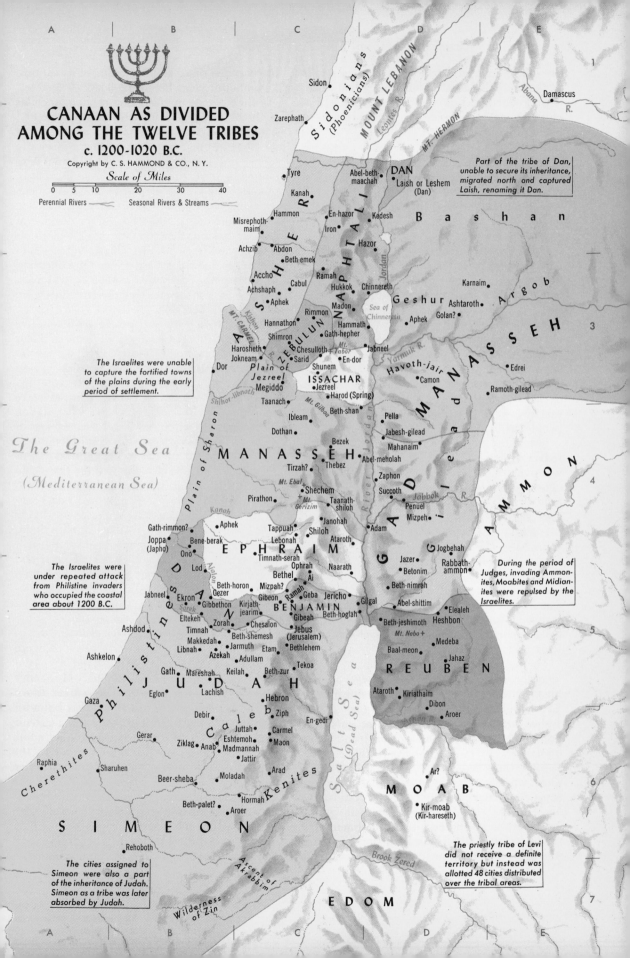

CANAAN AS DIVIDED AMONG THE TWELVE TRIBES
c. 1200-1020 B.C.

Copyright by C. S. HAMMOND & CO., N.Y.

Scale of Miles

0   5   10   20   30   40

Perennial Rivers ——   Seasonal Rivers & Streams ——

Part of the tribe of Dan, unable to secure its inheritance, migrated north and captured Laish, renaming it Dan.

The Israelites were unable to capture the fortified towns of the plains during the early period of settlement.

The Israelites were under repeated attack from Philistine invaders who occupied the coastal area about 1200 B.C.

During the period of Judges, invading Ammonites, Moabites and Midianites were repulsed by the Israelites.

The cities assigned to Simeon were also a part of the inheritance of Judah. Simeon as a tribe was later absorbed by Judah.

The priestly tribe of Levi did not receive a definite territory but instead was allotted 48 cities distributed over the tribal areas.

The Great Sea
(Mediterranean Sea)

MOUNT LEBANON
Leontes R.
MT. HERMON
Abana R.
Damascus

Sidon
Sidonians (Phoenicians)
Zarephath
Tyre
Kanah
Hammon
Misrephoth-maim
Achzib
Abdon
Beth-emek
Accho
Achshaph
Aphek
Cabul

ASHER

Abel-beth-maachah
En-hazor
Iron
Hazor

DAN
Laish or Leshem (Dan)

Bashan

Kedesh
Ramah
Hukkok
Madon
Rimmon
Hannathon
Shimron
Hammath
Gath-hepher

NAPHTALI

Chinnereth
Sea of Chinnereth

Karnaim
Geshur
Ashtaroth
Aphek
Golan?

Argob

MT. CARMEL
R. Kishon
Harosheth
Jokneam
Dor
Plain of Jezreel
Megiddo
Shihor-libnath
Taanach

ZEBULUN
Chesulloth
Sarid
Mt. Tabor
En-dor
Shunem

ISSACHAR
Jezreel
Harod (Spring)
Beth-shan
Mt. Gilboa

Jabneel
Yarmuk R.
Havoth-jair
Camon

MANASSEH
Edrei
Ramoth-gilead

Ibleam
Dothan

Bezek
Thebez
Abel-meholah

Pella
Jabesh-gilead
Mahanaim

Gilead

AMMON

MANASSEH
Tirzah?
Mt. Ebal
Shechem
Mt. Gerizim
Pirathon

Zaphon
Succoth
Jabbok R.
Penuel
Mizpeh

Gath-rimmon?
Joppa (Japho)
Bene-berak
Ono

Aphek
Tappuah
Lebonah
Taanath-shiloh
Janohah
Shiloh
Ataroth

EPHRAIM
Timnath-serah
Ophrah
Naarath
Adam

Jazer
Betonim
Rabbath-ammon
Jogbehah

Lod
Bethel
Beth-horon
Gezer
Mizpah?
Ai
Gibeon
Ramah
Geba
Jericho
Gilgal

DAN
Jabneel
Ekron
Gibbethon
Kirjath-jearim
N

BENJAMIN
Gibeah
Beth-hoglah
Beth-nimrah
Abel-shittim

Eltekeh
Ashdod
Timnah
Zorah
Chesalon
Jebus (Jerusalem)

Makkedah
Beth-shemesh
Libnah
Azekah
Jarmuth
Adullam
Etam
Bethlehem
Tekoa

Beth-jeshimoth
Mt. Nebo
Elealeh
Heshbon
Medeba
Baal-meon
Jahaz

REUBEN

Ashkelon
Gath
Mareshah
Keilah
Beth-zur

JUDAH
Lachish
Eglon
Hebron
Ziph
En-gedi

Ataroth
Kiriathaim
Dibon
Aroer

Gaza
Debir
Caleb
Juttah
Carmel
Maon

Gerar
Ziklag
Anab
Eshtemoh
Madmannah
Jattir
Arad

Raphia
Sharuhen
Cherethites
Beer-sheba
Moladah
Kenites

Ar?

MOAB
Kir-moab (Kir-hareseth)

Hormah
Beth-palet?
Aroer

SIMEON
Rehoboth

Salt Sea (Dead Sea)

River Jordan

Brook Zered

Wilderness of Zin
Ascent of Akrabbim

EDOM

To Shiloh, the first city built by the Israelites, the sacred Ark of the Covenant was borne, to be placed in the new tentlike Tabernacle. The sons of Levi, the priestly tribe, carried the Ark, which was covered by the veil, badger skins and a blue cloth.

seacoast to the Jordan, which was allotted to Manasseh. It included the beautiful Plain of Sharon, a fertile stretch eight to twelve miles wide, famous for its scarlet anemones (the biblical "lily of the valleys") and white narcissus, or "rose of Sharon." Immediately below it were three small parcels of land which provided homes for Ephraim, Benjamin and Dan. In the days that followed, this latter tribe was unable to take over the coastal plains which made up the bulk of its allotment. The portion in the hills being inadequate, a number of its members went to the headwaters of

the Jordan, seized the city of Laish (Leshem), changed its name to Dan and settled there.

The land which fell to Judah was bounded on the north by the Vale of Sorek and a curving line from Kirjath-jearim swinging just south of Jebus (Jerusalem) and continuing to the northern end of the Salt Sea. Its southern boundary was the Wilderness of Paran. The land between stretched from the Mediterranean to the Salt Sea and was made up of a rich coastal plain, where grain flourished, a hilly section called the Shephelah, where there were fine olive groves and vineyards, and a mountain range which fell abruptly down to the Salt Sea. The tiny tribe of Simeon lived within Judah's borders in the Negeb or "south country," sharing with Judah the cities in that extreme southern part of Canaan.

One other group still remained to be cared for — the Levites, or descendants of Levi. This whole tribe had been set aside as priests and servants of God, charged with the care of the Tabernacle and the sacred Ark of the Covenant. It was given rights in forty-eight towns scattered through the lands of all the tribes.

In return for his wonderful leadership, Joshua was assigned a town of his own, Timnath-serah in the hills of Ephraim, where he died aged one hundred ten years. Before he died Joshua established a religious center at Shiloh, about ten miles to the northeast in the same tribal area. Shiloh is supposed to have been the first city the Israelites ever constructed for themselves, and it was there that they erected a beautiful new Tabernacle to house the holy Ark of the Covenant. For many years pilgrimages were made to Shiloh by devout members of all the tribes.

The Israelites rebuilt many cities after assailing and demolishing them. They were shepherds, not mechanics or artisans, and unhappily their reconstruction work was shabby, and inferior to that which they had destroyed. This warrants a few comparisons between life as it had been and as it now began to develop.

CANAAN was a land of city-states, whose kings squabbled among themselves, even during the period when Egypt kept a firm hold on the land. There was a ruling class, an aristocracy, as in Egypt, and a lower class made up of serfs who were virtually slaves. The labor of the majority was at the beck and call of the few masters, and their cities were built by forced labor to whatever standards were demanded.

By contrast, the Israelite was a relatively independent person. He respected his tribal and family loyalties; beyond these he was a free man. In Israel at this time there was no corvée, no conscription of labor. So it was that, when the Israelites went to work as a group to rebuild a city they had destroyed, they worked together just long enough to meet the minimum requirements. Once these were fulfilled each man went about his own affairs again; the result was that Israelite towns were much less sturdy and well built.

It took these shepherds several generations to advance from tent dwellers and wanderers to city dwellers. They were not able to spend much time cultivating the gentler arts of peace; there was war, from within as well as from without. After the death of Joshua, during the period of the Judges, there were invasions from the east by the Ammonites, the Moabites and the Midianites.

It was the Midianites who brought the able Gideon to fame. With God's blessing and only three hundred men, he crushed their mighty forces. For this he was offered the kingship of Israel, an honor he refused because as a devout Hebrew he felt that the Children of Israel were to serve no earthly king; they were to serve only God (Judges 6:2-40; 7; 8:1-32).

The war against the Midianites was only one of many serious problems which beset the Israelites at this time. Famine in Judah drove Naomi and her husband, among others, into the land of Moab. Left a widow, Naomi returned home with her Moabite daughter-in-law, the devoted Ruth, who, married to Boaz, was to become the great-grandmother of King David and an ancestress of Jesus.

The Ark of the Covenant, made of acacia wood overlaid with gold, was believed to contain the tablets of the Law, the Covenant between God and Israel, the pot of manna and the rod of Aaron. Above the mercy seat between the two hovering cherubim, the Presence of God was believed to dwell as He communicated with His people.

For eighteen years the Ammonites held Israel east of the Jordan in subjugation, until dislodged by a "judge," or national leader and hero, Jephthah. During another eighteen-year period the Moabites under King Eglon harassed Israel, until Eglon was dispatched by the brave, left-handed Ehud. A little later there rose the threat of a Canaanite federation; its general, Sisera, was slain and his chariot corps hacked to pieces at Megiddo by an Israelite army recruited from the northern tribes. This exploit not only made a hero of the victorious Israelite leader Barak but also a heroine of the prophetess Deborah, who had prevailed upon Barak to raise the forces to overcome the enemy host.

While these events were going on there were also internal tensions — threats against the tribe of Reuben when its members erected a memorial altar within its own territory. The most serious internal trouble came toward the end of the period of the Judges, when the Benjamites were nearly blotted out for offering protection to the wicked people of Gibeah.

All this strife came about during that period in which, the Bible tells us distinctly, there was no king in Israel and everyone did as he thought best (Judges 21:25). But the neighboring Philistines posed a new threat to the Israelite tribes, forcing them to draw closer together and to select a king. The great feats that Samson performed against them — such as slaying a thousand Philistines with the jawbone of an ass, and pulling down their temple with his bare hands — foreshadowed this threat. Another invasion of Israel was about to come.

THERE are today a good number of earnest Christians who feel that the first five books of the Bible — the Books of Moses — are little altered from the form in which Moses composed them. There is nonetheless unmistakable evidence that through extensive editing the form in which we now know them was not achieved until long after Moses' time. In recent years it has been shown beyond doubt that the people known as the Philistines did not secure a foothold in the Holy Land earlier than the twelfth century before Christ. Thus when we find mention of them in Genesis (21:32) or Exodus (15:14), their inclusion should be looked upon as the expression of a later viewpoint, and as referring rather to the Canaanitish people occupying the seacoast plains which were

later taken over by the invading Philistines.

The "sea peoples," as the Egyptians called the Philistines, apparently originated in Caphtor, which is the island of Crete. From this mountain fastness they attacked Greece and also the eastern shores of the Great Sea (the Mediterranean). A horde of them swarmed down along that coast, supported by a fleet of ships offshore, conquering and gaining strength as they went, their final objective being Egypt and its great wealth. But the Egyptians under Rameses III were prepared, and they defeated and turned back these bold raiders in the year 1188 B.C. Those who escaped slaughter retreated up the coast into Canaan and established a five-city confederacy — Ekron, Ashdod, Ashkelon, Gaza and Gath — in the plains along the seacoast between Joppa and the wilderness of the Sinai Peninsula. The episodes involving Samson and the Philistines were only a forecast of the great strife which was to come between these well-organized, hard-fighting people and the loosely knit and highly independent Israelites. Because of the Philistines, God's Chosen People would be subjected to far more severe tests from within and without during the next several generations than they had been during the period of the Judges.

The theocracy formed at Mount Sinai was proving too ideal a government for imperfect men. Also the house of the High Priest Eli at Shiloh was doomed, because of his evil sons. So God called Samuel as a seer, or prophet, that he might hold the Chosen People together. His ministrations came none too soon, for the Philistines thrust their way into Israel and gave the Israelites a severe beating in two sharp battles. In addition, they seized the venerated Ark of the Covenant and carried it off with them as a battle prize. However, this revered trophy proved the source of much trouble to the Philistines; because of it they were cursed with illness. After keeping it for seven months, they willingly returned it.

Almost with one accord the elders of Israel began to plead with their new leader and priest, Samuel, to form them into a kingdom, so that they might compete more successfully with their hostile neighbors. While an arrangement of this kind had long been the divine intention (Genesis 17:6,16; Deuteronomy 17:14-20), the king was to have been a direct representative of the Lord — neither a political symbol nor an absolute worldly monarch. What the people

were now proposing looked very much like a transfer of faith from an almighty invisible God to a visible, if imperfect, king. Samuel patiently warned of what might happen to their freedom if a ruler were placed in power, but they continued their clamor, and the Lord finally consented. The heavenly choice was made known to the prophet Samuel; it fell to a handsome, brave and tall young man of the tribe of Benjamin — Saul, the son of Kish.

Shortly thereafter Samuel met this chosen of the Lord at the little city of Ramathaim-zophim (Ramah), fifteen miles east of Joppa. There he honored and anointed him. A short while later Samuel called the people of Israel together at Mizpah, about eight miles northwest of Jebus. By casting lots, they agreed upon Saul the Benjamite as their king. While some were anything but pleased by this choice (1 Samuel [1 Kings] 10:27), enough of them did follow him to beleagured Jabesh-gilead beyond the Jordan to drive off the besieging Ammonites. Soon after this victory, Saul was formally proclaimed king of the Israelites at Gilgal.

This first king of Israel took up residence in tiny Gibeah, whose name means "height."

The little town stood on an eminence some three miles north of Jebus. The remains of this place, Saul's royal city, were unearthed in the Tell el-Fûl, which means "hill of beans," an indication that the soil, unsuited to grains, is excellent for legumes. Even the pots and bowls from the kitchen of Saul's modest little palace have come again to light. Saul's throne room was only about fifteen by twenty-four feet; the double walls of the palace fortress enclosed a space less than forty by sixty yards. Life in this Gibeah of Saul was primitive! The Kingdom of Israel had most humble beginnings.

Whatever his personal ambitions may have been, necessity demanded that Saul be a true king. One of his first official acts was to institute conscription for military service and to establish a standing army, said to have totaled three thousand men. A routine action involving a part of this force under the leadership of Saul's eldest son, Jonathan, soon touched off another war with Israel's foes to the west, and a sizable Philistine force promptly invaded the hill country and pitched its camp at Michmash. The Israelites thereupon fled, some taking refuge in the Jordan Valley, and some going even beyond that river.

In rallying his forces at Gilgal and preparing to march against these invaders, Saul, deeply worried, committed the first of two serious and costly errors. Samuel had firmly promised Saul to appear before the battle and in a special religious service entreat the Lord in behalf of His people. But for some unexplained reason Samuel's arrival was delayed, and the volunteers began to grow restless and to desert the army in alarming numbers. Faced with this crisis, King Saul usurped priestly prerogative and himself conducted the sacrifice. Thereupon Samuel suddenly appeared, berated the king for his disobedience and presumption, and prophesied that the throne would pass from both him and his family. Saul was to be deprived of establishing a dynasty.

Saul's son Jonathan, moving up from Gibeah, finally defeated the invading Philistine forces, though their weapons, fashioned of the new metal, iron, were far superior to those of the Israelites. The Philistine smiths for many years had a monopoly in the production and working of iron, and withheld their knowledge from the Israelites (1 Samuel [1 Kings] 13:19-22). One of their ancient iron-smelting furnaces has been discovered in the Wâdī Ghazzeh to the south of Gaza.

Saul's second grave error, his failure to obey God, was not long delayed. After securing the southern border of the Promised Land by defeating the Amalekites, he failed to destroy them and their possessions completely as the Lord, through Samuel, had instructed. Upbraiding the king for this disobedience, Samuel departed for his home in Ramathaim-zophim and broke off all further contact with the man he had anointed as ruler.

After a number of years Samuel was instructed by the Lord to go to Bethlehem in Judah and there select a youthful shepherd lad, David, son of Jesse, who was the grandson of Ruth, and anoint him to succeed Saul as sovereign. Thus begins a most dramatic period, related in the Old Testament in greater detail than any other equal span of years, climaxed in the Golden Age of Solomon. There were many exciting years at the outset before this shepherd boy ascended first the throne of Judah and a little later that of all Israel.

Saul, who had grown ill — "an evil spirit from the Lord troubled him" (1 Samuel [1 Kings] 16:14) — first met his successor when the lad became his armor-bearer and court harpist. David's playing and singing soothed the king and roused him from his attacks of deep despair.

David stayed at Saul's court for some time, but finally returned to his old home and to his former life as a shepherd. It was not, in fact, until he wandered upon the battlefield in the Valley of Elah and slew the Philistine giant, Goliath, with his slingshot that he and King Saul were reunited and Jonathan, the king's son, became the close friend of David. His great popularity following this heroic act soon touched off Saul's violent jealousy; and later David, although he had become by then the king's son-in-law, was forced to flee for his life.

Quite naturally he sought refuge in the southern highlands, the land of Judah, which he knew so well and where he was destined to live, sometimes with as many as four hundred followers, as a sort of Hebrew Robin Hood. On his flight he stopped to secure food and the iron sword of his victim Goliath in the little priestly city of Nob within sight of the walls of Jebus. At Gibeah Saul soon knew the direction he had taken.

From Nob David hurried on to the Philistine city of Gath, some twenty-five miles west and a little south of his native Bethlehem, seeking an alliance with Israel's enemies. In the midst of his audience with King Achish the palace servants spoke of David's fame in his own land, sowing doubts about him in the king's mind. Fearful of the king, David pretended to be crazy and was allowed to depart. He gathered supporters about him and went to live in one of the numerous caves in those limestone hills. His choice was Adullam, about twelve miles from both Bethlehem and Hebron. As Saul appeared ready to attempt his capture, and his aged father and mother would thus be in much danger, David took them to Moab — where his family had roots, as is told in the Book of Ruth — and put them under the protection of its king.

By this time David was coming to be known as a "king" himself, even by Israel's enemies (1 Samuel [1 Kings] 21:10-11). Saul did make strenuous attempts to seize him; he would gladly have destroyed David and his whole family. David, on the other hand, did not want to kill Saul. He could have slain him easily on two occasions but did not do so. Once King Saul sought a few minutes' rest in a cave in the wilderness west of the Salt Sea, in which David was hiding to escape Saul's soldiers. As the

THE KINGDOM OF SAUL
c. 1020-1000 B.C.

Copyright by C. S. HAMMOND & CO., N.Y.

Scale of Miles

0 5 10   20   30   40

Perennial Rivers
Seasonal Rivers & Streams
Capitals
Israelite Forces
Enemies of the Israelites
Kingdom of Saul at its greatest extent

The Philistines invaded Israel through the Plain of Jezreel. The Israelites were defeated and Saul slain at Mt. Gilboa.

Saul defeated the Ammonites besieging Jabesh-gilead. For his triumph Saul was proclaimed king of all Israel.

Ramathaim-zophim Home of Samuel. Saul anointed here.

Jonathan's exploits at Michmash routed the Philistines.

Encounter of David and Goliath.

David, driven into exile by Saul, finally took refuge among the Philistines and settled in Ziklag.

Saul secured the southern border of Judah by defeating the Amalekites.

The Great Sea
(Mediterranean Sea)

SYRIAN
STATES
ZOBAH
Aramaeans
Bashan
MAACHAH
GESHUR
TOB
MOUNT LEBANON
MT. HERMON
Phoenicians

Damascus
Sidon
Zarephath
Ijon
Abel-beth-maachah
Dan
Tyre
Kanah
Kedesh
Karnaim
Hazor
Ashtaroth
Achzib
Chinnereth
Accho
Cabul
Aphek
Edrei
Rimmon
Hammath
Sea of Chinnereth
Havoth-jair
Camon
Shimron
Plain of Jezreel
En-dor
Shunem
Ramoth-gilead
Dor
Jezreel
Megiddo
Beth-shan
Taanach
Jabesh-gilead
Mahanaim
Ibleam
Dothan
Bezek
Thebez
GILEAD
Shechem
Succoth
Penuel
AMMON
Shiloh
Adamah
Rabbath-ammon
Joppa
Ophrah
Lod
Bethel
Michmash
Beth-horon
Mizpah?
Geba
Heshbon
Gezer
Gibeon
Raman
Mt. Nebo
Jabneel
Kirjath-jearim
Gibeah
Medeba
Ekron
Nob
Gilgal
Timnah
Jebus (Jerusalem)
Ashdod
Beth-shemesh
Bethlehem
Azekah
Socoh
Ashkelon
Adullam
Tekoa
Keilah
Gath
Dibon
Eglon
Lachish
Hebron
Aroer
Gaza
Ziph
En-gedi
Carmel
Maon
Gerar
Ziklag
MOAB
Raphia
Jattir
Ar?
JUDAH
Beer-sheba
Kenites
Hormah
Kir-moab (Kir-haresheth)
Aroer

PHILISTIA
Canaanites
Plain of Sharon
Cherethites
Wilderness of Judah
Salt Sea (Dead Sea)
River Jordan
MT. CARMEL
MT. GILBOA
Mt. Tabor
Mt. Ebal
Mt. Gerizim
Kishon R.
Yarmuk R.
Jabbok R.
Leontes R.
Abana R.
Arnon R.
Besor
Elah
Brook Zered

Amalekites

EDOM

Gibeah, Saul's little royal city not far from Jerusalem

weary ruler rested there, David reached out and sliced a piece of cloth from the hem of his robe, as evidence that he could just as easily have cut his throat. On another occasion David and his cousin Abishai stole into Saul's camp in the hills below Hebron in the dead of night and made off with the king's own spear. When David finally came to the throne it was not as an enemy but as an Israelite estranged by Saul.

Saul's pursuit of David was so relentless that David had to take refuge among the Philistines, and as their vassal he was assigned little Ziklag as his own city. Would he be forced to take up arms in the contest then in the making between the Israelites and these able farmers, artisans and soldiers of the seacoast plains?

Jealousy on the part of certain of the Philistine princes perhaps kept David from being thrust into this very unpleasant position. As the host of Philistia marched off to the north to engage Saul, the onetime shepherd boy and his Hebrew band accompanied King Achish. However, when the army paused at Aphek, the suspicious lords of the Philistines put pressure upon their king so that David and his party were hurriedly ordered back to Ziklag.

This time Saul accepted battle in the northern Plain of Jezreel, rather than in the central

highlands. His confidence was by now badly shaken. He had totally lost contact with God and felt that he was about to suffer serious defeat, losing his throne and his life. Could he perhaps get in touch with the prophet Samuel, who had once been his friend and who was now dead?

There was at En-dor, a settlement on the Hill of Moreh to the north of Jezreel, a female soothsayer and spiritualistic medium. At Saul's orders, he was taken to visit this woman of En-dor, who conducted a séance for him at which the spirit of Samuel appeared. A voice which Saul took to be Samuel's spoke most frightening words. Israel, it said, would be badly defeated by the Philistines on the following day, and the king and his sons would be slain. Promptly Saul fell in a faint.

These words proved to be only too true.

The battle was fought on Gilboa, a northeastern spur of the highlands as they drop away into the Plain of Jezreel. There the Philistine archers raised havoc with the Israelites, who fled the field. The mighty bowmen were able to annihilate three royal princes, and a final deadly shaft lodged in the body of the king himself. Poor Saul! He had lost his Lord. He was losing his kingdom. And he was ready, if his armor-bearer would kindly take it, to give up his life, rather than fall prisoner to his foes. His youthful aide refused to strike him down, so the pathetic first king of Israel had to fall upon his own sword to end his sufferings.

The following day King Saul's head was hacked off and taken away by the Philistines as a memento of victory, while his body and the bodies of the three sons were fastened to the walls of nearby Beth-shan, now a Philistine stronghold. At night these bloody cadavers were removed secretly and given decent burial by the grateful men of Jabesh-gilead, in return for Saul's aid to their city years before.

David, the outcast, wrote that most moving lamentation for his dead friend Jonathan and his king and father-in-law, for whom he still had admiration and affection (2 Samuel [2 Kings] 1:17-27). It is one of the finest examples of ancient Hebrew poetry. In it David calls upon the people of Israel to weep for Saul and Jonathan, who he says were "swifter than eagles ... stronger than lions," and whose valiant hearts never faltered. It ends with a deep echo from his heart: How are the mighty fallen and the weapons of war perished!

Ancient cedars of Lebanon remain to this day. From these forests the kings of Tyre brought logs to build the Temple of Solomon.

5. The Kingdom of David and Solomon

While contemporary Old Testament records are lacking, the Apostle Paul, who lived about ten centuries later, tells us that Saul reigned for forty years (Acts 13:21). In the Holy Land in New Testament times records seem to have been made by writing, with a pen and ink, on papyrus or prepared animal skins. In a dry climate such as that of Egypt, papyrus and leather provided a permanent material for records, but in the damp climate of the ancient Holy Land this was unfortunately not so; papyrus and leather slowly disintegrated even when carefully stored. As Jerusalem was twice totally destroyed, and probably thoroughly sacked and pillaged on several other occasions, most early records, except the closely guarded texts of the Holy Scriptures, have disappeared.

Accurate dating during the era of Saul's kingdom is almost impossible. Paul's notation of forty years for Saul's reign may be taken in the broad sense of "one generation," which would make it considerably less than forty years. Modern chronology places Saul's reign at about 1020-1000 B.C. The chronology of Ussher, with which so many are familiar, lags some fifty years behind at this point in Bible history.

So let it be assumed that Saul became king at Gilgal about 1020 B.C., at a time when affairs in Egypt were drastically changing. The high priests of Amun had seized the reins of government. Egyptian might and prestige quickly began to crumble, and during the next century and a half while they held power this land of the pharaohs was no longer a threat to its neighbors, including Israel.

By the time David came to the throne in 1000 B.C., international affairs were relatively quiet. It is true that a few of the smaller countries nearby challenged the badly weakened kingdom that Saul had left behind, but that was because they were not at first aware of the caliber of the new leader with whom they would have to deal.

David was in little Ziklag, far to the south, when word came of the disaster in the Plain of Jezreel. His response was characteristic of many of his acts from that time on. He sought the will of the Lord and was told to betake himself to Hebron, the Hittite settlement which had become a substantial city since Abraham first camped beside it hundreds of years before. With his two wives and his six hundred fighting men and their families, he moved about twenty miles northeast into the higher country. There, in sight of the Cave of Machpelah, in which the bodies of the founders of the Hebrew nation lay, David was anointed king of Judah.

What sort of person was this thirty-year-old man? He has been called a genius and is without doubt fully entitled to that description. On his gentle side, he was a poet, and a most able one, as shown by the magnificent eulogy he wrote at the death of Saul and Jonathan and by the seventy-three psalms traditionally ascribed to him. He was a competent musician as well; with his eight-string lyre (harp) he had brought his badly confused king and master, Saul, back to moments of reason. There is little doubt that he was a composer too, and that some at least of the tunes mentioned in the titles of his psalms were his own.

On the sterner side, David proved himself a real statesman; he found Israel little more than a loose federation of tribes and made it into a stable nation, well on its way to becoming an empire. Sterner still were his soldierly qualities, which so soiled his hands with blood that the Lord finally forbade him to build the Temple that had long been his great ambition. The tremendous store of material that he gathered for this sacred structure indicates great ability in still another direction — organization and business. Ruddy, handsome, and born to

command, this former shepherd boy was indeed the chosen of the Lord (Psalms 78 [77]:70).

There were problems ahead to try his mettle, such as the refusal of the northern tribes to swear allegiance to him. Instead they proclaimed Ishbosheth (Ish-baal, "man of Baal"), one of Saul's younger sons, king of Israel, and established a capital at Mahanaim, east of the Jordan. There he ruled for two fruitless years. At the end of that time he sought to wage war against David. He and his commander in chief, Abner, were assassinated and Saul's dynasty came to an abrupt end. In the year 993 B.C. the northern tribes traveled down to Hebron and anointed David king over all Israel.

These northern clans were, in part at least, vassals of the Philistines, and one of David's first tasks was to break this stranglehold. To extend his realm through Judah to the south and secure the main highway to the east, David wished to gain possession of the little city of Jebus. He organized his forces and stormed its stout walls. In the end he captured the city by cunning. The word rendered "gutter" in some English versions of the Bible (2 Samuel [2 Kings] 5:8) probably referred to a shaft cut through solid rock which led down from inside the city to the never-failing Spring Gihon. David's forces very likely broke through into this shaft. They were then within the walls, and the city was quickly theirs. Thus did the Jebusite stronghold begin its long history as the "Holy City," venerated to this day by three great living religions: Christian, Judaic and Moslem.

Jebus now became David's stronghold, the capital of Israel, and a threat to ambitious neighboring nations. It became known as Jerusalem, the City of David. Its walls were strengthened, and other fortresses were soon erected in Judah, apparently with the Philistines in mind.

One of David's great contributions was the orderly organization of the government of the kingdom. It is probable that during his reign the first regular records were kept.

Another move which had a profound effect was the league with the Phoenicians, principally with Hiram, king of the fabulous trading city of Tyre. The Israelites still lacked mechanical skills; the Tyrians, by contrast, were talented artisans; their ability with tools could help the Israelites offset the craftsmanship of

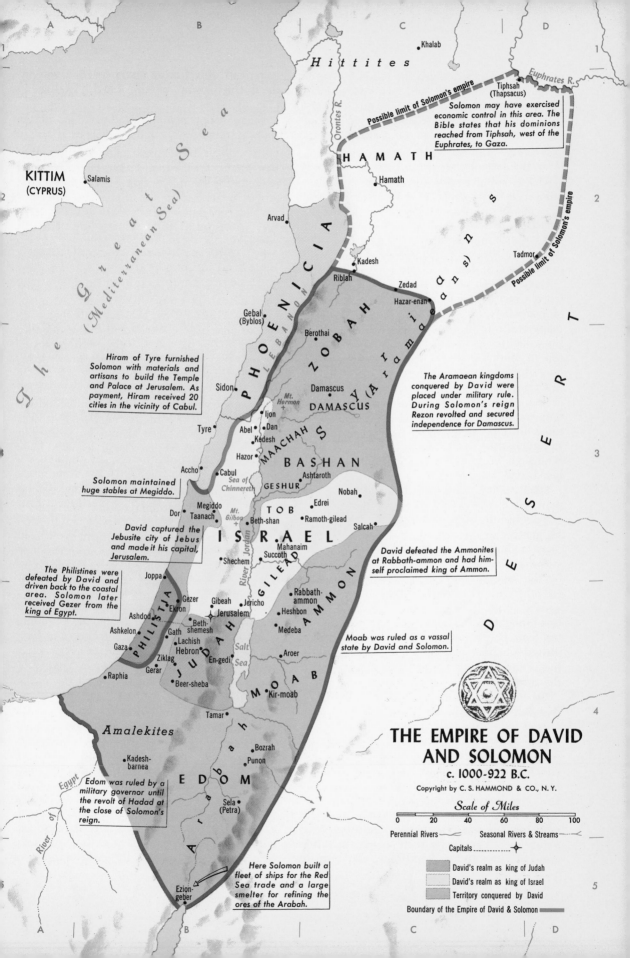

THE EMPIRE OF DAVID
AND SOLOMON
c. 1000-922 B.C.

Copyright by C. S. HAMMOND & CO., N. Y.

Scale of Miles

0   20   40   60   80   100

Perennial Rivers   Seasonal Rivers & Streams

Capitals

David's realm as king of Judah
David's realm as king of Israel
Territory conquered by David
Boundary of the Empire of David & Solomon

Hittites

Khalab

Euphrates R.

Tiphsah
(Thapsacus)

Possible limit of Solomon's empire

Solomon may have exercised
economic control in this area. The
Bible states that his dominions
reached from Tiphsah, west of the
Euphrates, to Gaza.

HAMATH

Hamath

KITTIM
(CYPRUS)

Salamis

Tadmor

Possible limit of Solomon's empire

Arvad

Kadesh

Riblah

Zedad

Hazar-enan

A   r   a   m   i   a   n   s

Gebal
(Byblos)

Berothai

Z
O
B
A
H

S
Y
(Aram

DAMASCUS

Damascus

The Aramaean kingdoms
conquered by David were
placed under military rule.
During Solomon's reign
Rezon revolted and secured
independence for Damascus.

Hiram of Tyre furnished
Solomon with materials and
artisans to build the Temple
and Palace at Jerusalem. As
payment, Hiram received 20
cities in the vicinity of Cabul.

Sidon

Mt.
Hermon

Ijon

Tyre

Abel   Dan

Kedesh

MAACHAH

Hazor

Accho

Cabul

Sea of
Chinnereth

BASHAN

Ashtaroth

GESHUR

Nobah

Solomon maintained
huge stables at Megiddo.

Megiddo

Dor   Taanach

Mt.
Gilboa

TOB

Edrei

Beth-shan

Ramoth-gilead

Salcah

I S R A E L

Mahanaim

David defeated the Ammonites
at Rabbath-ammon and had himself proclaimed king of Ammon.

David captured the
Jebusite city of Jebus
and made it his capital,
Jerusalem.

Shechem

River Jordan

GILEAD

Succoth

The Philistines were
defeated by David and
driven back to the coastal
area. Solomon later
received Gezer from the
king of Egypt.

Joppa

Gezer

Gibeah

Jericho

Rabbath-
ammon

AMMON

Ashdod

Ekron

Beth-
shemesh

Jerusalem

Heshbon

Ashkelon

Gath

JUDAH

Salt
Sea

Medeba

Moab was ruled as a vassal
state by David and Solomon.

Gaza

Lachish

Hebron

En-gedi

Ziklag

Gerar

Beer-sheba

Aroer

Raphia

M
O
A
B

Kir-moab

Tamar

Amalekites

Kadesh-
barnea

Bozrah

Punon

Edom was ruled by a
military governor until
the revolt of Hadad at
the close of Solomon's
reign.

E   D   O   M

Sela
(Petra)

River of Egypt

A
r
a
b
a
h

Here Solomon built a
fleet of ships for the Red
Sea trade and a large
smelter for refining the
ores of the Arabah.

Ezion-
geber

The Great Sea
(Mediterranean Sea)

the Philistines. The Phoenicians were the great traders of the ancient world, and they needed David's coöperation just as much as he needed theirs. So David and the people of Tyre continued to be allies. David invited them into his new city to build him a palace modestly spoken of as "a house of cedar."

At this moment of progress and peace, another matter demanded David's attention. The aggressive Philistines marched an army almost into his back yard — into the Valley of Rephaim a few miles southwest of Jerusalem. Promptly driven out, they returned a second time, only to be badly beaten; the survivors were pursued into their own land.

King David now undertook one of the most important missions of his reign; he made Jerusalem forevermore the spiritual and cultural center of Hebrew life. In a great religious procession, with joyous clamor and dancing, and with the sound of trumpets, harps, timbrels, cornets and cymbals, he brought the sacred Ark of the Covenant to Jerusalem, where a new Tabernacle had been erected to receive it. So great was the jubilation on that occasion that King David himself, dressed in a priestly garment made of linen, danced with all his might before the Lord (2 Samuel [2 Kings] 6:14).

Hardly had this been accomplished when the Philistines, growing desperate, took one final fling. This time David trounced them thoroughly and took possession of one of their royal cities, Gath. They gave little trouble from then on.

The subduing of the Philistines, however, raised disturbances in other directions. Neighboring nations, worried by the growing strength of Israel, grew tense. The Ammonites joined forces with the Syrians and attacked the Israelites. David defeated their combined armies. Moab next had to be crushed. Soon afterward difficulty arose with the land farther south, Edom. It was made a vassal state, and garrisons of Israelite soldiers were stationed throughout its length and breadth.

King David then discovered a way to great wealth — through the mines of Edom. Its iron was vital to any nation with a sizable army, while its copper, the basis of brass and bronze, was a most valuable commodity. Edom also lay in the path of trade routes from the huge Arabian peninsula. It served as a storehouse for spices and other valuables. David's allies the Phoenicians must certainly have wanted to trade with the East, and probably shared their profits with David in return for permission to cross through Israelite territory into Edom.

While King David's son Solomon would bring these business affairs to full fruit during his reign, the father very likely did far more than merely lay the foundation. The gifts David made to the Temple building fund represented an enormous fortune for those days. Since important caravan routes crossed Israelite territory, substantial tolls poured into David's coffers.

Certainly the royal establishment which came to center about David's "house" in Jerusalem (2 Samuel [2 Kings] 7:1-2) was in strong contrast to the simple court Saul had maintained at Gibeah. It was so elaborate that it began to take on the intrigue and low morality typical of the palaces of other eastern sovereigns at that period. David unhappily made his own contributions to these failings; his family had grown to include a wide assortment of wives and concubines and an array of children. As power and wealth accumulated, it was only human that there should be strife and contention in his family. David seems to have been a rather indulgent parent, and perhaps a trace too easygoing.

Also, David was growing older. The years of hardship as an outcast and outlaw were reflected in his health. As his grasp of empire and family affairs lost some of its firmness, a contest for power with his favorite son, Absalom, occurred. This handsome, agreeable and ambitious prince decided to try his wings. Other princes of that time frequently shared the throne with an aging parent, so why not he? Absalom may have been surprised at the popular support he obtained. In any event, by the time King David awoke to what was happening, Absalom and his followers were in a position to seize the government. The situation was, in fact, so serious that the sixty-two-year-old David hurriedly fled Jerusalem to escape assassination, taking refuge in the hill country east of the Jordan.

Caught off guard, with life and throne at stake, he now called forth his former sagacity and dispatch, rallied his forces, and prepared to meet the rebels headed by his much-loved son. There was a sharp encounter in a forest in Gilead in which the king, at the request of his generals, took no part. During this encounter, Absalom, caught by his long hair

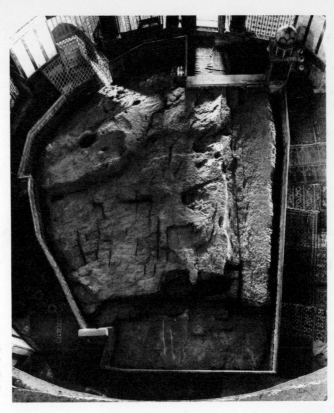

The stone threshing floor of Araunah which David bought as the base for his altar to the Lord is believed to be the rock now covered by the Dome of the Rock.

in the low-hanging branches of an oak as his frightened mule plunged beneath it, was slain by three arrows shot by Joab, David's commander in chief. The rebellion was at an end, but it took rather stern words from ruthless Joab to steady David, who, brokenhearted over the loss of his beloved son, lamented his death in words which have become immortal — "Absalom, my son, my son!" (2 Samuel [2 Kings] 18:33).

The return to Jerusalem was triumphant. Though King David was generally popular, he now had enemies who dared to oppose him openly. The following year there was another short-lived rebellion, led by the Benjamite Sheba. This uprising, crushed at Abel-beth-maachah, was one of those early expressions of the mutinous tendencies of the northern tribes which, a half century later, burst into open revolt and permanently divided Israel.

During these revolts David's martial spirit came again to the fore. His hired bodyguard, made up of valiant and mighty men of many nationalities, probably was strengthened. Also he very willfully and in opposition to his chief

officers took a military census of all the tribes. Some consider this to have been the first step in that old device of starting a war with other nations in the hope of quieting strife at home. But the Lord punished him for his imprudence; He sent a pestilence upon Israel from Dan to Beer-sheba which took the lives of seventy thousand men.

Seeing what misery he had caused, King David repented, and so the Lord stayed the hand of the Angel of Death, who, hovering over the threshing floor of Araunah the Jebusite, was about to strike the entire city of Jerusalem. In gratitude for the mercy God had shown him and his city, King David bought the threshing floor and erected an altar there. He gave the remaining years of his life to peaceful pursuits. Since the Lord had forbidden him to build the Temple, he could console himself by planning it and gathering the materials.

Illness now seized the once robust King David, old far beyond his years, and the Bible gives the impression that be became a semi-invalid confined to the palace. Once again, as when Absalom was seeking power, David's

Solomon's Temple, built by Phoenician artisans, contained the Ark of the Covenant in the Holy of Holies. Before it stood the great altar for sacrifices, and nearby the Molten Sea, the huge brass basin symbolizing the source of life. Ten lavers on wheeled stands carried water for washing utensils used for burnt offerings.

grip on national affairs slackened. Trouble followed, for he had at least two more ambitious sons.

One was Adonijah, who "exalted himself" and secretly plotted to seize the throne. Part of the court favored him, while another group headed by the prophet Nathan and King David's favorite wife, Bath-sheba, supported the latter's son, Solomon. David, it seems, had made a firm promise to Bath-sheba that this younger prince should succeed him. By skillful maneuvering Solomon was anointed king while his older half brother, Adonijah, and his supporters were celebrating an accession to the throne which never took place.

Following this coup, King David died. Then came days and weeks of intense violence; Solomon slew the leaders who opposed him, along with his aspiring half brother. For the next forty years, the throne would be his without further contest.

WHEN Solomon came into undisputed possession about 961 B.C., Israel was enjoying peace with most of her neighbors. He was called upon to subdue the city of Hamath, far to the north in Syria, and was later forced to take a firm stand with Damascus and Edom, but with these exceptions his entire reign proved to be one of uninterrupted peace. As recorded in the Bible,

all dwelt without fear, each man under his vine and under his fig tree, from Dan to Beer-sheba, all the days of Solomon (1 Kings [3 Kings] 4:25).

We do not know the exact extent of Solomon's empire to the north; it may have reached to the Euphrates. We do know what its other boundaries were. Its western line ran south along the Phoenician border as far as Mount Carmel. It then ran along the shore of the Mediterranean to Joppa, swung around Philistia south of Gaza and extended to the coast again, continuing to the wadi known as the River of Egypt. Where this river empties into the Mediterranean the boundary swung southeast as far as Ezion-geber at the head of the Gulf of Aqaba. From this port the line then stretched northeast along the edge of the Arabian Desert beyond far-off Damascus.

Because Solomon, like his father, needed Phoenician skills and trade, he renewed the league with Hiram begun some years before. While there seemed to be no special threat from Egypt, he cemented ties with that country by taking a wife from among its royal princesses. Thus did young Solomon become the son-in-law of the reigning pharaoh. Over the years Solomon would repeat this act of statesmanship many times: he would establish affinity with a land and seal the compact with a wife taken from its ruling family. During his reign he is said to have accumulated no less than seven hundred wives and three hundred concubines (1 Kings [3 Kings] 11:3). If such an estimate is accurate, his was a stupendous harem, undoubtedly the largest in all history.

Solomon's first consuming interest was to erect that Temple which his father, David, had planned but was denied permission to build. King David had designated the threshing floor bought from Araunah the Jebusite farmer as the site for the Temple. With the vast store of building materials and precious metals left by his parent, Solomon began the task without delay, employing special workmen from the city of Tyre. To build the great Temple to house the sacred Ark of the Covenant was a noble and glorious task, but to accomplish it Solomon made a move that contributed to a lasting breach in the Israelite nation. Needing an abundance of labor, he established the corvée, or impressment of the common people. They had been conscripted before in times of war and had willingly surrendered their freedom in the face of general alarm. Now to be dragged from their farms and homes in time of peace and led away for one month out of each three was bitter to them. The day of reckoning would be delayed, but it eventually came.

The Temple, built of marble, and roofed and lined with cedars of Lebanon and cypress richly carved and overlaid with gold, took seven long years to complete. Two cherubim were carved to stand guard before the Ark of the Covenant, ten gold candlesticks were wrought, and ten tables for shrewbread, and the altar for incense was constructed. A great altar of brass and a huge brass basin, the Molten Sea, had to be cast. This basin, supported by twelve great brass oxen, was fifteen feet in diameter and seven and one half feet in depth. There the priests washed their hands before sacrifices.

When all was completed, the Temple was dedicated in an impressive ceremony which is believed to have taken place in October of 950 B.C. (1 Kings [3 Kings] 8:2). This magnificent and holy building remained in continual use for about four centuries, until its destruction by Nebuchadnezzar in 587 B.C.

The "House of God" being finished, Solomon now turned his attention to more personal matters. An aristocracy had grown up, with a ruling coterie attached to the court. His own immediate household was large, and with these additional people, many of whom lived in the palace, his housing needs became acute. This is probably why he found it necessary to spend thirteen years erecting the complex of structures adjoining the Temple that made up "his own house." Also there was the planting of gardens and vineyards (Ecclesiastes 2:4-6), some perhaps at a rural retreat at Etam, seven miles south of the city, as Josephus relates, while some may have been in the high country far to the north.

In the earlier years of his reign, Solomon took considerable interest in religious matters over and above the effort expended in the creation of the Temple. He certainly assumed a most prominent part in its dedication ceremony, leading the nation in prayer and invoking divine blessing upon the assembled multitude, both of which were primarily priestly roles.

Despite manifold promises of peace, Solomon gave much attention to military preparedness. The army was maintained at full strength and kept in training, and the walls of Jerusalem were enlarged and strengthened. The breach in them effected by David's troops during its capture many years before had been only temporarily filled in; it is now believed that a tower fortress, probably the Millo of Solomon, was erected at that spot. Solomon may also have walled in the western hill of Jerusalem, as the remains of ancient stonework in that place have the character of other construction of his reign.

Whether the division of the country into twelve districts that cut across old tribal boundaries was military as well as political is not certain. The fact that they were supply districts seems to favor the view that they were part of a military plan. The greatest contribution to national defense was the fortification of several towns which were made into army posts. Best known among them was Megiddo, at the gap in the Mount Carmel ridge where the international caravan trail cut through from the Plain of Jezreel to the coastal flatlands of Sharon and Philistia on its way to Egypt.

Few ancient sites have had more thorough investigation than Megiddo. Rebuilt by Solomon, it became a most effective fortress city and the headquarters of twenty or more squadrons of his extensive chariot corps. The most interesting discovery there was the ruins of huge stables, laid out in systematic order along a broad, paved central street. The stalls were arranged on either side of paved runways which gave access to them. Each cubicle had a stone manger and a stone column, a roof support, with a hole through it for a tie rope. The stalls were most often in groups of twenty-four, which might indicate that, with two horses to a chariot, the corps was based upon squadrons of twelve chariots each. No less than four hundred fifty such stalls have so far been unearthed at this one site. The remains of Gezer, Hazor and the other fortified towns may not yield anywhere near the number of stalls needed to stable the horses for King Solomon's dashing corps of twelve thousand horsemen mentioned in the Bible; yet these ruins at Megiddo substantiate reports of a lively trade in horses with Egypt during this prosperous period (1 Kings [3 Kings] 10:26-29).

Solomon, either directly or through his associates, was soon very active in a whole array of business enterprises. Although they are merely alluded to in the Bible text, we know that his activities in this field were focused in the south. This was partly because of the wealth of minerals which could be mined in the Edomite dependency between the Salt Sea and the Gulf of Aqaba. The port of Ezion-geber at the northern end of the gulf eventually became the center of these undertakings.

There, possibly as a joint enterprise with Hiram of Tyre, Solomon built a copper smelter, a manufacturing plant and a shipyard. The smelter, most ingeniously designed and constructed, is one of the industrial wonders of the ancient world. Metal refined in it from ores partly roasted in the neighborhood of the mines was shipped either as ingots or as finished products — weapons, tools, fishhooks, nails and other goods.

There is evidence today of ancient copper-smelting operations of this sort in the Jordan Valley, in the area about Tell Deir 'allā, ancient Succoth. Wood from Bashan and Gilead, reduced to charcoal, fed the fires in many smelteries where copper was refined and fused into alloys. Molds for casting were made from the abundant native clay. It was there that craftsmen from Tyre turned out the building trim and ceremonial objects, some as large as the Molten Sea, for the Temple.

Vessels launched at Ezion-geber were engaged in trade along the shores of the Red Sea and possibly as far away as India, Ceylon and the eastern coast of Africa. The items brought home, such as spices, ivory, strange animals and incense, give a fair indication of how far these ships must have journeyed.

During this same period, the people of Tyre as well as other Phoenicians sailed through the Mediterranean, possibly venturing out into the Atlantic and up as far as the tin mines of Cornwall in the south of England. Solomon seems to have had a fleet of vessels accompanying them in trading operations in these western waters. The port of Tarshish (1 Kings [3 Kings] 10:22) may have been their most westerly port of call and is thought to have been on the island of Sardinia or in southwestern Spain outside the Strait of Gibraltar.

Overland transport of goods between Phoenician ports on the Mediterranean and the port

Model of the stables of Solomon at Megiddo

Traditionally known as "Solomon's Pools," these reservoirs bring water to Jerusalem even today. Some scholars date them 200 B.C.

of Ezion-geber serving the eastern ocean was probably quite heavy. This latter place, no doubt on the same site as the modern town of Elath, was a station on the King's Highway, and also the destination of many camel caravans coming from that huge spice chest, the Arabian peninsula. The land of Sheba, present-day Yemen, lay at the southwestern corner of this immense stretch of land, and the visit of its queen to the court of Solomon may have been for commercial as well as for political purposes.

The splendor of Solomon's court, the bounties of his table and the pomp and circumstance which evidently attended him reveal him as a true oriental potentate. Yet "Solomon in all his glory" developed two major defects.

One stemmed from the princesses he took as wives, who were principally the pledges of other monarchs held as hostages so that these rulers would keep the peace. To Hebrew eyes, these women were idolatrous heathen. Political necessity forced Solomon to erect shrines to their gods and to give the appearance of taking part in certain ceremonies with them when visiting dignitaries were at his court. For this apostasy and crass disloyalty "the Lord was angry with Solomon," and after his death the bulk of his kingdom was rent from the hands of his family (1 Kings [3 Kings] 11:9-13). In comparison to his father, David, Solomon displayed a very shallow religious spirit, casual and even opportune.

Solomon's second weakness was his excessive, sensual worldliness, expressed particularly in immoderate luxury. This imposed an onerous burden upon his subjects, the bulk of whom had but indifferent loyalty to him, and therefore weakened his kingdom. Yet the ruling clique which he had organized and placed in power was too strong and firmly entrenched for his enemies — and he had many — to hope to seize the throne during his lifetime.

So the Golden Age continued throughout his forty-year reign and brought widespread prosperity despite heavy imposts and levies. Taxes, especially heavy ones, are certain poison politically, and the king was far from being immortal. In fact, Solomon was an even younger man than his father when he died — possibly in his sixtieth year. And he had hardly been laid away "in the city of David his father" when the vengeance of the Lord, and of the outraged northern tribes, crashed down upon Jerusalem.

6. Israel and Judah

King Solomon's death marked the end of an era, followed by dramatic changes. The forty-year-old heir presumptive, Prince Rehoboam, whose mother had been an Ammonitess, was an arrogant, frivolous and stupid man. And although King Solomon had had seven hundred wives and three hundred concubines, there was no other prince with enough character and ambition to oppose Rehoboam and claim the throne.

His serious rival was Jeroboam the Ephraimite, who had at one time been Solomon's superintendent of forced labor. A prophet had forecast that this protégé of the monarch would one day be crowned king over ten of the Twelve Tribes. When this had been made known to Solomon, he had immediately sought to have this contender for honors slain. Therefore Jeroboam, like David in the days of Saul, had become an outcast, and had fled to Egypt.

The Libyan Shishak had recently seized the throne of Egypt and proclaimed himself pharaoh. He had managed to give refuge to Jeroboam without causing a breach with Solomon. Canaan had once paid substantial revenues into Egyptian coffers, and this new pharaoh surely had ambitions in that direction.

Solomon's funeral was scarcely over, and Rehoboam little more than hastily and perhaps secretly anointed king, when a call went out for all Israel to meet in solemn conclave at Shechem—yes, Shechem, not Jerusalem. The choice of this location near the tribal center of the nation foreshadowed trouble. So, too, did the speed with which Jeroboam raced home from Egypt to become spokesman for the northern tribes. Facing Rehoboam, insecure occupant of the throne, he demanded to know whether those Israelites living in the north, beyond Judah's borders, might expect more just, equitable and lenient treatment from him than they had received from his father.

The heir of the house of David stalled, and begged three days for soul-searching and consultation. The elders of Judah recommended that he promise far greater tolerance. His own friends, however, told him to be adamant. So on the third day he foolishly informed the tribal leaders gathered at Shechem that, if they thought his father had been rigorous, they might well be on their guard. He was their lawful ruler, and he intended to handle them as sternly as he knew how!

This statement was all the dissatisfied northern tribes needed to proceed with plans of their own. It was quite true that the decision had been made long since at the foot of Mount Sinai to form one indissoluble nation. But neither Rehoboam nor his father before him measured up to the high standards of royalty which had been set forth by the Lord (Deuteronomy 17:14-20). Let these people of Judah and their friends of the tribe of Benjamin go their way. The real kingdom would be built from the remaining Ten Tribes.

THE KINGDOMS OF ISRAEL AND JUDAH
c. 922-842 B.C.

Copyright by C. S. HAMMOND & CO., N.Y.

Scale of Miles

0   5   10   20   30   40

Perennial Rivers ....
Seasonal Rivers & Streams ....
Capitals ....
Egyptian & Syrian Attacks ......→

The Great Sea

(Mediterranean Sea)

In the reign of Baasha the cities of northern Israel were raided by the king of Damascus in league with Asa, king of Judah.

The Syrians waged almost constant war against Israel. They were held in check by Ahab until his death in battle at Ramoth-gilead.

The introduction of Phoenician cults following the marriage of Ahab with Jezebel caused violent reactions in Israel that eventually wiped out the house of Omri.

Samaria, fortress capital of Israel, was built by King Omri c. 870 B.C.

Elijah challenged the prophets of Baal at Mt. Carmel.

Moab was ruled as a vassal kingdom under Omri and Ahab. The Moabite Stone commemorates the victory of Mesha, king of Moab, over Israel and the return of Moabite independence.

Shishak, Egyptian pharaoh, raided the divided kingdoms, plundering Jerusalem in the reign of Rehoboam.

During the reign of Jehoshaphat, Judah regained control over Edom.

Damascus
Abana R.

Sidon
Zarephath
Tyre
Ijon
Abel-beth-maachah
Dan
Kedesh
Hazor
Accho
Cabul
Chinnereth
Karnaim
Ashtaroth
GESHUR
Sea of Chinnereth
Aphek
Yarmuk R.
Bashan
Edrei
Ramoth-gilead

MOUNT LEBANON
Leontes R.
MT. HERMON
PHOENICIA
S y r i a n s
A S S Y R I A N S

Dor
Megiddo
Taanach
MT. CARMEL
Kishon
Plain of Jezreel
Shunem
Jezreel
Beth-shan
Ibleam
Dothan
Mt. Tabor
Hammath
Havoth-jair
Jabesh-gilead
Mahanaim
Tishbe
Sochoh
Samaria
Mt. Ebal
Tirzah?
Abel-meholah
Shechem
Mt. Gerizim
Succoth
Penuel
GILEAD
River Jordan
Jabbok R.
AMMON
Rabbath-ammon

Plain of Sharon

I S R A E L

Joppa
Aphek
Zeredah
Jeshanah
Janohah
Shiloh
Zemaraim
Bethel
Jericho
Gilgal
Lod
Beth-horon
Mizpah?
Geba
Ramah
Jabneel
Gezer
Aijalon
Ekron
Gibbethon
Ashdod
Timnah
Zorah
Beth-shemesh
Azekah
Socoh
Etam
Adullam
Jerusalem
Bethlehem
Tekoa
Ashkelon
Gath
Mareshah
Beth-zur
Hebron
Gaza
Lachish
Adoraim
Z000
Debir
Ziph
En-gedi
Gerar
Ziklag
Beer-sheba
Raphia

PHILISTIA

J U D A H
Wilderness of Judah
Cherith
Mt. Nebo
Elealeh
Heshbon
Medeba
Baal-meon
Ataroth
Dibon
Aroer
Arnon R.
Ar?
M O A B
Kir-moab
(Kir-haresheth)

Salt Sea (Dead Sea)

Valley of Salt
Brook Zered

E D O M

Walls were the main defenses of biblical towns. Lachish, one of the chief cities of Judah, was fortified by Rehoboam with a second wall and a moat.

As King Rehoboam announced his fatal decision that day at Shechem, Jeroboam and his followers cried out: What further interest have we in this house of David? Our heritage is in no way dependent upon any descendant of Jesse's! To your own tents, men of Israel! And as for you, you sons of David, attend to your own affairs!

Rehoboam, faced with the immediate loss of four fifths of his kingdom, now sought to put up a bold front and a show of strength. Choosing his tax collector, Adoram, no doubt a belligerent man, he ordered him to tell the mutinous tribes what might happen to them. It was only after they had stoned this hated emissary to death that the pretentious king came to his senses. These people made it very evident they wanted no part of him. So he had his chariot wheeled out and, jumping aboard, hurried off down the highland trail to the safety afforded by the stout walls of Jerusalem. There the men of his own tribe and part of the tribe of Benjamin accepted him as head of the dominion his worthy grandparent David had at first ruled — the Kingdom of Judah.

The ten other tribes promptly proclaimed Jeroboam king of Israel; and he in turn chose their place of meeting, Shechem, as his capital. Knowing that trouble was coming, he immediately strengthened its fortifications. He was right. King Rehoboam quickly regained his courage, or perhaps his audacity; he planned war to force his former subjects back into the fold. But the Lord, through one of His prophets, ordered him to cease. The prophet said that the division of the kingdom had been ordained on high and was the penalty for his father's shortcomings, so there was no attempt at civil war.

Jeroboam, it appears, had not been a unanimous choice. Sensitive to the attitudes of many of his people, he established a second, alternate capital at Penuel, where long ago father Jacob had wrestled with the Angel of the Lord. Such a move might please the groups living east of the Jordan and also might dissuade Syrian forces, then gathering strength in Damascus, from casting covetous eyes on this area.

Now, because King Jeroboam needed religious as well as political loyalty, he took a drastic step. To counteract the Temple at Jerusalem, which acted as a magnet in drawing great numbers of pilgrims from the northern tribes, he set up shrines at two old sanctuaries at the extreme limits of his land. The first was at Bethel, about twelve miles up the trail above Jerusalem, and the other at far-off Dan, at the foot of Mount Hermon. As Aaron had done long ago at Mount Sinai, he set up at each shrine a golden calf. Addressing the people, he said that it was too far for them to go to Jerusalem, and he repeated the very words Aaron had spoken when he set up the golden calf at the foot of Mount Sinai: Behold thy gods, O Israel, which brought thee out of the land of Egypt (1 Kings [3 Kings] 12:28 and Exodus 32:4).

Heathen influences now grew stronger and, while it is true that the worship of Yahweh (Jehovah) was not completely abandoned, the people of the Kingdom of Israel, as the northern kingdom came to be called, were led more and more into the worship of false gods. Jeroboam assigned priestly duties to "the lowest of the people," so that the Levites who had served as priests now took refuge in Judah. This new throne which Jeroboam had helped to set up posed many problems.

WHILE these things were going on in the northern kingdom, King Rehoboam of Judah was compounding difficulties of his own. Despite the glorious Temple in the midst of his handsome capital, he and many of his subjects turned apostate and began setting up temple towers, idols and pagan groves throughout his land. In the fifth year of his reign, the Egyptians under Pharaoh Shishak (Sheshonk) attacked Jerusalem itself and carried off a huge amount of treasure, including some from the Temple.

Finally, after seven fruitless years, Rehoboam gave place to his son Abijam, who sat on the throne of Judah but two years and was succeeded in turn by a son of his, Asa. This resolute man was to rule for no less than forty years.

The first years of Asa's reign were peaceful, and he rid the land of much of its idolatry and other despicable practices. Even the queen mother was deposed for erecting an idol. Then, suddenly, an Ethiopian host out of Africa stormed into Judah, and only by dint of the greatest effort, and with the Lord's aid, was Asa able to drive the enemy away.

MEANTIME, in Israel, Baasha had become king by slaying Jeroboam's son Nadab after the latter had reigned less than two years. He began to fortify Ramah, within the borders of Judah, almost within sight of Jerusalem. Asa, too greatly weakened by the war with the Africans, was incapable of seizing this Israelite outpost and had to go hurriedly in search of aid. In return for a part of the remaining Temple treasures, Ben-hadad I, Syrian king of Damascus, was prevailed upon to at-

Kings of Israel and Judah

(for later kings see page 82)

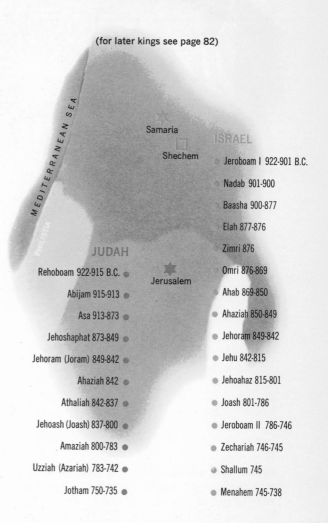

MEDITERRANEAN SEA

PHILISTIA

Samaria

Shechem

ISRAEL

JUDAH

Jerusalem

JUDAH	ISRAEL
Rehoboam 922-915 B.C.	Jeroboam I 922-901 B.C.
Abijam 915-913	Nadab 901-900
Asa 913-873	Baasha 900-877
Jehoshaphat 873-849	Elah 877-876
Jehoram (Joram) 849-842	Zimri 876
Ahaziah 842	Omri 876-869
Athaliah 842-837	Ahab 869-850
Jehoash (Joash) 837-800	Ahaziah 850-849
Amaziah 800-783	Jehoram 849-842
Uzziah (Azariah) 783-742	Jehu 842-815
Jotham 750-735	Jehoahaz 815-801
	Joash 801-786
	Jeroboam II 786-746
	Zechariah 746-745
	Shallum 745
	Menahem 745-738

tack the northern border of the Kingdom of Israel. This stopped work at Ramah and opened the caravan route to the north to traffic again.

In the years that followed, the Syrians proved to be a curse; once they had tasted the pleasure and profit of victory over the Kingdom of Israel their armies visited that land again and again.

King Baasha of Israel was no better than Jeroboam, yet he managed to retain the throne for twenty-three years. His son, the confirmed

Above: Ruins of the wall built by Omri and Ahab around the palace and courtyard at Samaria, capital of the Kingdom of Israel.

Right: The hill site of Samaria.

drunkard Elah, lasted only a year. While he was carousing, the commander of one of the two wings of his chariot corps, Zimri, slew him and took the crown. But the army proclaimed Omri, its commander in chief, as king, called off a siege against the Philistines then in progress, and hurried back to Tirzah, which was now the capital. There was a sharp tussle, and, when the palace in which he was hiding was threatened, Zimri set it afire and perished in the flames. He had ruled Israel for only one short week. Thus did three of the new nation's first five kings meet violent death.

Omri, who now ascended the throne, had already proven his military capabilities, for he had subjugated Moab during Baasha's reign. A vigorous ruler, he occupied an insecure throne during his first five years; an aspirant, backed by about half the people, proved a continuing threat. This contender finally died, and Omri, feeling a greater sense of security, set to work to give the Kingdom of Israel a completely new and permanent capital, the city named Samaria.

Excavations at its site have turned up many interesting facts. It was probably the most splendidly located city in all the land, situated as it was on a hill in the center of a beautiful valley completely surrounded by low mountains. It was a luxurious metropolis destined for long use. It served until destroyed by the Maccabees, was rebuilt by Herod the Great, and remained important well down into the period of the Crusades. The construction work of the early town was of most excellent quality, probably the work of Phoenician artisans. This testifies to the close alliance then in force between the people of the Kingdom of Israel and those of the upper seacoast, a league which would yield strange and pernicious fruit during the reign of Omri's son Ahab.

There was a league, too, with the Syrians, but whether it was voluntary or compulsory is uncertain. We know that merchants from Damascus had their own trading quarter within Samaria's walls, but it is probable that this was a concession granted under pressure. It now appears that the city was hardly completed before Ben-hadad I, with his Syrian cohorts, was again in the land. He had taken three towns in the extreme north on his previous visit, and on this second invasion he may have worked his will upon Omri.

What Damascus seems to have been especially interested in at first was control of the important trading cities and farming areas to the east of the Jordan between the river and the King's Highway. These biblical Syrians, also known as Aramaeans, had been filtering into that area and settling there. This region had been the first of the allotments made to the tribes of Israel some centuries before. Before the Israelites, there had been still earlier occupants. This important portion of Omri's realm was, therefore, a tinderbox, and hazards prompted him to make a strong alliance with the Phoenicians.

While this king of Israel was adjudged by religious standards probably the most wicked of them all, he did manage to imprint his name indelibly upon the records of some other nations. His vassals, the Moabites, remembered him all too well, while the Assyrians, looming as an immense threat off to the northeast, still called the Kingdom of Israel "the house of Omri" a century after his death.

The alliance which King Omri of Israel made with the Phoenicians was sealed by the marriage of the king of Tyre's daughter, the strong-willed, somewhat masculine princess Jezebel, to his son and heir presumptive, Prince Ahab, a marriage which would produce one of the most dramatic tales in all the wondrous Bible story. The nature of Jezebel's contributions to the affairs of the northern kingdom during her wavering husband's nineteen-year reign was such that her name even today is the

These Samarian ivories, from King Ahab's "houses of ivory" condemned by Elijah, include the famous medallion of the infant Horus, Egyptian sun god. They adorned thrones and couches.

65

The unflinching prophet Elijah pitted the power of the Lord against the heathen god Baal, whose worship was decreed by King Ahab and his pagan queen, Jezebel.

proverbial synonym for a shameless, immoral woman.

As Jezebel's regal father had first been a priest of Astarte, the voluptuous Phoenician goddess, Jezebel had grown up in a ritualistic atmosphere and had become a devoted worshiper of Baal. This pagan "master" or "lord of the earth" was also a weather god, whose right arm hurled lightning bolts, whose voice was thunder, and who, when he tore open the clouds, let life-giving rain pour upon a thirsty land. The legend concerning his death and resurrection had strong appeal for a still fairly primitive and largely agricultural people. He supposedly died with the close of spring's "latter rains," when a torrid thirsty sun began to bake and scorch the earth. Then, with the onset of the "former rains" in the fall, he came alive again and gave fertility to another growing period.

Baal worship had a colorful, impressive ritual, conducted in elaborate temples adorned with Phoenician art, and apparently enriched with what in that day passed for very stirring music. This deity, together with such female symbols of sex and fertility as the goddesses Ashtoreth, Asherah and Astarte, touched a mystic chord deep within the being of many an Israelite of both the northern and the southern kingdoms.

Even in this present day and age, our religious interests are strong or weak according to our attachment to a community or parish church. And in those early times, the nearby "high place," or local temple of Baal, in contrast to a Temple far removed from all but residents of Jerusalem, gave heathen ways a strong competitive pull in the kingdoms of both Israel and Judah.

To please his queen who swayed him so readily, Ahab built a sanctuary for Baal at Samaria, while somewhere hard by he laid out an "Asherah," or sacred grove. These desecrations did more "to provoke the Lord God of Israel" than the acts of all his predecessors on the throne. In addition, Jezebel took the law

suddenly Ahab and Jezebel were confronted by that most formidable of all men of God, Elijah the Tishbite. He was a gritty, unflinching character but much favored by the Lord. Once, during a dire drought sent as a punishment to Ahab, the Lord commanded the ravens to feed Elijah, and when the hand of the Lord was upon him he could outrun the king's best chariot horses (1 Kings [3 Kings] 17:1-8; 18-46).

There was strife at once between the royal pair and this hairy prophet clad in a girdle of leather, and it came to a dramatic climax on the summit of Mount Carmel. There Elijah pitted the power of God against that of the heathen idol Baal. Fire from heaven vindicated Elijah; it consumed his offering. Under the influence of this miracle, the people turned upon the heathen priests of Baal, and all four hundred fifty of them were killed.

When Jezebel, stunned by this setback, took a solemn oath to slay the Tishbite before the next day dawned, Elijah fled the land. He later returned to foretell the violent end of Ahab and Jezebel.

Baal, the Syrian god of thunder and lightning, from a relief at Ugarit in Syria

into her own hands and declared war on the priests of Yahweh. This indomitable creature slew every one of them she could hunt out and seize.

Another incident in which Jezebel played the principal role, and which shows how Israelite religious and moral thinking was suffering at her ruthless hands, was the dastardly affair concerning Naboth's vineyard. Ancestral property had an almost religious significance to God's Chosen People and could not be lightly parted with, whereas to the Phoenicians it was as fluid and transferable as merchandise. King Ahab, therefore, could understand why Naboth refused to sell him his vineyard, but Jezebel could not. Thinking that Naboth was being insubordinate, she was determined to get the vineyard for her husband. She had Naboth falsely accused of blasphemy against "God and the king" and then caused him to be stoned to death (1 Kings [3 Kings] 21:1-14).

Such shocking disregard for Israelite ways could not be allowed to go unchallenged, and

7. Damascus, the Warring Neighbor

Just how many kings of Damascus called Ben-hadad appear in the Bible is uncertain; there were at least four. The name means "son of Hadad," a deity familiarly called Baal and the counterpart of the Assyrian Rimmon, both gods of rain and storm, of thunder and lightning. These Syrian, or Aramaean, monarchs were the descendants of wanderers from the Syrian desert who had eased their way into the plains and hill country running south from the base of Mount Hermon as far as the valley of the Yarmuk. There they had sunk their roots and ceased their roving, and had grown ambitious and envious of their neighbors. The number of peoples with similar characteristics and tendencies which the land bridge has harbored since the beginning of recorded history is considerable.

The first of the kings of Damascus to be mentioned in the Bible was the contemporary of Baasha of Israel and Asa of Judah. We have seen how he harried the first, when rewarded by the latter. Since he seized the towns of Ijon and Abel-beth-maachah and the shrine at Dan, and ravaged the area west of the upper Jordan, the Syrian invasions technically begin with this Ben-hadad I.

The kings of Damascus were thorns in the sides of both Israel and Judah during quite a long period. Ahab was harassed by them for a number of years, but then suddenly a victory was his. He met Ben-hadad II's forces at Aphek in Bashan and, while the Syrian host covered the country on every side and the soldiers of Israel were only like "two little flocks" of kids, the Israelites won the battle (1 Kings [3 Kings] 20:25-30).

Yet Ahab dared not pursue the enemy, slay his chief adversary and cut his army to pieces. There was just then the threat of trouble from beyond Damascus, and from a foe so much more potent than the Syrians that discretion outweighed any desire to take complete advantage of his success. Ahab's army and people took strong exception to their king's next act and one of the prophets berated him harshly. Yet it was among his sanest moves. He made a quick, earnest peace with his opponent, Ben-hadad II, entered into a covenant with him and sent him home as a friend.

Ahab's diplomatic maneuver was not accomplished one moment too soon, for word now came, probably rushed down over the caravan trails, of dismaying happenings to the north, involving that foe beyond Damascus. The Assyrians ruled vast tracts of land to the north and east of the Syrians. Their king, Shalmaneser III, had attacked Carchemish, the capital of a Hittite kingdom on the west bank of the Euphrates River. This victorious colossus was now headed for Israel. An alliance called the Syrian League was formed to oppose the Assyrians and included Damascus, Hamath, twelve coastal cities, and other nations, as well as "Ahab the Israelite."

Eleven members of this confederacy hurriedly mobilized their forces and met the Assyrian onslaught at Karkar, about two hundred fifty miles north of Samaria. There, in 853 B.C., a battle was fought, and although it was inconclusive the Assyrians' progress was stayed. Shalmaneser led his host all the way back to his home base at Nineveh. Ben-hadad of Damascus and Ahab of Israel had both taken part as allies, the latter leading some ten thousand men and two thousand chariots.

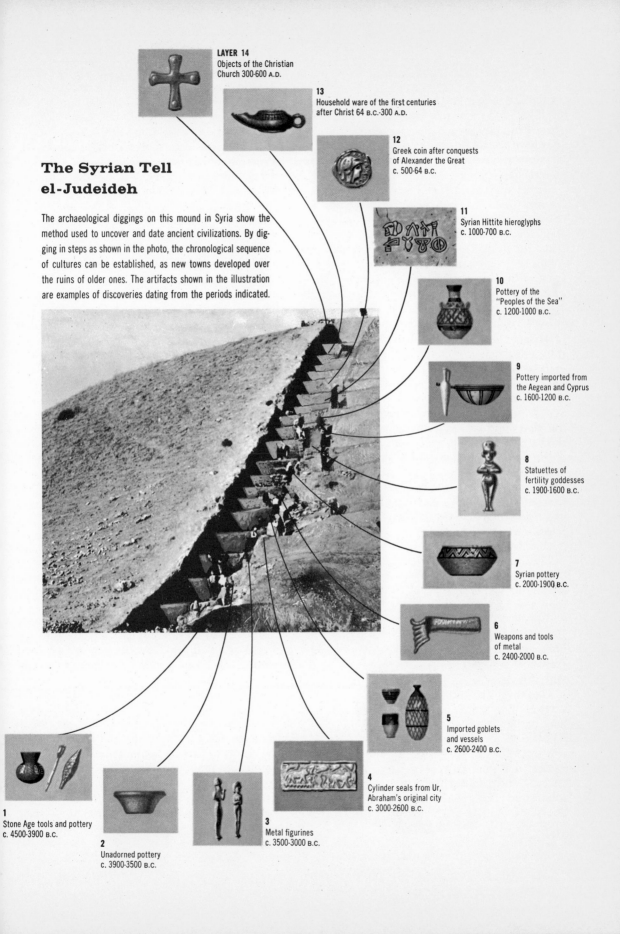

The Syrian Tell el-Judeideh

The archaeological diggings on this mound in Syria show the method used to uncover and date ancient civilizations. By digging in steps as shown in the photo, the chronological sequence of cultures can be established, as new towns developed over the ruins of older ones. The artifacts shown in the illustration are examples of discoveries dating from the periods indicated.

LAYER 14
Objects of the Christian Church 300-600 A.D.

13
Household ware of the first centuries after Christ 64 B.C.-300 A.D.

12
Greek coin after conquests of Alexander the Great c. 500-64 B.C.

11
Syrian Hittite hieroglyphs c. 1000-700 B.C.

10
Pottery of the "Peoples of the Sea" c. 1200-1000 B.C.

9
Pottery imported from the Aegean and Cyprus c. 1600-1200 B.C.

8
Statuettes of fertility goddesses c. 1900-1600 B.C.

7
Syrian pottery c. 2000-1900 B.C.

6
Weapons and tools of metal c. 2400-2000 B.C.

5
Imported goblets and vessels c. 2600-2400 B.C.

4
Cylinder seals from Ur, Abraham's original city c. 3000-2600 B.C.

3
Metal figurines c. 3500-3000 B.C.

2
Unadorned pottery c. 3900-3500 B.C.

1
Stone Age tools and pottery c. 4500-3900 B.C.

In the third and again in the eleventh year following, the Assyrians would make other unsuccessful attempts to overrun the kingdoms of the Syrian League, but Ahab would not be called upon to face them on these occasions. Many years later his son's assassin, Jehu, would be among those who would pay tribute to this same Shalmaneser.

Israel and Syria had been allies against a common enemy, but peaceful relations between them were short-lived. Unsettled conditions east of the Jordan again bred war. This time Judah managed to get involved. Jehoshaphat, the sound, able ruler of the kingdom to the south, happened to be on a state visit in Samaria. Ahab, anxious to regain the lost city of Ramoth-gilead, east of the Jordan on the King's Highway, prevailed upon his counterpart from Jerusalem to accompany him on a raid against this valuable and strategic town.

Jehoshaphat insisted that the will of the Lord be consulted before they set forth, and so Ahab assembled some four hundred prophets of Baal. Parrotlike, this huge assemblage gave wholehearted approval and unqualified assurance of success. The king of Judah, completely devoted to the Lord, wanted no part of these fraudulent seers. Ahab knew of only one man of God still in his land, Micaiah, and he hated him fervently for prophesying evil concerning him. However, since Jehoshaphat was determined to hear the

Moabite warrior, from a stele in the Louvre

truth, Micaiah, this sole representative of the Living God left in Israel, was called. When pressed by Ahab to tell him nothing but the very words of the Lord, the man promptly prophesied Ahab's impending doom.

And that is precisely what happened. Ahab rode into battle disguised so that he would not furnish a ready target, but a Syrian bowman, by merest chance, lodged an arrow in the cleft between the shoulder joints of the king's armor. There had been nineteen evil years in his reign, and now the Kingdom of Israel had a new king, the ineffectual Ahaziah.

Moab had long been a vassal state of the Kingdom of Israel. Now that war had weakened the northern kingdom and Ahab was no more, the Moabites revolted. One of the interesting heritages from antiquity is the Moabite Stone, discovered about a century ago. On it is engraved the record of that land's shepherd king, Mesha, who proudly led his people to freedom.

No doubt it delighted this little monarch to hear that dogs had actually licked up the slain Ahab's blood by the pool in Samaria, just as the prophet Elijah had foretold. And a few years later, he must have been further edified to learn that the depraved Queen Jezebel, who had outlived her husband, had met the revolting end also prophesied for her by Elijah. While leaning out of a window berating Jehu, famous charioteer and commander of Israel's host at Ramoth-gilead, for having killed her son Jehoram, she was thrown to the street by several eunuchs and trampled to death by Jehu's horses, and her flesh was eaten by dogs (2 Kings [4 Kings] 9:10, 30-36).

Jehoshaphat, king of Judah, managed to reach Jerusalem safely following Ahab's death. There he ruled for one more year before completing his very commendable twenty-four-year reign. He is credited with always having done that which was right in the sight of the Lord; his chief mistake was the failure of a grand commercial venture. Like his great-great-grandfather Solomon, he too built a trading fleet to bring home gold from elusive Ophir, but it suffered shipwreck before it ever got out of its home port of Ezion-geber (1 Kings [3 Kings] 22:48).

While Elijah, greatest of the nonwriting prophets, outlived Ahab, he was carried on high in the fiery chariot before Jezebel was hurled to her fate. His mantle fell to another

The Moabite Stone, longest nonbiblical document dealing with Bible lands and times, names many places and events described in the Bible.

steadfast person, also a nonwriting prophet, Elisha. The miraculous acts of this remarkable man fill four and a half chapters of the Bible; two of them involve Syrian matters, evidence that Damascus and Samaria had much in common.

While fear of the sudden reappearance of the Assyrians probably discouraged the Syrians from engaging in full-scale hostilities against the Kingdom of Israel, the kings of Damascus did keep up their predatory operations. Raids for the taking of booty or slaves were common; they were annoying, and were perhaps repaid in kind, but did not cause the breaking of relations between the two kingdoms, at least not for long.

The little maid stolen out of Israel who turned up among the slaves in the home of Naaman, the commandant of the armed forces in Damascus, is a case in point. Her new master was a leper in a society where that frightful disease did not make one an outcast. Yet to be freed of its loathsome burden was worth almost any effort or price. This Israelite child was so

convincing regarding the curative powers of Elisha, the man of God at Samaria, that the Syrian general started off in search of healing. He bore a letter from his king, Ben-hadad, to the king of Israel, so he was not turned back at the border. Neither was he kept under watch of any kind. It is true there were a few uncertain moments at the palace, for the letter Naaman bore seemed so strange to the king of Israel that he thought it a hoax, perhaps a means of fomenting real trouble. Elisha quickly straightened the matter out and arranged for the miraculous cure of this foreigner, and the whole affair passed off peaceably. In deep appreciation, Naaman renounced idolatry and became a worshiper of the True God.

Finally Ben-hadad, at a time when there were no immediate threats of attack by the Assyrians, marched his troops to Samaria and laid siege to it. So tight was the cordon thrown about the city that there was no access to it from the outside at all. Food supplies quickly began to give out, and surrender seemed close. Then a miracle took place, as Elisha had predicted. The Lord made the enemy host hear a din like the clatter of chariots and horses, and the tread of marching feet. The one thought among the Syrian besiegers was that the Hittites and Egyptians had been hired to attack them from the rear. Fear seized them and lent speed to their limbs, and they went hurrying off home to Damascus (2 Kings [4 Kings] 7:6-7).

These insistent and aggressive Syrians continued to make trouble for many years for Israel and lands to the south, forcing them to suffer much from their oppressions. However, there were periods of comparative peace when people could travel from one land to the other. It was during such a period, while Elisha was visiting in Damascus, that a very dramatic incident took place. Ben-hadad II, who was seriously ill, sent a messenger named Hazael to Elisha to ask the prophet whether he would recover. Looking steadfastly at Hazael, Elisha replied that Ben-hadad would not succumb to his illness but that he would die even so, and that Hazael would mount the throne. Hazael hurried back to the palace and, dipping a thick cloth in water, pressed it upon Ben-hadad's face until he was dead; he then proclaimed himself king of Syria, thus fulfilling Elisha's prophecy.

Under their new king, Hazael, the Syrians

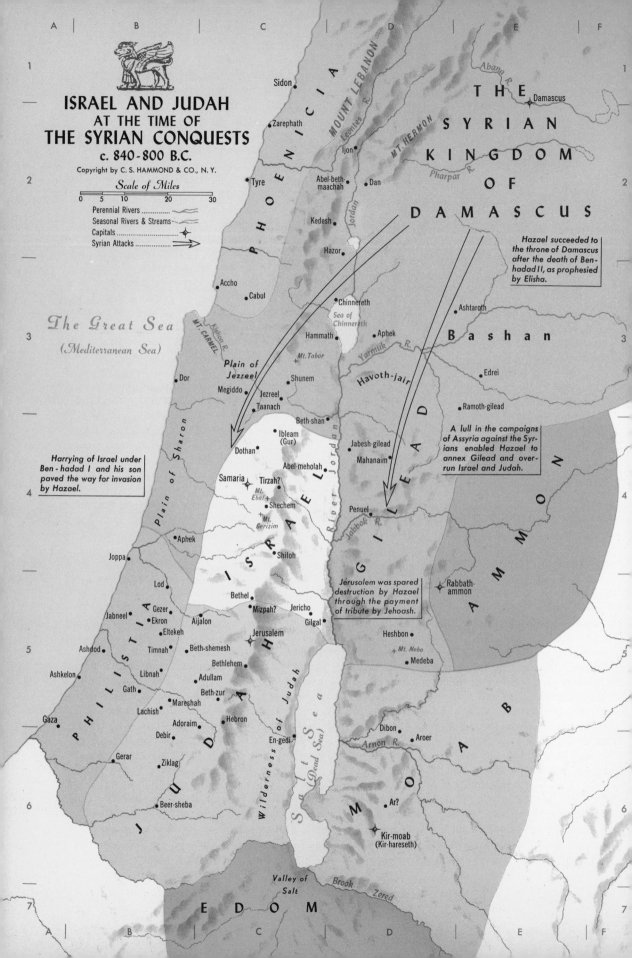

ISRAEL AND JUDAH
AT THE TIME OF
THE SYRIAN CONQUESTS
c. 840-800 B.C.

Copyright by C. S. HAMMOND & CO., N.Y.

Scale of Miles

0   5   10   20   30

Perennial Rivers ....
Seasonal Rivers & Streams .....
Capitals ....✦
Syrian Attacks ....➔

THE

SYRIAN

KINGDOM

OF

DAMASCUS

Hazael succeeded to
the throne of Damascus
after the death of Ben-
hadad II, as prophesied
by Elisha.

A lull in the campaigns
of Assyria against the Syrians enabled Hazael to
annex Gilead and over-
run Israel and Judah.

Harrying of Israel under
Ben-hadad I and his son
paved the way for invasion
by Hazael.

Jerusalem was spared
destruction by Hazael
through the payment
of tribute by Jehoash.

The Great Sea
(Mediterranean Sea)

• Damascus

Abana R.

MOUNT LEBANON
Leontes R.
MT. HERMON
Pharpar R.

P H O E N I C I A

• Sidon
• Zarephath
Ijon •
• Tyre
Abel-beth- •
maachah
• Dan
Jordan
• Kedesh
• Hazor

• Accho
• Cabul
Chinnereth
Sea of
Chinnereth
• Ashtaroth

MT. CARMEL
Kishon R.
Plain of
Jezreel
• Hammath
Aphek •
Yarmuk R.

B a s h a n

Mt. Tabor
• Dor
Megiddo •
• Shunem
• Jezreel
• Taanach
Havoth-jair
• Edrei

Plain of Sharon
Beth-shan •
• Ramoth-gilead
• Ibleam
(Gur)
• Dothan
• Jabesh-gilead
River Jordan
• Abel-meholah
• Mahanaim
• Samaria Tirzah? •
Mt.
Ebal+ • Shechem
+Mt.
Gerizim

I S R A E L

G I L E A D

A M M O N

Jabbok R.

• Aphek
• Shiloh
• Penuel
• Joppa
• Lod
• Bethel
• Jericho
• Rabbath-
ammon
• Jabneel • Gezer Mizpah? •
• Gilgal
• Ekron Aijalon •
• Eltekeh
• Jerusalem
• Heshbon
• Ashdod Timnah •
• Beth-shemesh
+Mt. Nebo
• Medeba

P H I L I S T I A

Wilderness of Judah

• Ashkelon • Libnah
• Bethlehem
• Gath • Adullam
Salt
• Beth-zur
• Lachish • Mareshah
• Gaza • Adoraim
• Hebron
• Debir
• En-gedi
Dead Sea
• Dibon
• Aroer
Arnon R.

J U D A H

• Gerar
• Ziklag

M O A B

• Beer-sheba

• Ar?

Valley of
Salt
Brook
Zered

• Kir-moab
(Kir-haresheth)

E D O M

continued their attacks against the Kingdom of Israel. During one of their campaigns they not only seized its lands east of the Jordan River but also overran the northern part of the Kingdom of Judah, threatening Jerusalem. The Holy City was spared only after it had given Hazael all the portable treasure from the people's homes and the Temple.

WHAT WERE these ancient kingdoms like — Judah, Israel, Damascus and the larger states? They were absolute monarchies; the king had supreme power and the members of the ruling family sought to retain the throne generation after generation, by the use of force and violence whenever necessary. The ruling dynasty was often challenged by bold men thirsting for power, especially in Israel, where the dynasties of Jeroboam, Baasha and Ahab were uprooted one after another in less than a century. Then Jehu, the furious charioteer who had been responsible for Jezebel's death, forced his way to the throne by wiping out the house of Ahab in fulfillment of Elijah's prophecy, and established a dynasty that lasted almost a hundred years.

Absolutism and the struggle for power were the prevailing way of governing in the Orient in ancient times. The Bible story from David to the fall of Jerusalem is sprinkled with assassinations and other acts of ferocity.

Most of these instances are much alike; however, one is unique, involving the only woman ever to rule as queen in either Israel or Judah. She was Athaliah, princess royal of the northern kingdom and a daughter of the wicked Jezebel, whose masculine courage she inherited in abundance. She married King Jehoram of Judah, and her son Ahaziah succeeded his father as king. He was slain by Jehu of Israel because through his mother he had some claim to the northern throne.

Immediately after her son's death, the unscrupulous Athaliah had all of his male children slain; only one escaped, an infant, Jehoash (Joash), who had been hidden by an aunt. Seizing the throne, the doughty Athaliah reigned for five years, when she was killed in a rebellion of the priests in favor of young Jehoash.

Jehoash was crowned when but seven years old and appears to have been married and the father of a son when fourteen or fifteen. He reigned in Judah for almost four decades, only to die in bed at the hands of his own servants while suffering a severe illness.

Amaziah son of Jehoash, had conducted the government during his father's illness, and managed to seize the throne of Judah after the assassination. The murderers were put to death but their children spared, in conformity with Mosaic Law (Deuteronomy 24:16).

These were not the only troubles confronting the young king. His Edomite vassals to the southeast had revolted, and so he hired 100,000 fighting men from the Kingdom of Israel and set forth to put down the uprising. On the advice of a prophet he dismissed these Israelite mercenaries along the way and marched on with only his own troops. It was a daring thing to do, but God was on his side and he captured the Edomite capital, Sela.

He now misjudged his role, and carried away Edom's idols and set them up for his gods. Then, because the hired troops of Israel, homeward bound, had plundered several cities of Judah, Amaziah, flushed with his recent victory, started a war with Joash, king of Israel. He was roundly defeated at Beth-shemesh, taken prisoner there and dragged home to Jerusalem. A portion of that city's wall was broken down and much treasure and many hostages were carried off to Samaria.

Amaziah had reigned many years when a conspiracy against his life drove him from Jerusalem. He sought refuge in Lachish, but his enemies pursued him and slew him there. His years on the throne had been uneasy ones, yet much like those of many another oriental potentate in that ruthless age.

THE TWO little kingdoms on the land bridge knew a few years of great prosperity during the eighth century before the Christian era. Once again, as in the time of David and Solomon, there was a period free from major wars. Egypt was occupied within her own borders, while the Assyrians were involved with neighboring peoples and domestic concerns. Even the Syrians stayed at home. The peaceful times enabled Phoenician Tyre to found one of the great cities of antiquity—Carthage, on the north coast of Africa.

This flourishing period came to fruition during the reigns of two able kings, Jeroboam II of Israel and Uzziah of Judah. Jeroboam II, who ascended the throne about 786 B.C., was the son of Joash, and third in descent from that furious charioteer, Jehu. Uzziah, sometimes called Azariah, was the grandson of Jehoash of Judah. Jeroboam had been king of Israel for several years when sixteen-year-old Uzziah took over the rule of Judah.

Although his father, Joash of Israel, had been able to defeat Judah and had bested the Syrians three times, regaining the cities lost to them earlier, Jeroboam took over the northern kingdom in a sorry state. The religious life of this politically able ruler fell so far short of the standards recognized by compilers of the Books of the Kings that they devoted only seven verses of text to his forty-year reign.

Jeroboam managed to subdue the persistent Syrians, eventually capturing Damascus, even though this was rendered possible only because of repeated Assyrian attacks on Syria. Jeroboam also restored the border of his kingdom from Hamath to the Salt Sea (2 Kings [4 Kings] 14:23-25). During his reign Israel reached its greatest extent and achieved more prosperity than it had since the death of Solomon. Even Judah, largely under the northern kingdom's economic domination, benefited by the good times.

There is some question as to whether any particular advantages flowed to the small farmers and shepherds who composed the bulk of the people, or whether the upswing merely lined the pockets of a class which some writers have called a robber nobility. Such a caste had been developing, particularly in Samaria, for a number of generations. Certainly the ruins of the royal palace show this to have been a most luxurious period. Clay invoices covering shipments of wine and oil to the court indicate extravagant living; beautiful objects carved from ivory and embellished with gold and fine jewels are evidence of great wealth. Tribute from conquered areas and burgeoning commerce, together with taxes on the produce of fields and flocks, advanced the well-being of the privileged classes of the northern kingdom.

The expanded domain had been forecast by the prophet Jonah of Gath-hepher, the same Jonah who, after disobeying God's command to go to the wicked city of Nineveh and preach, was cast into the sea by the sailors of the ship in which he was fleeing to Tarshish, and was swallowed by a whale. Three days later, in answer to his prayers, God allowed the whale to cast him up upon the land; thoroughly chastened, Jonah then went to Nineveh in far-off Babylonia as the Lord had commanded.

There was another man of God called Amos, a humble farm laborer from the hill country south of Bethlehem, whose voice was heard in Israel during the days of Jeroboam. Leaving his rural home in Tekoa, the fiery Amos made his way north, beyond his own country, and

Walls of Damascus, mentioned in three chapters of the Old Testament, still guard the world's oldest city, inhabited since prehistoric times.

A | B | C | D

Assyrian power in Syria at this time was limited, allowing minor states to flourish unmolested until the coming of Tiglath-pileser III.

Khalab (Aleppo)

Euphrates R.

A S S Y R I A N

E M P I R E

Orontes R.

Karkar

HAMATH

Hamath

KITTIM (CYPRUS)

Salamis

Kition (Phoenician colony)

G r e a t   S e a
(Mediterranean Sea)

The Great Sea

Arvad

S Y R I A

Tadmor (Palmyra)

Kadesh

Zedad

Hazar-enan

Jeroboam II restored the borders of Israel from Hamath to the Salt Sea, as prophesied by Jonah.

Gebal (Byblos)

Berytus

Berothai

KINGDOM OF DAMASCUS

Sidon

Mt. Hermon

Damascus

Tyre

Ijon

Abel   Dan

Damascus, weak from the Assyrian invasion of 805 B.C., was defeated by Joash of Israel and his son Jeroboam II.

Kedesh

Hazor

Accho

Karnaim

Sea of Chinnereth

Aphek

D E S E R T

P H O E N I C I A

L E B A N O N

Gath-hepher

Dor   Megiddo

Taanach   Ibleam

I S R A E L

G I L E A D

Edrei

Ramoth-gilead

Israel enjoyed outward prosperity and success but, as Amos depicted, was inwardly corrupt and wicked.

Samaria

Shechem

River Jordan

Joppa

A M M O N

The Philistines were conquered by Uzziah (Azariah), king of Judah.

Bethel

Rabbath-ammon

Jabneh   Ekron

Gilgal

Heshbon

Ashdod

Jerusalem

Medeba

Ashkelon

Gath   Tekoa

Gaza

Lachish   Hebron

Salt Sea

P H I L I S T I A

Gerar

Beer-sheba

J U D A H

M O A B

Raphia

Kir-moab (Kir-haresheth)

Bozrah

EGYPTIAN

Kadesh-barnea

Punon

Egypt

KINGDOM

E D O M

A r a b a h

Sela

**ISRAEL AND JUDAH
AT THE TIME OF
JEROBOAM II
c. 786-746 B.C.**

Copyright by C. S. HAMMOND & CO., N. Y.

Uzziah regained control of the Arabah and fortified Ezion-geber.

River of Egypt

Ezion-geber (Elath)

Scale of Miles

0   20   40   60   80   100

Perennial Rivers   Seasonal Rivers & Streams

Capitals

Israel and areas governed by Israel

Judah and areas governed by Judah

Limits of territory under political or economic control of Jeroboam II preached near the shrine of the golden calf at Bethel. He pictured Jeroboam as a powerful and wealthy king ruling over prosperous people. Yet to a man such as Amos with a strong moral and ethical sense, these were evil times, and bitter indeed are his sermons in the nine chapters of the Bible book bearing his name. He bluntly attacks members of the court clique at Samaria. The wives he likens to cows, and he berates them for their demands on their husbands, which forced the latter to oppress the poor.

Amos points out the number of *gibborim* — strong men — the king kept by him to tyrannize the freedom-loving shepherds and farmers. The small landholders, burdened with taxes, were ruthlessly exploited by the city's moneylenders. The society pictured is much like that which prevailed in the Canaanite cities when the Children of Israel entered the Promised Land some five centuries before.

The desert *mishpāt* — the customs and the sense of justice which had prevailed among God's people as tribesmen — was breaking down. Their concept of morality was decaying, and they were forsaking Yahweh for a host of pagan deities and cults. The cities were dominating the rural areas, and the way of life was growing sinful, with the poor and the lowly suffering greatly. And here was dauntless Amos, from the Kingdom of Judah, thundering denunciations at the ruling classes of the Kingdom of Israel. Small wonder he was accused of treason and threatened with expulsion.

Still, his was not the only voice speaking in protest at conditions in the flourishing land of the Ten Tribes. The other was a native of this northern kingdom, the fine-fibered, sensitive, poetic Hosea. While he did not emphasize so strongly the economic upheaval which had taken place, he was conscious of the nation's sinful ways and made a series of impassioned pleas for national repentance and reform.

WHAT of conditions in Uzziah's Judah? Although his forty-one-year reign is given far more space in the Books of the Kings than is Jeroboam's, some of the best impressions of conditions within his kingdom come from the writings of two prophets, Isaiah and Micah. Judah was also enjoying newfound wealth, and this prosperity, as in Israel, was not benefiting the many nearly as much as it was corrupting the few. Both Isaiah and Micah warned the people against continuing their evil ways, and both predicted that, if they did not reform, the Assyrians would sweep down from the north and lay waste their land.

Micah said that no good men were left, that all lay in wait for blood, that a man's enemies were in his own house and that every son was set against his father and every daughter against her mother. He predicted that Samaria would fall and Jerusalem become a heap of rubble, plowed under like a field, and that the people would be carried away as captives.

Isaiah believed the same but was more hopeful. He looked forward to the coming of an age when all men would put aside their evil ways and follow the One and Only True God. It was Isaiah who proclaimed: "They shall beat their swords into plowshares," and "nation shall not lift up sword against nation."

So great was the luxury and splendor that to the people of the time it seemed the pattern for all the foreseeable future. There was crass indifference to the threatening force of Assyria building up beyond the limits of these two monarchies on the little land bridge. Even Amos, the country boy turned prophet, had an infinitely better understanding of what was going on in the world at large than did the Hebrew princes. A life-and-death struggle was ahead, yet there was a sharp falling off in the stamina needed to meet it.

Murder followed murder. Zechariah, son of Jeroboam II, ruled Israel only a few months before he was slain by an aspirant called Shallum; his death marked the end of the dynasty of Jehu. Shallum in turn was assassinated after one month by Menahem, who ruled for eight years. They were lean, bitter years. Of considerable significance, they deserved but eight verses in the opinion of the compilers of Bible text. It was during this reign that the inevitable happened.

The biblical Pul, who was Tiglath-pileser III, led a gigantic Assyrian host to the south, confronted Samaria, and exacted a crippling tribute of one thousand talents of silver, or just under two million dollars. In our own time this may seem almost a paltry sum, but twenty-seven hundred years ago it was sufficient to start a kingdom on a downward course.

This first visitation of the Assyrians was a bitter experience for the Kingdom of Israel. The Kingdom of Judah was not molested; but her turn would come.

The winged bull with a king's head guarded the throne room of Sargon II. Carved from limestone weighing forty tons, it stands some sixteen feet high.

8. The First Great Empire: Assyria

The highly interesting tenth chapter of Genesis contains a description of a prehistoric empire, ruled by Nimrod, a great-grandson of Noah. The first city mentioned, and no doubt the principal city of the empire, was Babel, or Babylon, one of the most ancient towns noted in the Bible text. This seat of Nimrod's power was apparently also a very early center of the Semitic peoples. Asshur, the son of Noah's first-born son, Shem, came from there and with his descendants moved north along the Tigris River, making their home on its banks between the tributary streams Great Zab and Little Zab. There a kingdom rose, dominated by the town of Ashur, the remains of which have been found at Qal'ât Sherqât, about sixty miles downstream from another famous ancient city called Nineveh.

Ashur and its environs are believed to have been the place of origin of Assyria and of a

The barbarous Assyrians, under the savage Ashurnasirpal, with strange and terrible weapons moved south over Syria.

people destined to make their name a synonym for ruthlessness. They built the first great war machine, created the first extensive international empire, and finally perished through exhaustion brought on by military excesses. In its early years Ashur was evidently subject to Babylon and under the control of governors appointed by the kings of that city-state, which lay about two hundred seventy-five miles to the south on the Euphrates River. Scholars have found it exceedingly difficult to separate the two great empires which ultimately grew up about Ashur and Babylon, for both geographically and historically their relationship was closely interwoven.

While Babylon may have dominated Ashur in early historical times, and conquered it during the reign of Hammurabi (1728-1686 B.C.), Ashur's power grew greater after that. Finally, about 1290 B.C., at the time of the Exodus from Egypt, Babylon surrendered to Ashur. During the next seven centuries, with relatively brief interruptions, Ashur and its domains, or Assyria, as it was then called, would be the leading power in the East.

At the end of the twelfth pre-Christian century, King Tiglath-pileser I greatly extended the Assyrian Empire. He conquered the Hittites who occupied the upper Euphrates Valley to the west, and triumphed over the Aramaeans, or Syrians, to the southwest; he pushed his influence as far as the shores of the Mediterranean, and forced the Egyptian pharaoh to acknowledge his powerful position and send tribute to Assyria, as Assyria had been forced to pay tribute to Egypt during the reigns of the two previous pharaohs.

This period of Assyrian ascendancy was rather short-lived; the empire crumbled rapidly after Tiglath-pileser's death. For the next two centuries Assyria was forced to attend to affairs within her own boundaries. Israel, during this untroubled time, experienced its Golden Age under David and Solomon.

Assyrian power rose again with the accession of Ashurnasirpal II in 883 B.C. His campaigns were well planned and executed, and waged more relentlessly than those of any previous Assyrian monarch. The lands to the northeast and northwest were burned, pillaged, and forced to pay heavy annual tribute. But this new king was a builder as well as a warrior; during his twenty-four years on the throne magnificent palaces, temples and other structures were erected. The ancient city of Calah, whose ruins lay between Nineveh and Ashur, was chosen as his capital; it was rebuilt and greatly beautified.

The remains of Ashurnasirpal's Calah, hidden beneath the Mound of Nimrod, were uncovered by the young Englishman A. H. Layard in 1845. At that time, Assyria, of

which all traces had been completely lost for centuries, began to emerge once more. Fortunately some of the ancient palaces at Calah had remarkable libraries, filled with carefully kept records, inscribed in cuneiform characters on small tablets of baked clay which are practically indestructible. It took a number of years for the key to Assyrian writing to be discovered. When at last it was possible to translate the wealth of documents which had been found, light was thrown upon the history of Assyria and Babylon and many points in Bible text were verified.

One major objective of the Assyrians down the years was the conquest of Egypt. In order to achieve this, it was necessary to clear away all opposition along the land bridge through Syria and Israel. While the forays recorded in the Books of the Kings were in part for plunder, they were also to open up this pathway to the ultimate objective, the fabled cities on the banks of the Nile. And the incidents mentioned in the Bible are confirmed among the exploits of the Assyrian kings. In the records of the military accomplishments of Ashurnasirpal, that monarch says, "From Aleppo [in north

Syria] I launched the attack and crossed the Orontes ... I marched from the Orontes ... I conquered the cities ... I caused much slaughter, I destroyed, I devastated, I burned. I took their fighting men prisoners and impaled them on sharpened stakes in full view of their cities. I settled Assyrians in place of them ... I bathed my weapons in the Great Sea."

On this campaign the Assyrians collected huge plunder of gold and silver, and also of the more serviceable metals, lead and copper. They exacted heavy tribute of the coastal cities of Tyre, Sidon and Byblos, and what they did there had a profound effect further south. Even that hard-bitten soldier, King Omri, realized that discretion was the better part of valor. So he drew two talents of silver, the equivalent of about $3900, from the royal treasury, bought the most readily defended hill in the northern kingdom from its owner, Shemer, and set about building that beautiful and heavily fortified capital, Samaria, which has already been described.

Again, as in a previous period of dominance, Assyria demonstrated its major weakness as a world power. Although the Assyrian people

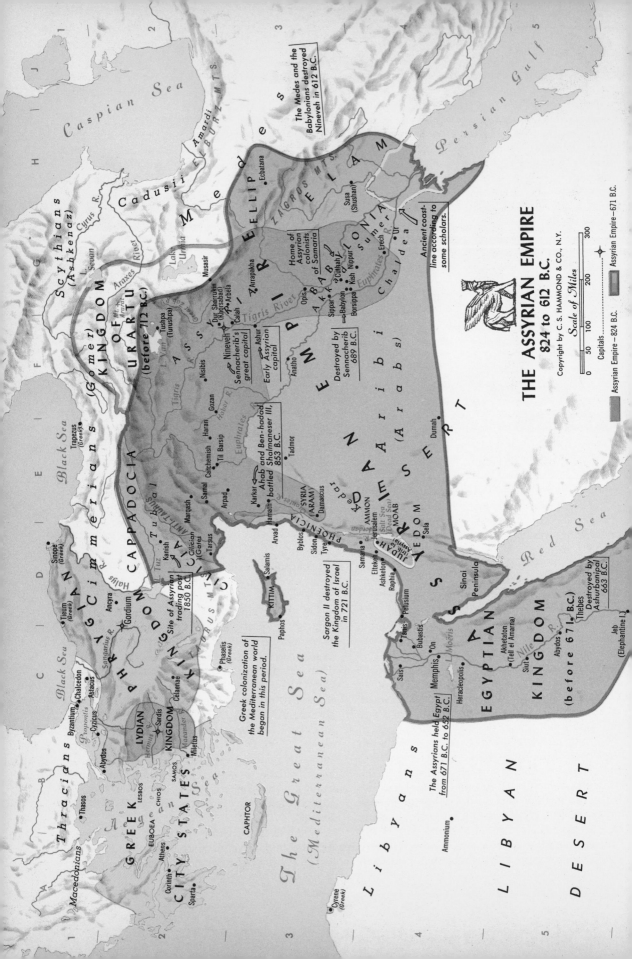

THE ASSYRIAN EMPIRE
824 to 612 B.C.

Copyright by C. S. HAMMOND & CO., N.Y.

Scale of Miles

0   50   100   200   300

Capitals ◆

▬ Assyrian Empire – 824 B.C.
▬ Assyrian Empire – 671 B.C.

Caspian Sea

Black Sea

The Great Sea
(Mediterranean Sea)

Red Sea

Persian Gulf

The Medes and the Babylonians destroyed Nineveh in 612 B.C.

Home of Assyrian colonists of Samaria

Destroyed by Sennacherib 689 B.C.

Ancient coast-line according to some scholars.

Ahab and Ben-hadad battled Shalmaneser III, 853 B.C.

Sargon II destroyed the Kingdom of Israel in 721 B.C.

Greek colonization of the Mediterranean world began in this period.

Site of Assyrian trading post 1850 B.C.

The Assyrians held Egypt from 671 B.C. to 652 B.C.

Destroyed by Ashurbanipal 663 B.C.

Scythians *(Ashkenaz)*

Cimmerians *(Gomer)*

KINGDOM OF URARTU *(before 712 B.C.)*

MEDES

ELAM

EMPIRE

AKKAD · BABYLONIA · Sumer · Chaldea

Aribi *(Arabs)*

ASSYRIA

SYRIA (ARAM)

PHOENICIA

JUDAH

Ass'n

AMMON · MOAB · EDOM

DESERT

CAPPADOCIA

PHRYGIAN KINGDOM

LYDIAN KINGDOM

GREEK CITY STATES

Thracians

Macedonians

EGYPTIAN KINGDOM *(before 671 B.C.)*

LIBYAN KINGDOM

LIBYANS

DESERT

ZAGROS MTS.

ELBURZ MTS.

TAURUS MTS.

ANTI-TAURUS

CILICIA

SINAI · Peninsula

KITTIM

SAMOS

LESBOS

EUBOEA

CHIOS

CAPHTOR

Ecbatana

Susa (Shushan)

Kish · Nippur · Erech · Ur

Opis · Sippar · Cuthah · Babylon · Borsippa

Ashur · Early Assyrian capital

Nineveh · Sennacherib's great capital

Dur Sharrukin (Khorsabad)

Calah

Arbela

Arrapkha

Anatho

Hamath

Tadmor

Dumah

Sela

Mt. Ararat

Tushpa (Turushpa)

L. Van

Musasir

Nisibis

Gozan

Haran

Carchemish

Til Barsip

Samal

Arpad

Marqash

Karkar

Arvad

Byblos

Sidon

Tyre

Damascus

Samaria

Jerusalem

Eltekeh

Ashkelon

Raphia

Pelusium

Tanis

Bubastis

On

Sais

Memphis

Heracleopolis

Akhetaton (Tell el Amarna)

Siut

Abydos

Thebes

Jeb (Elephantine I.)

Ammonium

Cyrene (Greek)

Sparta

Corinth

Athens

Abydos

Miletus

Samos

Sardis

Celaenae

Phaselis (Greek)

Tarsus

Kanish

Cilician Gates

L. Tuz

Gordium

Ancyra

Sinope (Greek)

Trapezus (Greek)

Cyzicus

Astacus

Chalcedon

Byzantium

Tieium (Greek)

Thasos

Paphos

Salamis

Lachish

Sevan

Urmia

L.

Lake Urmia

Cadusii

Amardi

Araxes River

Cyrus R.

Tigris River

Euphrates

Khabur R.

Halys

Maeander

Sangarius R.

Hermus

Nile

Moeris

Araxes R.

Propontis

Pe'or

Dead Sea (Salt Sea)

Jordan

Red Sea

proved to be effective soldiers, they lacked political sagacity and ability. The governors appointed to rule the conquered territories must have been inept, or weak, or both. Unlike the later Romans, Assyria bled herself white through military campaigns directed time after time at the same regions, in which she should have been undisputed mistress for long, peaceful and prosperous periods.

This lack of political wisdom is well illustrated by Shalmaneser III, who followed Ashurnasirpal and came to the throne in 859 B.C. Although he had a long reign of thirty-five years, no less than twenty-six of them were filled with almost continuous fighting. He made a lunge at Syria and Palestine in 853 B.C. and was stayed in his advance at Karkar near the Orontes River in Syria. It was there that King Ahab of Israel, together with others of the Syrian and Phoenician confederacy, opposed this monster from the banks of the Tigris.

The Assyrians also lacked the ability to keep order at home. This same Shalmaneser, who had fought his way almost to the southern border of Syria, must have been as humiliated as he was incensed when, only a few years before his death, he had to put down an uprising in his own palace, led by his son Ashurdaninapal. This upheaval was sufficient to give even the firmly held provinces such as Babylon an opportunity to mutiny. The next monarch, Shamshi-Adad V, spent his twelve years' reign in one campaign after another attempting to reconquer formerly subjugated lands.

The following century was filled with just such efforts of Assyria's rulers struggling to hold their kingdom together. Yet the ambition to dominate remained, and when a usurper came to the throne in 745 B.C. he ushered in an era filled with famous rulers.

The first king in this remarkable galaxy was Tiglath-pileser III, known in the Bible as Pul, and by the Babylonians as Pulu. Five months after he had seized the throne he was off to the wars. His first objective was Babylon, and soon that land was brought under direct control of the Assyrian throne. Both there and in other restless dependencies to the east, deportation on a large scale was inaugurated. Native populations were mixed with foreigners brought sometimes great distances from their home countries. The purpose behind this device was to temper national consciousness — to break up special groups and with them the will to resist.

Lands and provinces to the north and northwest next demanded Tiglath-pileser's attention. He needed income and, as the tributaries in Syria and the Holy Land were withholding their annual payments, the mailed fist was needed in that quarter too. With a wealth of past experience — and errors — to draw upon, the army was reorganized, and Assyria now began a century and a half of virulent warfare. In a purely military sense, Assyrian achievements have been admired by the best strategists ever since their extensive records were rediscovered in the past century.

A few years before Tiglath-pileser came to the throne, some eighteen hundred miles to the west a city was founded, according to venerable legend, by the twins Romulus and Remus, sons of the god Mars. This was Rome, which one day would rule the Western world.

King Jehu of Israel kneels before Shalmaneser III, king of Assyria. He paid tribute to the Assyrians to secure protection from King Hazael of Damascus.

Kings of
Israel and Judah

(for earlier kings see page 63)

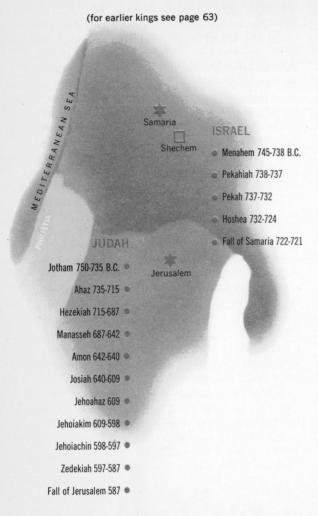

MEDITERRANEAN SEA

PHILISTIA

Samaria

Shechem

ISRAEL

Menahem 745-738 B.C.

Pekahiah 738-737

Pekah 737-732

Hoshea 732-724

Fall of Samaria 722-721

JUDAH

Jotham 750-735 B.C.

Jerusalem

Ahaz 735-715

Hezekiah 715-687

Manasseh 687-642

Amon 642-640

Josiah 640-609

Jehoahaz 609

Jehoiakim 609-598

Jehoiachin 598-597

Zedekiah 597-587

Fall of Jerusalem 587

Seven centuries later its ability to govern would be far superior to that of the Assyrians. Yet its legions were probably never made up of better or more audacious soldiers than the well-trained horde that finally set out with Pul in command, seeking to right matters on the land bridge. The period of prosperity for the kingdoms of Israel and Judah had ended; Jeroboam II of Israel and Uzziah, king of Judah, had been dead for several years.

After Pul's successes in the north of Syria, the move to the south met with no serious resistance, and one city and country after another became vassal of his invincible host. Even

the stout walls of Samaria, whose foundations Omri had laid over a century before, did not seem nearly adequate, and the Kingdom of Israel surrendered without resistance. As mentioned earlier, its king, Menahem, bought peace and the retention of his throne for one thousand talents of silver, or about $1,950,000, a tremendous amount for those days. This impost is recorded in 2 Kings [4 Kings] 15:19-20, and also in the annals of Pul's reign, in which it is admitted very briefly: "I received tribute from Menahem of Samaria . . . Like a bird, alone he fled and submitted to me."

Menahem seems to have collected this huge sum by assessing some sixty thousand of his subjects fifty shekels each. This would have been about the going price of a good pair of oxen or donkeys, or a male slave, or a small house and a bit of surrounding land. It was indeed a burdensome tax. And as taxes are never popular, it bred an uprising in the land. The revolt was headed by an army officer, Pekah, who slew Menahem's son, Pekahiah, and took possession of the throne.

The Assyrian grip on Samaria began to falter at once. Tiglath-pileser had built up his army, but apparently had not improved the Assyrian manner of governing captive nations. There was trouble, too, in Damascus, where Rezin, king of the Syrians, began to plot organized resistance through a defensive league. It was in reality a renewal of the same old confederation, the Syrian League, which had on a previous occasion stemmed the Assyrian advance.

All the little countries hurried to join — all, that is, except the Kingdom of Judah, whose ruler, Ahaz, was paying tribute to Assyria, preferring to buy peace rather than to win freedom through violence. Rezin was determined that Assyria should have no allies in the area and persuaded Pekah, the king of Israel, to accompany him to Jerusalem, putting it under siege.

King Ahaz, however, could not be forced to yield. He sent emissaries galloping off to the north begging for Assyrian aid, the plea being accompanied by lavish gifts of silver and gold stripped from the Temple and the palace. The Bible record of this transaction has its brief counterpart in Assyrian chronicles: "I received tribute from Jauhazi [Ahaz] of Judah."

In 734 B.C. Assyrian cohorts were again at the gates of Damascus. Just how long that city withstood siege is not certain, but it seems to have been a rather brief time. Rezin, the king, was slain, the noblemen were impaled upon stakes, the city itself was ransacked, if not burned, and towns and villages in sixteen surrounding districts were leveled. Some eight hundred citizens, probably those of leading families, were led away to servitude.

It was only about one hundred miles by trail down to Samaria; and either later that same year, or early the next, Tiglath-pileser moved south, reducing to impotence the countryside through which he passed. One province after another felt the grinding heel of Assyrian might. Great numbers of the people were marched away to the north and east, while Assyrian governors were put in charge of the remnants of the population.

It was now the turn of "Bet-Omri," or the Kingdom of Israel, to be invaded. The outlying districts fell easily. The Assyrian records of this particular campaign state very briefly: "All its people I took away to Assyria." Actually the "all" did not include the people of Samaria itself, but referred to the other cities and towns in the northern kingdom, taken over and organized into Assyrian provinces. The area was subjected to utter disruption, and heavily depopulated through deportation. It was a ghost country in comparison to the land which had risen to such plenty and luxury under the second Jeroboam.

Though the capital, Samaria, was spared, it was not without trouble. Another conspiracy flared up, and the usurper Pekah was assassinated at the hands of one Hoshea, a puppet of the conquerors. And so Samaria, while not completely subdued, was shorn of its power and so weakened that it might at any time be disposed of completely.

Assyria was now mistress from the Persian Gulf around the great Crescent to the very borders of Egypt. That ancient land along the Nile, bereft of the shield afforded by the cities of Syria and the Israelite kingdoms, realized its turn might come within a few years. It therefore set its representatives to work exploring means of rebuilding these buffer states.

Conditions in the Assyrian Empire seem to have gone on with little change during the remaining six or seven years of Tiglath-pileser's reign. But there was the customary stir and test of strength following his death. Hoshea in Samaria withheld his annual tribute and hastily

entered into an agreement with the Egyptian pharaoh, So, or Sewe. It was a bold move and a desperate one. The new Assyrian sovereign, Shalmaneser V, who took the throne in 727 B.C., did not temporize with such disloyalty; his forces were soon assaulting the walls of Samaria. To the great credit of its people, the city held out stubbornly through three long years. Actually it withstood the siege better than did the Assyrian king, for before the city capitulated he was dead; one of his generals, probably his brother, now came to the throne, taking the illustrious name of Sargon II.

This monarch in later centuries was to remain for a long time something of a mythical character; his name was unknown except in the Bible text. Then, in the year 1843, a French consular agent and scholar, Paul Emile Botta, uncovered his palace at Dur Sharrukin (Khorsabad) just north of Nineveh, close to the Tigris. This proved a remarkable find, especially as important events in the king's reign appeared in legends inscribed on the palace walls.

One of these inscriptions includes this very illuminating bit: "At the beginning of my rule, in the very first year I reigned . . . I set siege to and conquered Samaria . . . I carried away into captivity 27,290 persons who lived there; I took fifty fine chariots for my royal equipment." Other recovered records add that he

Sargon II, conqueror of the Kingdom of Israel, who deported the Ten Lost Tribes

later rebuilt Samaria, making it even greater than before. In the conquering Assyrian manner, people from other lands were then brought in and settled there, so that the population might be mixed. A governor was placed over the people of this new province, and tribute and taxes were "imposed upon them as upon the Assyrians."

These facts closely parallel those found in the Bible passage of 2 Kings [4 Kings] 17:3-6, which relates that the king of Assyria took Samaria and carried the people "away into Assyria" and placed them in Halah, and on the Habor, the river of Gozan, and "in the cities of the Medes." In the 24th verse of this chapter it is explained how those who had been led away were replaced by Syrians and other unfortunates uprooted in distant lands and herded in from as far away as Babylon and Cuthah. The Kingdom of Israel, which had lasted for two hundred years, had now come to an end, in 721 B.C., and the members of the Ten Tribes who had been hurried off to Assyria became the Lost Tribes, for they have never again emerged in world history.

The mixture of peoples in and about Samaria came to be known as the Samaritans, and their numbers were far less than those who had peopled this highland area before the coming of the Assyrians. There were so few of them that lions began to multiply in the land. And since these people worshiped many false gods, the Lord used these beasts as a scourge against them. The poor discouraged people finally resorted to the Assyrian king for aid and guidance, and he sent them a priest of Israel from among the captives he had taken. This holy man established a shrine at Bethel and sought to instruct his charges in the worship of Yahweh. But their idolatry was too ingrained; they combined the worship of God with that of their many idols.

The ruin and wretchedness spread by the Assyrians affected many lands. Nevertheless, some of the victims came back to life. Damascus, Babylon, Sidon, Memphis and one or two others went on to still greater fame. Samaria continued to exist, but its glory was permanently dimmed, and its wickedness, which was great in the sight of the Lord, lastingly sapped its vitality. For years the greatest of Israelite cities, it was from this time on just another hill town in the central highlands. The Lord's will had been worked upon it at the hands of the first real empire builders, the ambitious, barbarous Assyrians.

WHAT HAVOC time had wrought in the land of promise! How hopefully its conquest had begun, when a new and sternly disciplined generation of Israelites had moved in out of the wilderness and sought its subjugation under the capable leadership of Joshua. How great had been the promise after it had been welded into a true kingdom by the firm hand of David. Then, during the days of Solomon, prosperity had showered down upon it; there had been a Golden Age.

But even as Solomon reigned, seeds of discord had sprouted and developed into a lush growth. And with his death the kingdom had split in two. Now the northern kingdom, made up of the greater portion of the domain promised to God's Chosen People, had passed back into heathen hands.

Only the tiny Kingdom of Judah remained, a little oval block running from a few miles above Jerusalem south to Kadesh-barnea and from the Salt Sea to just west of Lachish. It embraced hardly more than one fourth the area of present-day Belgium. In fact, it was a mere trace of the kingdom passed along by David to Solomon; and even this remnant was virtually a possession of the Assyrians.

Hezekiah, its king, continued the role of vassal assumed by his father, Ahaz, and records of his annual payments of tribute may still be read on the numerous clay tablets unearthed in Assyria. He and his people found the burden unbearable, and he resolutely hoped in some way to lighten this load. The Assyrian Empire extended down to the west of Judah; it included certain of the Philistine cities, and when rioting broke out in Ashdod Hezekiah was greatly encouraged, believing that freedom was in sight. But when a number of neighboring cities and peoples formed a confederacy to combat the enemy, for some unknown reason he carefully avoided direct involvement, although he did connive and lend encouragement behind the scenes.

Egypt, at that time ruled by an Ethiopian dynasty of kings, was very apprehensive, and was making many worthless promises in the hope of stimulating resistance to the Assyrians on the part of her northern neighbors. The ruling pharaoh may well have been Shabaka, next to the last of these Ethiopians, and it is

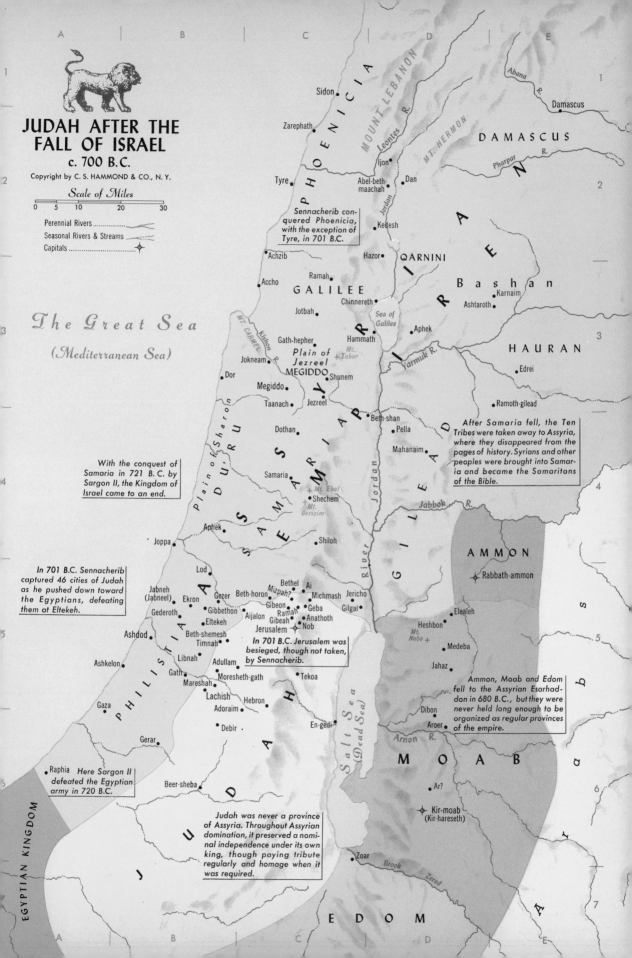

JUDAH AFTER THE FALL OF ISRAEL
c. 700 B.C.

Copyright by C. S. HAMMOND & CO., N.Y.

Scale of Miles

0 5 10 20 30

Perennial Rivers ....
Seasonal Rivers & Streams ......
Capitals ....

The Great Sea

(Mediterranean Sea)

Sennacherib conquered Phoenicia, with the exception of Tyre, in 701 B.C.

After Samaria fell, the Ten Tribes were taken away to Assyria, where they disappeared from the pages of history. Syrians and other peoples were brought into Samaria and became the Samaritans of the Bible.

With the conquest of Samaria in 721 B.C. by Sargon II, the Kingdom of Israel came to an end.

In 701 B.C. Sennacherib captured 46 cities of Judah as he pushed down toward the Egyptians, defeating them at Eltekeh.

In 701 B.C. Jerusalem was besieged, though not taken, by Sennacherib.

Ammon, Moab and Edom fell to the Assyrian Esarhaddon in 680 B.C., but they were never held long enough to be organized as regular provinces of the empire.

Judah was never a province of Assyria. Throughout Assyrian domination, it preserved a nominal independence under its own king, though paying tribute regularly and homage when it was required.

Here Sargon II defeated the Egyptian army in 720 B.C.

Place names

Sidon
Damascus
Zarephath
DAMASCUS
Abana R.
Pharpar R.
MOUNT LEBANON
Leontes R.
MT. HERMON
Ijon
Tyre
Abel-beth-maachah
Dan
PHOENICIA
Kedesh
QARNINI
Achzib
Hazor
Accho
Ramah
GALILEE
Bashan
Karnaim
Chinnereth
Ashtaroth
Jotbah
Sea of Galilee
Aphek
MT. CARMEL
Kishon R.
Gath-hepher
Hammath
Mt. Tabor
HAURAN
Jokneam
Plain of Jezreel
Edrei
Dor
MEGIDDO
Shunem
Megiddo
Yarmuk R.
Taanach
Jezreel
Ramoth-gilead
Beth-shan
Dothan
Pella
Mahanaim
SAMARIA
Jordan River
GILEAD
Samaria
Mt. Ebal
Shechem
Mt. Gerizim
Jabbok R.
Aphek
AMMON
Joppa
Shiloh
Rabbath-ammon
Plain of Sharon
DOR
Lod
Bethel
Ai
Mizpah?
Michmash
Jabneh (Jabneel)
Ekron
Gezer
Beth-horon
Geba
Jericho
Gibeon
Ramah
Anathoth
Gilgal
Gederoth
Gibbethon
Aijalon
Gibeah
Elealeh
Eltekeh
Jerusalem
Nob
Heshbon
Ashdod
Beth-shemesh
Mt. Nebo
Medeba
Libnah
Timnah
Gath
Adullam
Moresheth-gath
Tekoa
Jahaz
Ashkelon
Mareshah
Dibon
Gaza
Lachish
Hebron
Aroer
Adoraim
MOAB
Debir
En-gedi
Arnon R.
Gerar
Salt Sea (Dead Sea)
Ar?
Raphia
Kir-moab (Kir-haresheth)
Beer-sheba
JUDAH
PHILISTIA
Zoar
Brook Zered
EGYPTIAN KINGDOM
EDOM
ISRAEL

likely that he had a large diplomatic force at Jerusalem trying to influence Hezekiah.

The Assyrian intelligence system had a full complement of spies and informers, and word of the defections in Philistia and Judah was rushed back to headquarters on the Tigris as fast as the camel post could make the long journey. Assyria launched another series of invasions, which ultimately were to end disastrously for her.

There were apparently three waves of invasions, the first coming while Sargon was still upon the throne, but led by a tartan, *turtanu,* or commander in chief, who may have been his son, Sennacherib. This perhaps involved only one army corps; the main forces were busy to the north and east of the homeland. The visitation very likely lasted three or four years, and it is the one recorded in Isaiah [Isaias] 20:1.

During the next ten years several notable occurrences took place. One was the death of Sargon, which resulted in a wave of restlessness, sweeping the empire from one end to the other. Sennacherib quickly took over the throne, so no major revolt occurred.

In Judah, the life of King Hezekiah was threatened, not by a conspiracy but by a "boil." While there is little enough on which to base a diagnosis, some doctors believe this affliction to have been the deadly bubo of bubonic plague, a not uncommon and often fatal disease in the East. Hezekiah's competence in handling the kingdom was sorely needed, and, as he had always been very devout and had fought idolatry, God spared Hezekiah's life and granted him an additional fifteen years (Isaiah [Isaias] 38:4-5).

The "sign" which the Lord had manifested in this healing of His servant was immediately used to further a little intrigue. A delegation arrived in Jerusalem from Merodach-baladan, then king of Babylon. After congratulating Hezekiah on his recovery, the group disclosed its true purpose; it invited him to take an active part against the Assyrians by joining in a confederacy made up of the rulers of Babylon, Edom, Egypt, Moab, Philistia and Phoenicia. The Judean king was much elated, and foolishly took the ambassadors on a tour of his treasuries, showing what wealth Judah still possessed.

Hezekiah's act aroused heavenly displeasure, and Isaiah quickly sought out his king and prophesied to him the word of the Lord: the people and the remaining treasure of Judah would someday be carried off to captivity in Babylon, the very city from which the delegation had come. In spite of this warning Hezekiah joined the alliance.

Well aware of the conspiracy that was going on, the Assyrians started their main campaign against the Philistines, subduing the Phoenicians en route. With these invincible forces once more on the march, terror struck all. There was a rush of ambassadors to the Assyrian king's tent, including representatives from Ammon, Ashdod, Edom and Moab, eager to compromise. Some of the coastal towns, however, held out and later were punished.

At last Sennacherib was able to turn east into Judah, where he threw his siege troops against Lachish. Thinking perhaps to save Jerusalem from similar treatment, Hezekiah sent word to Sennacherib, confessing his faults and defections and asking the invaders to name the price of peace and amity. The Assyrians quickly complied. The sum amounted to about $1,500,000; even the gold leaf had to be stripped from the Temple doors (2 Kings [4 Kings] 18:14-16).

Sennacherib accepted the huge tribute sent to him by Hezekiah, but he had no intention of letting Jerusalem escape all punishment. After Lachish had been reduced and the main stage of this second invasion got under way, Jerusalem received immediate attention. Suddenly the Assyrian multitude was before its gates; as described in Byron's classic words, "The Assyrian came down like the wolf on the fold." A *rab-saris,* or court officer of Sennacherib, bawled out a dire warning to the representatives of Hezekiah, who stood upon the wall to hear his words. What would, or could, the king now do?

His remarkable cure, plus the exhortations of the man of God Isaiah, seems to have strengthened Hezekiah's faith in Yahweh; he stoutly refused to admit these Assyrian troops sent to garrison the city. The main Assyrian army was just then embroiled at Libnah, and when Sennacherib heard of Hezekiah's defiance he dispatched messengers with letters threatening vengeance. But as his own situation at the moment was highly critical — a major battle against the Egyptians was threatening — Jerusalem would have to wait.

The Assyrian forces fell back to Eltekeh,

about twenty miles west of Jerusalem. There Sennacherib met the combined forces of Egypt and Ethiopia and defeated them. Turning upon nearby Ekron, he added it to his list of conquests. While Sennacherib's inventory, like other similar lists, may be exaggerated, he

Sennacherib's attacks on the cities of Judah appear in the bas-reliefs of Nineveh, and are described in cuneiform on the famous clay prism (right).

Banquet scene of Ashurbanipal, last of the great Assyrian kings

claims to have taken a total of forty-six fortified cities and towns in Judah alone, from which he led away into bondage a reported 200,150 persons. He also plundered the countryside of countless horses, camels, donkeys, mules and sheep.

He would most certainly have gone on and leveled Jerusalem had not disaster just then struck him a paralyzing blow. A plague broke out in the ranks of his army and killed, according to the Bible account, 185,000 of his warriors in a single horrible night (2 Kings [4 Kings] 19:35). He had no choice but to gather together his few remaining men and hurriedly retreat. Jerusalem was thus miraculously spared.

Troubles in Babylon now demanded Sennacherib's attention, and Judah was to know a few quiet years, during which Hezekiah died in peace. He was succeeded by his twenty-two-year-old son, Manasseh, whose reign was to prove at first as evil and revolting as his father's had been just and good. He rebuilt the altars to Baal which his father had torn down; he believed in enchantments and dealt with soothsayers and wizards, all of which were an abomination in the eyes of the Lord.

It appears that Manasseh continued as a vassal of Assyria; two Assyrian kings, Esarhaddon and Ashurbanipal, have left records of tribute payments made by him. It was probably the latter who caused the brash young man to be led captive to Babylon. While there, Manasseh repented of his gross wickedness, and the Lord therefore restored him to his kingdom. He ruled for the incredible period of forty-five years, the longest term any king of Judah held that throne.

He was succeeded by his young son, Amon, who followed the bad habits his father had practiced during his younger years. His servants had had quite enough of him after two years and slew him. The people of the land then quickly dispatched the assassins and placed Amon's eight-year-old son, Josiah, on the throne.

Josiah's reign was to prove one of the finest in the history of the little Kingdom of Judah. During his immature years he was virtually a ward of the High Priest Hilkiah, who had great influence upon the formation of his religious attitudes. While still a young man he sought to make his life and that of his court conform to the Law of God, and he set about suppressing idolatry not only in his kingdom but also to the north in what had once been the Kingdom of Israel. All this was very pleasing to the Lord and to the prophet Jeremiah, who was just beginning his long mission as a man of God.

Josiah was about twenty-six years old when he gave orders for the repair and refurnishing of the Temple, during which an ancient copy

a changed world stage. Assyria was by this time no longer in the unquestioned position of power it had held earlier in this same century. At that time it had extended its empire widely; Esarhaddon had been able to seize Memphis in Egypt in 671 B.C., and eight years later Ashurbanipal had pushed the conquest on up the Nile as far as Thebes. This latter ruler, however, seems to have been a somewhat less vigorous soldier than his forebears; it was during his reign that weakening influences began to take hold of the Assyrian Empire.

With his death in 626 B.C. the situation grew worse. Pressure from within and without mounted in volume and strength. A new nation, the Medes, had arisen under the ruler Cyaxares in the mountains east of the Tigris Valley, while within the empire the Babylonians were increasing in power and threatening to break away. Finally in 612 B.C. a force made up of Medes, Babylonians and their allies fell upon Nineveh, the fabulous Assyrian capital. While it was under siege the Tigris flooded and carried away parts of its walls, rendering it indefensible. The city was laid waste with such thoroughness that for ages it was completely lost sight of and became something of a myth.

From the vantage point of today it is quite evident that, with the fall of Nineveh, the first great empire had come to an inglorious end. But at the time there were fears that this military goliath was not truly dead and might suddenly rise again, and so Assyria continued to influence the Kingdom of Judah for some time to come.

of the Law was discovered in a chamber. Its reading profoundly impressed not only the young king but his subjects as well. A second campaign for the elimination of every conceivable form or vestige of idolatry was set in motion, and the Passover celebration is said to have had greater religious fervor than any since the time of Samuel.

Although Josiah had reigned thirty-one years, he was only thirty-nine when Egyptian armies under Pharaoh Necho began to move north over the land bridge on their way to help their old enemies the Assyrians against a common enemy, the rising Babylonian state. Josiah, a vassal of Assyria like his father, grandfather and great-grandfather before him, hated the Assyrians and wanted to see them destroyed. Hoping, therefore, to prevent the Egyptians from joining the Assyrians, he gathered together his small army and met them at Megiddo in 609 B.C.

During the battle a well-placed arrow dealt King Josiah a mortal wound. Hastily transferred from his own chariot to another, he was hurried back to Jerusalem, sixty miles away, but he had no more than arrived there when he died. This was a great loss to his faltering kingdom, and all Judah and Jerusalem mourned for him, including the prophet Jeremiah.

Stern days of reckoning for Judah were once again at hand. They would occur, however, on

All that is left of Nineveh, called "the great city" by the Hebrews, a site so vast that its excavation may never be completed

9. Bondage in Babylon

King Josiah of Judah had hoped to prevent the Egyptians under Pharaoh Necho from joining with the Assyrians. He had failed. But his hopes had not been completely in vain, for when the Egyptians finally reached the Euphrates they and the Assyrians were defeated by the Babylonians in a battle close to ancient Haran. A few years later, in 605 B.C., Necho's forces were cut to ribbons in a battle at Carchemish on the upper reaches of the Euphrates. This defeat was so complete that Necho was driven back into Egypt and, according to 2 Kings [4 Kings] 24:7, he "came not again any more" out of his land.

Following the fall of Nineveh and the expulsion of the Egyptians, the Assyrian Empire was split between the conquering Medes and Babylonians. The Medes took over lands to the north and northwest, while to the Babylonians fell the territory to the south and southwest.

These Babylonians were also known as Chaldeans; they were a people who had settled earlier around "Ur of the Chaldees." From 625 B.C., when the Chaldean Nabopolassar came to the Babylonian throne, he had waged vigorous war against the Assyrian overlords, and the empire he built was known as the Chaldean, or New Babylonian, Empire.

In the division of lands between the Medes and Chaldeans, Nabopolassar claimed Syria and the Holy Land. But he was already advanced in age and in no mood for the long journey to inspect his greatly enlarged domain. Nabopolassar had a very able son, who had led his forces to victory over the Egyptians at Carchemish, and who bore a name that was the despair first of Hebrew chroniclers and later of their English translators—Nebuchadnezzar. The aged king placed his son at the head of a vast army and sent him toward the provinces far to the west and south.

In the very midst of this expedition, word reached Nebuchadnezzar that his father had died. So he hurried back to Babylon, leaving his army in the hands of his able generals. Affairs at the capital claimed his attention for a time; Judah and some of the other vassal states were left in peace.

For several years Jerusalem faithfully forwarded its tribute to Babylon. Then it revolted. It revolted in spite of the persistent and forceful warnings by the prophet Jeremiah that it should accept its new master as a just punishment from the Lord for its grievous sins: for

As the captive Israelites arrived in Babylon, they were struck dumb by its magnificence—the massive walls, the palace of hanging gardens and the wondrous Tower of Babel.

worshiping false gods and for straying from the sacred laws.

Money proved as much of a consideration with Judah's new overlord, Nebuchadnezzar, as it had with his Assyrian predecessors. So he was soon in the Holy Land, where Jehoiakim, Josiah's eldest son, was on the Judean throne. Before the great Babylonian king and his armies reached Jerusalem Jehoiakim died, and it fell to his son, Jehoiachin, to surrender the Holy City. This new king was exiled to Babylonia together with the remainder of the nobility of Judah and the artisans and soldiers. Nebuchadnezzar then placed Josiah's second-youngest son, Mattaniah, on the throne as a puppet king. His name was changed to Zedekiah by his captors, and he was left to reign over the remnant of his people.

Cruel treatment of the people of Jerusalem only intensified Judah's hatred of the Babylonians. Jeremiah's dire warnings that opposition to Nebuchadnezzar would lead to the captivity of all the people and the complete destruction of Jerusalem went unheeded. When, in the ninth year of his reign, Zedekiah revolted, the Babylonians quickly attacked the city walls. The heaviest battering rams and siege equipment were brought up. The city proved to be too strong to be taken by open assault, so a series of fortifications was erected in a ring

GREAT EMPIRES OF THE SIXTH CENTURY B.C.

Copyright by C. S. HAMMOND & CO., N.Y.

Scale of Miles

0   100   200   300   400   500

Capitals
Limits of the Persian Empire c. 500 B.C.
Persian Royal Road
Red Sea-Nile Canal Built by Darius I

The Persians under Cyrus the Great overthrew the Medes, conquered Lydia and Babylonia to fulfill the prophecy of Daniel.

Darius I extended the Persian Empire into Europe. Attempts to subjugate Greece by Darius I and Xerxes I failed as the Greeks won at Marathon and Salamis.

An edict of Cyrus in 538 B.C. allowed the Jews to return to their homeland.

The New Babylonian (Chaldean) Empire brought an end to the Kingdom of Judah with the destruction of Jerusalem in 587 B.C.

Pharaoh Necho defeated Josiah of Judah at Megiddo but was driven out of the Holy Land after being defeated by Nebuchadnezzar at Carchemish (605 B.C.).

Egypt came under Persian rule after Cambyses defeated Psamtik III at Pelusium in 525 B.C.

MEDIAN EMPIRE (612-550 B.C.)

NEW BABYLONIAN EMPIRE (612-539 B.C.)

KINGDOM OF LYDIA (670-546 B.C.)

KINGDOM OF EGYPT (26th DYNASTY 663-525 B.C.)

about it, and a withering siege dragged on for months.

The appearance of an Egyptian army in the vicinity drew the Babylonians away for a time and brought hope to the beleaguered city. The food supply had long been exceedingly low, but the people now held on, hoping the Egyptians might raise the siege. When their stores were finally exhausted, Zedekiah and his fighting men managed to slip out of the city during the night. Picking their way gingerly through the line of surrounding forts, they hurried off to the east toward the Jordan Valley.

Word of their escape soon reached the Babylonians, and a detachment was sent in pursuit. On the plain of Jericho, Zedekiah was captured, having been almost completely forsaken by his officers and men. Nebuchadnezzar had taken up residence in the town of Riblah, north of Damascus, and this last king of Judah was dragged there in fetters, tried and condemned. One by one his sons were brought in and slain in his presence. His eyes were blinded; in fetters he was led off to Babylon and there thrown into prison for the rest of his days. No doubt remained that these new rulers of the world were as brutal as the Assyrians had ever been.

Jerusalem had held out for two years. It was now defenseless, and the people, except the very poorest, were marched off to captivity. The Temple and all important buildings were put to the torch, and the walls were leveled. The Kingdom of Judah was at an end — and Jerusalem, the Holy City, lay in ruin for the next fifty years. All was as Jeremiah had prophesied. Like the people of the Kingdom of Israel a century and a half before, the last of God's Chosen People had now become merely pawns in a pagan world.

It was to Babylon, capital of the Chaldean Empire, that the captives from Judah were led into bondage. And it was at this time that they began to be known as Jews, meaning those belonging to the Kingdom of Judah. Afterward this term would be applied to all Israelites, all Hebrews, wherever they were dispersed throughout the world.

How many of them were led away? At an earlier date, Sennacherib the Assyrian claimed that he deported a total of 200,150 from Judah, which is probably a gross overstatement. Nebuchadnezzar and his officers and governors sent off, over a twenty-three-year period, four different contingents, of which one group is believed to have been 11,000. Scholars have estimated that in all perhaps 50,000 were removed by Nebuchadnezzar, although there may have been many more, for numerous Judean cities ceased to exist from that time.

Nebuchadnezzar's Babylon was a beautiful, imposing and unforgettable city. So great is the area of the ancient site of Babylon that excavations there to date have been limited to the section containing the temples, palaces and government structures. The city was very well laid out, with broad streets intersecting at right angles, and must have been astounding to the men and women transported from compact, jumbled Jerusalem. Some of these avenues paralleled the continuous quay, or dock, along the riverfront, while others ran to great gateways in the handsome walls which could be closed by heavy bronze gates.

Chief among these broad thoroughfares was the one given the apt name of Procession Street. It began at the famous Ishtar Gate in the north wall, and down it the images of the gods were either borne or trundled on huge floats during the festival celebrating the new year. Near the Ishtar Gate, several vast palaces faced on this avenue. The second of these embodied one of the seven wonders of the ancient world, the famous Hanging Gardens. As this main artery continued toward the south, it crossed a small canal which flowed through the very center of the city, and then came to the principal temple, a towering ziggurat, visible for great distances in that flat, river-bottom land. After passing this imposing structure, the avenue then swung sharply to the west toward the Euphrates, which it crossed on a fine bridge supported by stone piers.

The river was of great importance to the welfare of Babylon, and was ever busy with fleets of circular gufas — small craft built of framework like a canoe, yet perfectly round, and covered with greased animal hides. They were not unlike the gufas which ply the waters of this same river today. Herodotus tells of many other peculiarities of the Babylonians, especially of carved walking sticks, and of how men of importance wore, suspended on a cord about their necks, the cylinder seal with which they affixed their official signatures to legal documents.

How did the Israelites fare in the new land? Many had left their homes no doubt expecting annihilation, much as had their cousins, the

Named for the goddess Ishtar, the Ishtar Gate of Babylon was more famous and beautiful than any other gate of ancient times. Animals in bas-relief, still in existence today, adorned the walls.

people of the Kingdom of Israel, nearly a century and a half before. Jeremiah had foretold that their bondage would be for a period of seventy years, but this was of questionable comfort for those torn from their homes. In Isaiah [Isaias] 47:6, it is implied that a few suffered harsh treatment, but by and large the Jews were in no sense mistreated in Babylonia. In most cases they enjoyed a wide variety of privileges. Not only were they allowed to build houses and to have servants, but they could also enter business. There is an open question as to how many had previously had any part in trade and commerce in Judah; probably not very many. Just where the bulk of the refugees lived in Babylonia is not certain; if it was in

the capital city itself, they were in the great industrial and trading center of that day. Many tried their hand at business, and some of them grew wealthy.

Other careers were also open to them. They were not denied even the highest places in the state, as the story of Daniel clearly indicates. This Jewish lad was put through the royal training school for government service, and after serving as governor of the province of Babylon became one of the three presidents, or rulers, of the entire land.

Fortunately, too, the Jews were allowed to have their priests, their prophets and their teachers with them; otherwise many might very well have been seduced by the great pantheon of Babylonian gods and goddesses and the colorful rituals and exciting magic which accompanied mass worship in that country. Under the leadership of the great prophet Ezekiel, and perhaps others of similar caliber, there appears to have been a religious awakening of large proportions. During the long years of the Captivity, the worship and religious interest of the Jews were given a new direction and a much more personal touch.

As there was now no Temple as a national center, small groups gathered regularly for instruction and devotions. Thus the synagogue, or assembly, came into being. When the opportunity came for some of the deportees to return to Jerusalem, they took back with them a heightened religious sense which was to serve them well. The religious fervor born at this time and the creation of synagogues were to have a profound and beneficial influence in keeping Jewish identity inviolate down through the ages to the present.

The religious feelings of the time are perhaps well exemplified by Job, a man who many scholars believe lived at that period somewhere in the northwestern section of the Arabian Desert between the Holy Land and the Euphrates. The story of how he was brought to ruin by one misfortune after another and of how, sitting amidst a heap of ashes and covered with boils, he still refused to surrender his deep faith in God is unfolded in the Book of Job. It constitutes the longest and finest poetic work in the Wisdom Literature of Israel. Twenty-five centuries have not diminished its emotional impact.

Under the teaching of their religious leaders the Jews in Babylonia began to understand that their captivity was truly to last but seventy years, and an attempt was made to focus attention, particularly of the young, upon the hoped-for return. Ezekiel strongly emphasized this return to the homeland, and much of his Book in the Bible is apparently a compilation of the highlights from a multitude of sermons he preached in the hope that a new, a disciplined and a better-prepared generation might one day leave the spiritual wilderness of Babylon, recapture the Promised Land and make Jerusalem a Holy City indeed. Many scholars believe that another unnamed priest and prophet wrote what are now Chapters 40

Out of Media came the deliverers of the captive Jews of Babylon.
Bas-relief of Mede and Persian warriors, palace of Persepolis

through 66 of the Book of Isaiah at this same time and for the same purpose. Some believe that he took the place of the deceased Ezekiel, who died about 565 B.C. It was this unidentified priest or prophet who first named the man who would make the return to Jerusalem possible.

The name of this "shepherd" of the lost sheep of Israel was Cyrus. He was the son of Cambyses, king of Anshan, and was destined to found the great Persian Empire. About 558 B.C. he ascended the throne of Anshan, a little desert principality beyond the Elamite country on the eastern edge of Babylonia. Destiny was to smile broadly upon him and grant him intelligence and competence equal to the great tasks assigned him. The remote area where he was born and ascended an unimportant throne played but a small part in world affairs. But to it he brought a consuming ambition and an organizing genius which was to make it mistress of a greater part of the world than any nation had previously been able to control.

Cyrus' first move was within family bounds; he forcibly annexed the kingdom of Media, ruled by his grandfather Astyages. Then, in 550 B.C., he seized Achmetha, or Ecbatana, the Median capital. This would become a treasure city and the summer residence of the Persian kings. After four years, Cyrus and his armies moved far to the northwest against the Lydian Empire and at Pteria conquered Croesus, its last ruler, noted for his fabulous wealth. The capital of Lydia, Sardis, was seized later that same year. It was another seven years before Cyrus was ready to attack the kingdom of the Chaldeans; finally, in 539 B.C., he marched on Babylon.

Nebuchadnezzar had then been dead for twenty-three years, and the throne had come into the hands of a scholar and connoisseur, Nabonidus. As this king was ill, his son Belshazzar became co-regent. Owing to this divided rule, the government and defense of the great capital had fallen into decay. Now the fear of invasion by the Medes and Persians was very real, dictating a new design of the city's fortifications. One addition was the Median Wall, which ran from near Opis on the Tigris to the outpost town of Sippar on the Euphrates. Another wall of defense ran just below the city, which stood on the eastern bank of the Euphrates and, with its inner and outer ramparts, formed a huge right-angled triangle. A somewhat more limited space along the riverbank was surrounded by still a third wall, which formed a citadel surrounding the temples, palaces and government structures.

Babylon was the most important city in the world at that time, the metropolis that Cyrus would have to conquer in order to establish his empire. How he succeeded in taking it was told by the famous Greek general and historian of the next century, Xenophon (though modern historians maintain that the city's gates were opened from within and no fighting occurred). Xenophon maintained that the Babylonians had ample time to prepare for the coming attack, as the usually sane Cyrus had spent most of the summer of the year 539 B.C. foolishly revenging himself upon the River Diala, or Diyala, which flows down from the Kurdistan highlands into the Tigris. It had drowned one of his favorite horses, and in rebuke the emperor-in-the-making had had the stream divided into no less than three hundred sixty-five channels. The Babylonians, fortunately for him, had grown soft, too self-satisfied in their reliance on their strong fortifications.

They merely laughed when Cyrus had a deep trench dug around the city, believing that he was planning to starve them out. This was ridiculous! Had they not a full twenty years of provisions on hand? They were easily deceived; the Persians were not now whiling away their time, but waited patiently for a night most vividly described in the Book of Daniel, when the leaders of the city were busy with their feasting and the terrifying fingers of a man's hand wrote a message in glowing letters on the palace wall. It read: *Mene, Mene, Tekel, Upharsin.* And Daniel, the Hebrew, he who had interpreted many dreams for Belshazzar, was called in to reveal its meaning. From it Belshazzar learned the fate awaiting his land. The mysterious words meant: God has numbered your kingdom and finished it. You are weighed in the balance and found wanting. Your kingdom will be divided and given to the Medes and the Persians.

That night the besiegers drained the Euphrates into their trench and entered the city through the dry bed of the river. They then threw down the gates, and the city's defenses were rendered worthless. The diverted river wrought much havoc, traces of which are still visible in the ruins of the inner walls. Babylon was readily subdued.

Frieze of Persian warriors from palace of Artaxerxes I at Susa. Son of the great Xerxes, this king granted Nehemiah permission to rebuild the walls of Jerusalem.

10. The Persians Restore Judah

Cyrus had conquered the city of Babylon by a most surprising strategy. Still more remarkable occurrences came with this quick transfer of Chaldean power to the mighty Persian.

To the astonishment of the conquered, there was no mass slaughter of the inhabitants, no herd of unfortunate people marched away into captivity. Even the gods of Babylon were left undisturbed. With great tolerance, Cyrus allowed life to proceed without violent alteration, in marked contrast to the ways the Assyrians and the Babylonians themselves had practiced toward conquered peoples. His vision of empire was completely different from that of others, for Cyrus hoped for a commonwealth of self-governing dominions, under the beneficent control of a clement emperor. Trade and the advantages of peace throughout the world were to be enjoyed by all.

His prompt decree that all nationals captive in the city and surrounding country might return to their homelands extended of course to the Jews. Their Captivity thus came to an end early in the year 538 B.C., and the event for which their leaders had long been preparing took place. The Jews of the Exile were not destined for obscurity like the Ten Lost Tribes. They were to go on and on, living a long, full history hardly exceeded by that of any other people. Yet the inhabitants of restored Judah were still pawns in a pagan world for the greater part of the ages ahead.

Sheshbazzar, a prince of Judah, was appointed by Cyrus as the governor. His task was to oversee the organization of the trek to Judah and to get it under way, an effort which, according to Persian methods and customs, called for tact and diplomacy. Actually Sheshbazzar was only the political head of this new colony, or province, and for actual leaders of the Jews he chose two men. One was a prince of the house of David whose name was Zerubbabel, and the other was Jeshua, grandson of possibly the last of the High Priests to serve in the Temple. The details of assembling the party that would make the journey and the accomplishment of this long trip itself were left in their hands.

Now that the way was opened, how many Israelites would go? How different this period of bondage had been from the one suffered by their forebears centuries earlier in Egypt! Leaving the land of the pharaohs had meant fleeing from slavery. But for many, leaving Babylon meant leaving newfound opportunities and a fuller life. The great majority, too, had never known Judah at first hand, for only a very few of those who had been deported were still alive and longed to return to their homes. A second and even a third generation had come into being during the Captivity, and it was from among these that the returning colony would be chosen.

The Bible account gives the impression that the Israelites were not too eager to leave Babylon, yet at two points in the text a total of 50,000 people is given (Ezra [1 Esdras] 2:64-65; Nehemiah [2 Esdras] 7:66-67). Many of these must have perished or deserted on the way, for descriptions of happenings in Jerusalem during the next century or more hardly account for that many people.

How far was it from Babylon to Jerusalem? The distance across the blistering, waterless desert of Arabia is five hundred thirty miles as the crow flies. By way of the caravan trails, the only practical course for so large a party, it was about nine hundred miles. With the best of luck and management the journey would have taken six months. Ezra made the same pilgrimage many years later, at the head of a far smaller group, spending four months en route. It was no "Sabbath day's journey." Many possessions must have been left behind, and all of the people walked, for the 8136 horses, camels, mules and asses mentioned in the Bible would have been burdened with food, goods and the great quantity of Temple vessels and implements which had been graciously returned to the Jews by Cyrus.

These travelers seem to have reached their destination well before the onset of the autumn rains. This was fortunate, as autumn is the time of plowing and planting in the Holy Land, and unless a grain crop had been sown then for spring harvesting there would have been certain famine during the coming year. One of their first common efforts was to erect an altar, built upon the very site — the threshing floor of Araunah — on which David had constructed an altar centuries before, and where countless sacrifices had been made through the years when Solomon's Temple had stood on or near that spot. According to tradition it is the place where Father Abraham had sought to offer young Isaac as a sacrifice to God. The new altar was perhaps a rather crude affair, but that did not matter, for once again the worship of the Lord was centered on Zion, His "holy mountain." The altar was dedicated in October of that memorable year, 538 B.C.

According to the enthusiastic plans made in the far-off land of the Captivity, this altar was to have been the first step in the prompt rebuilding of the Temple. But these people, born in the warmer climate of Babylon, needed houses. Tents were not sufficient during the winter season now upon them. They must wring a living from the lean and reluctant land. Whatever religious enthusiasm they had brought with them evaporated quickly in the face of the grim realities confronting them. The comforts and plenty of the land of Captivity had had a softening effect. There was

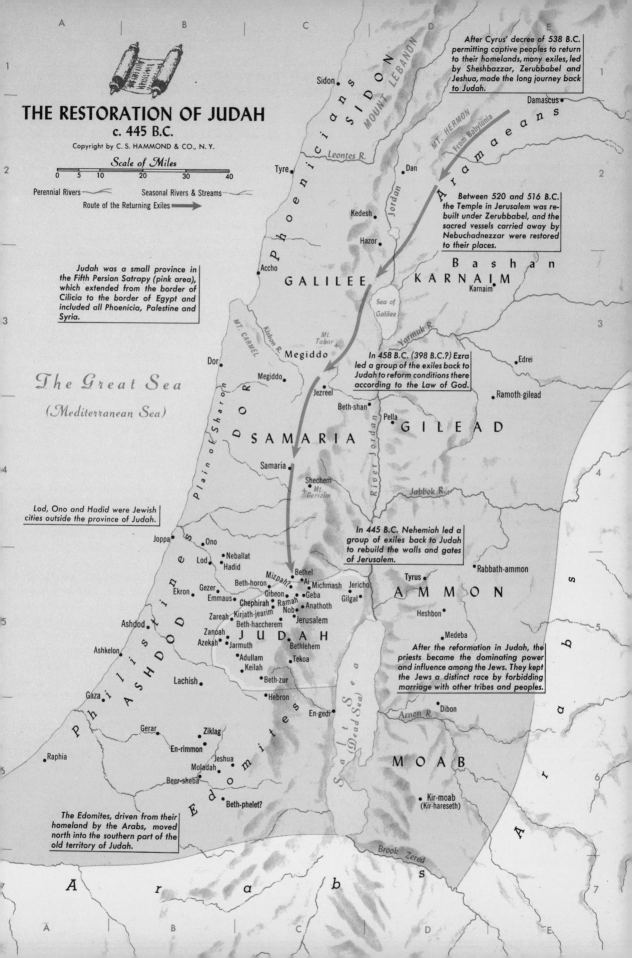

THE RESTORATION OF JUDAH
c. 445 B.C.

Copyright by C. S. HAMMOND & CO., N. Y.

Scale of Miles

0 5 10 20 30 40

Perennial Rivers

Seasonal Rivers & Streams

Route of the Returning Exiles

After Cyrus' decree of 538 B.C. permitting captive peoples to return to their homelands, many exiles, led by Sheshbazzar, Zerubbabel and Jeshua, made the long journey back to Judah.

Between 520 and 516 B.C. the Temple in Jerusalem was rebuilt under Zerubbabel, and the sacred vessels carried away by Nebuchadnezzar were restored to their places.

Judah was a small province in the Fifth Persian Satrapy (pink area), which extended from the border of Cilicia to the border of Egypt and included all Phoenicia, Palestine and Syria.

In 458 B.C. (398 B.C.?) Ezra led a group of the exiles back to Judah to reform conditions there according to the Law of God.

Lod, Ono and Hadid were Jewish cities outside the province of Judah.

In 445 B.C. Nehemiah led a group of exiles back to Judah to rebuild the walls and gates of Jerusalem.

After the reformation in Judah, the priests became the dominating power and influence among the Jews. They kept the Jews a distinct race by forbidding marriage with other tribes and peoples.

The Edomites, driven from their homeland by the Arabs, moved north into the southern part of the old territory of Judah.

The Great Sea
(Mediterranean Sea)

SIDON · Sidon · Damascus
MOUNT LEBANON · Phoenicians · Leontes R. · MT. HERMON · Aramaeans · From Babylonia
Tyre · Dan · Kedesh · Hazor · Jordan
Accho · GALILEE · Bashan · KARNAIM · Karnaim
MT. CARMEL · Kishon R. · Mt. Tabor · Sea of Galilee · Yarmuk R. · Edrei
Dor · Megiddo · Megiddo · Jezreel · Beth-shan · Pella · GILEAD · Ramoth-gilead
DOR · SAMARIA · Samaria · Shechem · Mt. Gerizim · River Jordan · Jabbok R.
Plain of Sharon · Joppa · Ono · Neballat · Hadid · Mizpah? · Bethel · Ai · Michmash · Jericho · Tyrus · AMMON · Rabbath-ammon
Lod · Beth-horon · Gibeon · Geba · Gilgal · Heshbon
Ekron · Gezer · Emmaus · Chephirah · Ramah · Nob · Anathoth
Zareah · Kirjath-jearim · Jerusalem · Medeba
ASHDOD · Ashdod · Zanoah · Beth-haccherem · JUDAH
Ashkelon · Azekah · Jarmuth · Bethlehem · Tekoa
Adullam · Keilah · Salt Sea (Dead Sea)
Gaza · Lachish · Beth-zur · Hebron · En-gedi · Arnon R. · Dibon
Philistines · Gerar · Ziklag · En-rimmon · Jeshua · MOAB · Arabs
Raphia · Moladah · Beer-sheba · Edomites · Beth-phelet? · Kir-moab (Kir-haresheth)
Brook Zered · Arabs

friction with the handful of Israelites who had lived on in Jerusalem and the surrounding country; and the people of Samaria to the north and the Edomites to the south were, if anything, antagonistic rather than friendly. It was two years before any further work on the Temple was undertaken.

It was hardly under way when trouble rose again. The Samaritans, that mixture of peoples who were descendants of those brought in by Sargon II when he took the city of Samaria almost two hundred years before, felt they should have a part in the building and use of this Temple. Zerubbabel and Jeshua overruled them. Cyrus, they insisted, had commanded the Jews to rebuild the Temple, and it would be contrary to orders to extend the privilege to others. The Samaritan leaders promptly exerted political pressure, and the work was brought to a halt.

While this opposition continued, the great Cyrus died. He was followed by his son Cambyses, who, though he reigned but a short time, managed to conquer Egypt and add it to the empire. At his death, the throne was seized by a pretender. Many of the different lands of the empire now attempted to break away. It was Darius, a member of another branch of the royal house that ruled over the Medes and the Persians, who killed the pretender, suppressed the rebellion, saved the empire and mounted the throne.

According to Chapter 6 of Daniel, Darius was not at first sympathetic to the Jewish cause. Although he raised Daniel to a high position, when Daniel defied the king's decree against worshiping God he was thrown into the lions' den. When God delivered Daniel, Darius had a change of heart.

The Jews of Jerusalem appealed to the new king for the right to continue work on the Temple. Darius ordered a search of the vaults at the Median capital at Achmetha (Ecbatana) for the original authorization. There a scroll inscribed with Cyrus' edict was found, and so in the third year of Darius' reign work on the Temple got under way again. After four years and a great deal of urging by the prophet Haggai, this second "House of God" was completed. The year is now generally believed to have been 516 B.C. (Ezra [1 Esdras] 5:6–6:15).

The new structure, which came to be known as Zerubbabel's Temple, was perhaps a trifle larger than Solomon's Temple, but far less magnificent and well built. Some of the few who were old enough to recall the first Temple were rather blunt and bitter in their criticism. Nevertheless, its walls were gilded and it housed a large store of treasure. There is an inventory in the Bible which lists 5400 gold and silver vessels such as chargers, basins, bowls and knives which had been taken by Nebuchadnezzar from Solomon's Temple and returned by Cyrus. All this, like the citizens themselves, existed in an unprotected city. The walls were still in the condition in which they had been left when the city was devastated seven decades before. It would be another seventy years before Jerusalem would be properly fortified. Yet the worship of Yahweh in a "House" of His own had been restored, and that was a real achievement.

In spite of the fact that many Jews had returned to the Promised Land from Babylon, the "scattering," which had been threatened in the time of Moses for all who departed from the Law of the Lord (Leviticus 26:33-37; Deuteronomy 4:27-28; 28:64-68), was now well advanced. The captivity of the Ten Tribes, and then of Judah and Benjamin, had contributed a great deal to the fulfillment of those prophecies. The Ten Tribes had been almost completely assimilated, and many of the people of Judah who had been taken to Babylon chose to remain there. There may even have been some emigration from Judah into other lands, particularly Egypt, after the restoration was in progress.

Some of the Jews in foreign places achieved considerable prominence; one maiden, whose Hebrew name was Hadassah, became the favorite wife of the Persian king Xerxes I. Bible readers know this famous couple as Ahasuerus and Esther. Esther was the cousin and adopted daughter of a certain man named Mordecai, and it was she who frustrated a plot instigated by the evil prime minister Haman to kill all the Jews in the empire. Haman was finally hung on a gallows he had erected for Mordecai, who then became prime minister in his stead. Esther's great contribution in behalf of her people is celebrated to this day during February or March by the festival of Purim, which terminates with lighthearted rejoicing and is perhaps the most colorful of all Jewish holidays. If Xerxes and Ahasuerus are actually one, as scholars now generally agree, then the lovely Esther became queen about 486 B.C.

So courageously did Esther exhort her king and husband, Xerxes I, that she delivered her people from destruction at the hands of their enemies. The Hebrew name of Esther was Hadassah.

The palace at Persepolis, a capital of the Persian Empire built by Darius I, father of Xerxes, with a magnificence greater than Babylon

Xerxes died in 464 B.C. and was succeeded on the Persian throne by his third son, Artaxerxes Longimanus, or "the long-handed." There was perhaps that period of uneasiness and rebellion which sometimes came with a change of rulers. If this was so, it probably accounts for the fact that the new king at first refused requests made of him for the rebuilding and strengthening of the city of Jerusalem.

Ezra, a priest of the colony of Jews still living in Babylon, promoted such an "awakening" among those to whom he ministered that finally, during the seventh year of his reign, Artaxerxes commissioned Ezra to go to Jerusalem on an inspection tour. He was to inquire into the civil and religious conditions among the people and see if they were abiding by the teachings of God's Law. He was also permitted to lead a new company of more than seventeen hundred Jewish exiles back to Judah.

After four months of traveling, Ezra and his group arrived safely at Jerusalem. New holy vessels and other utensils for use in the Temple were presented to the priests, sacrifice was offered, and Ezra delivered Artaxerxes' orders to the governors of neighboring provinces. Then he began an examination of local affairs.

He was highly disturbed over one condition: the men of Jerusalem, including some priests, had married foreign women. Since this was in direct opposition to the Law of Moses, Ezra openly attacked them and induced many to put away their "strange wives."

According to the sequence of events of the books of Ezra and Nehemiah, formerly reckoned by the Jews as but a single book, there now ensued a quiet period. About thirteen years intervened between Ezra's arrival in Jerusalem and the arrival of Nehemiah, another conscientious man, hopeful of bringing about vast improvements in conditions in the tiny Judean homeland.

Nehemiah had risen to an elevated and responsible position in the Persian court. He was the cupbearer to King Artaxerxes; his duties consisted of pouring wine into the royal cup and offering it to the king. Since Nehemiah was in a position to poison the sovereign, it was truly a post of trust. That such confidence was invested in a foreigner is the strongest possible recommendation for Nehemiah and his complete reliability.

Stationed at the Persian court, Nehemiah saw any and all people visiting there from Judah, and he was deeply grieved to hear of the state of ruin which still prevailed at Jerusalem. He finally asked and received permission from Artaxerxes to go there and rebuild the city wall. So great was the king's trust in Nehemiah that he not only granted him permission but also appointed him governor of Judah, giving him a cavalry escort and letters to the various Persian satraps along the way. The year was 445 B.C.

As our Bible now stands, Nehemiah would have found Ezra ministering in Jerusalem upon his arrival. By this older, traditional opinion the priest Ezra would have been there for thirteen years. But scholars who have given much time to the study of this question now believe that a fairly late editing of the Bible resulted in a change in the original order of the text, and that Nehemiah actually preceded Ezra. The date for Ezra's mission to Jerusalem may have been as late as 398 B.C., and it may have been made under another king, Artaxerxes II.

Whatever the date of Nehemiah's arrival, he managed to keep his main purpose secret for several days; he went about at night carefully examining the shattered and demolished walls. Then, after the third night of inspection, as the new governor he called the people together and disclosed his plan. Aid was willingly given. Some of the leading citizens offered to bear the expenses of restoring particular sections of the wall.

Neighboring Gentile tribes, such as the Arabs and Ammonites, were much disturbed and did their best to hamper the work, but Nehemiah quickly proved that he could not be frightened off, nor turned from his purpose. He ordered all those working on the wall to have weapons close at hand. While this was inconvenient and disturbing, the Gentiles' hostility spurred the men forward, according to the Bible, in only fifty-two working days the fortifications were restored. The historian Josephus disagrees. He claims that it took a full two years and four months to complete the task.

With the Temple and the walls rebuilt, enthusiasm mounted, and a religious revival followed. During a fervent ceremony Ezra read the Law of Moses to the people of the colony. Many of them had never heard it before in its entirety, and it had a profound effect upon them. Nehemiah prevailed upon the chief men to join him in a most solemn compact to worship Yahweh, and Him alone.

After governing at Jerusalem for about twelve years, Nehemiah journeyed back to the court of the Persian king. It was not long before he asked to return once again to Judah. He had his commission as governor extended and was back in the city in the highlands that same year, 433 B.C. He may have governed there during the remainder of his life, which, according to the historian Josephus, was a very long one. However, a letter discovered in Egypt in recent years indicates that by 419 B.C. Nehemiah was no longer governor.

Zerubbabel, Jeshua, Ezra and Nehemiah: these four men labored unceasingly that Jerusalem might be restored to its former glory as the center of all political and religious life of the people of Judah. As the fifth pre-Christian century drew to an end, the prospects had brightened materially.

Aerial view of Susa, winter residence of Xerxes I, showing ruins dating from 4000 B.C. to 1200 A.D., including the palace Esther lived in

Alexander the Great as he appears in a mosaic at Pompeii

11. Alexander and the Grecian Era

Up to the fourth pre-Christian century, the influences which had helped to shape conditions in the Holy Land had had their origin for the most part within the Fertile Crescent, or in the highlands immediately beyond its eastern point. It was in this latter area that Persian power had its beginnings, and it was from there that it spread not only into Egypt but across the Bosporus and the Hellespont into Thrace. At the time during which the Bible pictures Esther as Xerxes' favorite wife, that king threw

two pontoon bridges across the narrow Hellespont and, in 480 B.C., gained a foothold in Europe. Ancient records describe his army as a million strong; modern estimates indicate that it could have been only about 180,000.

After crossing the Hellespont, Xerxes moved west to Thermopylae, where he defeated Leonidas and his handful of Spartans and their allies. He then burned Athens and was about to take possession of all of Greece when the Athenians, who had fled to the island of Salamis just east of their city, forced him into a naval battle. The Persian ships were so utterly defeated that most of Xerxes' land forces had to flee back into Asia. Persia's attempt upon Europe had been dramatic, but short and costly.

One of the European countries that Xerxes crossed was Macedon, the mountainous area to the north of Greece. This little land remained unimportant until, in 359 B.C., its throne was seized by an able, crafty young man named Philip. After reorganizing the Macedonian army and perfecting the celebrated infantry formation known as the Macedonian phalanx, he managed, during the next twenty years, to bring the Greek states under his domination. He became so powerful that at a congress held in Corinth in 337 B.C. he was elected the commander of the allied Greek forces gathered to invade Persia and seek vengeance for the crimes that Xerxes had committed against Greek sanctuaries.

In the spring of the following year, Philip sent a vanguard of 10,000 men over the Hellespont to prepare for the liberation of the Persian-held cities of Asia Minor. In midsummer of 336 B.C. he was assassinated. He was succeeded by his twenty-year-old son, who came to be known as Alexander the Great. This young man had been educated by no less a teacher than Aristotle, and his father had made him, at sixteen, regent of Greece. He was accomplished both as a ruler and as a general by the time he ascended the throne.

In 334 B.C. Alexander crossed into Asia with some 30,000 foot soldiers and about 5000 cavalry. His position was at first uncertain but was much strengthened by a decisive victory over the Persian forces near Zelea, along the banks of the Granicus, a mountain stream emptying into the Propontis. The following year, at Issus in Syria, seventy-five miles east of Tarsus, Alexander met the army of Darius III and destroyed it so completely that the Persian king took to his heels, leaving his harem of many wives behind.

Moving on toward the south, Alexander then took over Syria, subdued Tyre by siege, and overcame the inhabitants of the Philistine city of Gaza. It was perhaps during the interim between these last two actions that a deputation of the leading citizens of Jerusalem, headed by the Temple High Priest, appeared before the young conqueror and arranged for their city to be spared.

Alexander's next objective was Egypt, where he was welcomed as the vanquisher of the now hated Persians. This new liberator, who had many of the fine characteristics of the Persian conqueror Cyrus, was rapidly annexing the empire that warrior had built. One of his great achievements in the land along the Nile was the founding of the city of Alexandria. For centuries to come it was destined to be a center of art, science and learning, a refuge for Jews, and also a stronghold of Christianity.

With Egypt now his vassal, Alexander the Great was ready to proceed with his chief objective, to complete the conquest of the Persian Empire. For several years he was busy fulfilling this dream, conquering all that lay before him. Beyond the easternmost reaches of Cyrus' empire, his army even penetrated distant and mysterious India. But, far from home and caught in a rainy season, his troops refused to go any farther and he was forced to turn back. The year was 324 B.C. He did not, however, give up his hopes of further conquests. The following year, at Babylon, while he was busily making plans for transporting his troops by sea around the Arabian peninsula, he fell sick of a fever and died, aged but thirty-two years.

What was to become of the vast empire Alexander the Great had conquered? Having no bonds to tie it together beyond the personality and will of the dead king, it was readily broken apart. A group of Alexander's army commanders, who became known as the Diadochi, or successors of the late monarch, took the situation into their bloody and brutal hands and partitioned the empire. Years of fighting and jockeying for power among them ensued, during which Alexander's mother, half brother, wife and posthumous son were murdered.

Antigonus Cyclops, the one-eyed Macedonian general, had western Asia Minor as his original share. He hoped to become lord of all Asia, and was on the way to that goal when the other Diadochi combined to prevent this and protect their own realms. The map on page 106 shows their holdings at the height of Antigonus' power, when he had proclaimed himself king and expanded his domains to include nearly all of Asia Minor and Syria. A few years later he was defeated and slain by a coalition of the other Diadochi in the battle of Ipsus, 301 B.C., and the spoils were once more divided.

THE EMPIRE OF
ALEXANDER THE GREAT
323 B.C.
AND THE KINGDOMS OF
ALEXANDER'S SUCCESSORS
c. 305 B.C.

Copyright by C. S. HAMMOND & CO., N.Y.

Scale of Miles

0   100   200   300   400   500

Alexander's Route
Nearchus' Voyage
Major Battles Fought by Alexander
Limits of Alexander's Empire 323 B.C.

Kingdom of Antigonus Cyclops
Kingdom of Seleucus
Kingdom of Ptolemy
Kingdom of Lysimachus
Kingdom of Cassander

Prior to the Battle of Ipsus 301 B.C.

The lion's share of Antigonus' territory was added to that of a king who was already shaping an empire that would reach from Thrace to India. This was Seleucus Nicator, who had served as a general in Alexander's army and had shared in the original partition of his empire. His real power had begun when he became ruler of Babylonia in 312 B.C., a date which marks the beginning of the Seleucid era. He proved to be a beneficent king, patron of the arts and sciences. He founded the Grecian city of Antioch in Syria in 300 B.C. and made it his capital.

One more piece of the jigsaw puzzle of the new kingdom was the realm that fell to one of Alexander's most trusted Macedonian commanders, Ptolemy I. He founded a dynasty which, during the next three centuries, would have twelve other kings bearing his name. His was the kingdom of Egypt, with Alexandria for its capital, a city which during the ensuing years would be principally Grecian in culture. Ptolemy had attempted to seize Palestine in 320 B.C., entering Jerusalem by taking advantage of the Sabbath rest. But he did not secure complete possession until after the death of Antigonus Cyclops in 301 B.C. Even then Ptolemaic rule of the Holy Land was to be strongly contested by the Seleucids in the century to come.

During this difficult time many Jews migrated from Judaea (as Judah was now called by its Greek rulers) to Cyrene, in north Africa, and especially to Alexandria. There they dropped the use of Hebrew and of Aramaic, the international Semitic tongue which they had brought back from Babylon, and spoke only Greek. Losing knowledge of Hebrew, they could no longer follow the readings from the Scriptures in their synagogue services.

Ptolemy II, known as Philadelphus, was very proud of the great library at Alexandria and attempted to bring together there the finest writings of all nations. According to legend he expressed much interest when he was told of the sacred literature of the Jews. Getting in touch with the High Priest in Jerusalem, he made arrangements to have Jewish scholars come to Egypt, to translate into Greek these holy writings, or Torah, as they were called. It is reported that seventy-two learned scribes assembled on the island of Pharos just offshore from Alexandria, where, in seventy-two days, they translated the entire Law.

This was of great service to the Jewish people, who were already widely scattered through a world in which Greek was becoming the common tongue. It was also to have a profound effect upon the New Testament. Jesus and His Apostles frequently quoted from this Septuagint version; of the hundreds of quotes from the Old Testament found in the New Testament over half were derived from the Septuagint. As evidence of the Septuagint's extensive use in early Christian times, there is the report of the chance encounter between Philip the Evangelist and the Ethiopian eunuch (Acts 8:27-30), wherein the latter, as he drove along in his chariot toward his home far away in Africa, was reading from the Septuagint.

In 223 B.C., about fifty years after this translation was made, Antiochus III, surnamed the Great, became king in Syria, continuing the Seleucid dynasty. Being ambitious, he overran the lands to the south, seeking to wrest lower Syria, Phoenicia and Palestine from Egypt. The reigning monarch in Alexandria at that moment was Ptolemy IV, called Philopator, a most debased creature. He was suspected of having killed his father to gain the throne, and his first act after becoming king was to murder his own mother and younger brother; his whole reign was made up of such horrible acts. Antiochus thought that one so depraved would be easy prey. But to his surprise his Syrian forces were roundly defeated by Philopator's troops at the battle of Raphia, twenty miles below Gaza, in 217 B.C.

Philopator thus entered Palestine and, being in the vicinity, he visited Jerusalem and insisted on offering sacrifice in the holy Temple for his victory. This was an abomination to the Jews. When they prevented him from further profaning the Temple by entering the Holy of Holies, he was enraged. On his return to Egypt he started a pogrom, attempting to assassinate every Jew in the city of Alexandria.

After Philopator's death in 203 B.C., Antiochus again invaded the Holy Land, and in 198 B.C. was victorious at the battle of Panias, adding Palestine to the Seleucid Empire. He now turned his ambitions upon Europe. He made a successful invasion of that continent and got as far as the famous pass at Thermopylae, only to meet with a sorry defeat at the hands of a new and rising power, Rome. He hurried back into Asia, where his army was again decisively vanquished at Magnesia, near

Coin with portrait of Ptolemy II and his wife

Ephesus, by another Roman army under the general Scipio. This major setback in 190 B.C. marks the first direct contact between the peoples of the Bible lands and the Romans, who were destined to dominate the remainder of Bible times.

The Romans dictated a most disastrous peace following the battle at Magnesia. In addition to the payment of an enormous tribute, Antiochus was forced to send twenty hostages to Rome as proof of his goodwill toward his conquerors; one of these men was his own son. His name was Antiochus Epiphanes, and he was to spend fifteen years in the Eternal City as a pledge, first for his father and then for his brother. At last in 175 B.C., when his brother died, the Romans allowed him to return to Syria and assume the throne as their vassal. It was the policy of the Romans from then on to harass and weaken the Seleucid Empire in every way.

In spite of all this, Antiochus Epiphanes was active and venturesome, and sought to extend and build up his domain as much as possible. He was most unfortunate in always antagonizing the people he ruled. This was especially true of the Jews. They had put all political ambitions behind them at the time of

To the Greek city of Alexandria, built on the Mediterranean, Ptolemy II summoned Hebrew scholars to translate the Scriptures into Greek. They retired to work on the nearby island of Pharos, whose lighthouse was one of the seven wonders of the ancient world.

Gerasa, forty miles southeast of the Sea of Galilee, in its time the most elegant city of Palestine. This oval forum may have been built by Greek survivors of Alexander's wars.

their return from Babylon and were willing to be vassals providing their overlord did not attempt to dictate or interfere in their religious matters. But Antiochus' needs were so great that he was driven to desperate means.

Before he dared think of attempting to throw off the Roman yoke, all the various groups within his domain must be more closely welded together. In his opinion, the greatest possible unifying force was Grecian thought and the Grecian way of life. It was particularly necessary that all, no matter what their nationalities or beliefs, adopt a common faith. Since he was an absolute monarch in his land, his first step toward unification was to issue an edict to that effect. Little did he realize the intense loyalty to God felt by the Jews, especially since the days of Ezra and Nehemiah. He was immediately in conflict with them over their faith.

Syrian emissaries were quickly dispatched to Judaea with explicit orders to stamp out Judaism and in its place establish the worship of the greatest of the deities of the Greeks, the supreme sovereign of the universe, Olympian Zeus. These men sought to do a thorough job. The Temple was robbed, and then a statue of Zeus, or Jupiter, as he was known to the Romans, was set up in the Holy of Holies. All the sacred books that could be found were burned. Circumcision, the rite of initiation into the covenant privileges of the family of God and the token of the sacred

covenant, was forbidden on pain of death. So, too, were any and all attempts to sanctify the Sabbath or celebrate the arrival of the new moon, a custom which had come down through the ages from the days of the patriarchs. The sacrifice of swine, a most abhorrent act to all Jews, became mandatory. As a result of these offensive regulations the terrors of religious persecution enveloped Jerusalem and all other Jewish communities in Judaea.

To add to these difficulties, the Syrian king sent his chief tax collector into Judaea, accompanied by an armed force which could not be resisted. This Apollonius, due one day to meet death at the hands of the avenger of his deeds, stripped all possible spoil from the city; then, setting it afire and destroying homes and other buildings, he sought to render it completely defenseless by tearing down its walls. He ordered a massacre of its inhabitants, drove many women and children off into slavery and herded away the animals as food for his soldiers.

Not only had Antiochus Epiphanes profaned the Temple of God, but he had antagonized the Jews forevermore. It was a heavier blow than had been dealt them by either the Assyrians or the Babylonians, so heavy in fact that for a time they were completely dazed. But within a year courage began to return, and resistance to the Syrian oppressor grew in the little devastated land. One of the most spectacular periods of Jewish history lay just ahead.

12. Revolt of the Maccabees

The "abomination of desolation" hovered over the Temple in Jerusalem as a result of the religious indignities instituted by Antiochus Epiphanes. But Jerusalem was not alone. The same indignities were imposed upon every town and hamlet of Judaea. Idols of the pagan Zeus, or Jupiter, were set up in all public places. Altars were built before the doors of houses, and those who valued their lives offered prescribed sacrifices upon them regularly. Those who did not obey the decree of the king and make an open display of their zeal were seized, publicly whipped and then slain.

The condition was intolerable. Resistance began to build up, and one of the first to give it frank and open expression was an aged priest called Mattathias. His name meant "gift of Yahweh," and such indeed he proved to be. He belonged to a family of distinction, prominent in the affairs of the small town of Modin, seventeen miles northwest of Jerusalem. Suddenly a Syrian official appeared in that community and called upon Mattathias to use his influence in establishing idolatrous worship there. The old man not only resisted this officer but, when the Syrian made preparations for offering a heathen sacrifice, he promptly slew the intruder.

Knowing that there would be violent reaction and savage redress from the Syrians, Mattathias and his five sons fled into the hills and hid in the caves with which the area abounded. Other devout Jews, inspired by the spirit of revolt, now began to join them. Although the old priest died in the following year, 166 B.C., he bequeathed the cause to his five brave sons. The rebels chose the third son, Judas, as the new leader.

While the late Mattathias and his sons bore the family designation of Hasmonaeans, this newer head of the clan received the surname of Maccabaeus, which was soon transferred to other members of the group. Although its meaning is not wholly certain, it is thought to have come from *maqqaba,* a hammer.

Under Judas Maccabaeus' leadership the revolt spread rapidly, and in a short time he had a sufficient number of armed men to meet and defeat the Syrians in open battle at Emmaus. Actually, Roman pressure — the indirect cause of the conditions which had brought about the Jewish rebellion — now

*With spears and farmers' tools the Jews, under Judas Maccabaeus, stormed
the walls of Jerusalem and drove off the Syrians who defiled the temple.*

helped the Jews in their fight for freedom. The enormous tribute demanded of Antiochus by Rome compelled the Syrian king to take the bulk of his army and march off to the East on a money-raising campaign. This left Syria with but a few soldiers on hand for use in an emergency.

Before leaving for the East, Antiochus had turned over the government at Antioch to a functionary and general of the army named Lysias, with specific instructions to quell any and all Jewish uprisings. Trusting the direction of the troops at first to others, this man finally decided to take command himself, only to be defeated at Bethsura (Bethzur) with heavy losses (1 Machabees 4:27-34).

Judas Maccabaeus now retook Jerusalem. The statue of Zeus was removed from the Holy of Holies and all the pagan implements of sacrifice were destroyed. The Temple was then purified, and daily sacrifices and worship were restored. This was the occasion for a joyous celebration, which became an annual affair known as Hanukkah, or the Feast of Dedication (John 10:22).

Word of the disaster which had befallen Lysias was hurriedly borne to Antiochus, who started immediately for home. Death caught up with him on the way and removed one of the Jews' most somber enemies.

Turmoil now disturbed the Syrian capital. Lysias seized the government and ruled in the

Statue of Zeus (Jupiter) found at Caesarea. Throughout Judaea, Syrian overlords pressed the Jews to worship before such idols at public altars.

name of Antiochus' nine-year-old son, Antiochus Eupator, in spite of the fact that the late king had appointed a courtier named Philip to act as regent during his son's minority. This situation, of course, worked for the benefit of the Jews; Lysias had to devote considerable time and attention to the claims of Philip, who was with the Syrian army in Persia.

According to the statement in 2 Machabees 11:34-36, another piece of good fortune for the Jews came to pass. Two Roman envoys, probably on their way from Alexandria to the Syrian capital at Antioch, offered to use their influence there in behalf of the people of Judaea. Evidently they kept their word, for a short-lived peace resulted.

The Syrians, however, were determined to gain the complete subjugation of their Jewish vassals, and so in the very next year, 162 B.C., another army appeared out of the north. Judas Maccabaeus and his men did their best to stop this horde, but the Syrians pressed on and put Jerusalem under siege. Conditions within the city quickly became critical, and it would soon have been forced to surrender had there not been a sudden change in Syrian plans. News

reached the besiegers that the regent Philip was returning from Persia at the head of an army, prepared to fight for his rights. The siege was called off, and the young Antiochus Eupator, on the advice of Lysias, granted the Jews complete religious liberty if they would keep the peace. The situation in Judaea now returned to what it had been before Antiochus Epiphanes had tried to force the worship of Zeus upon the Jews.

One very disturbing factor remained. It centered about the High Priest Alcimus, who had been appointed to that post by Antiochus Eupator. This man was entirely Greek in thought and sympathies, and thus loathed by the pious Jews. A plea to remove him might have been made to the child king, but affairs in Antioch suddenly became very tense. The child king was dethroned and slain by his cousin, who then took the crown as Demetrius Soter. This man, like his uncle the former king Antiochus Epiphanes, had been held in Rome as a hostage. Hearing of the death of Antiochus Epiphanes and the rivalry which had arisen between Lysias and Philip, he had made his escape and headed for Antioch. Arriving there, he seized the kingdom; and in addition to disposing of the child Antiochus he did away with Philip and Lysias too.

While the new king, Demetrius Soter, granted certain religious liberties to the Jews, his approval of the High Priest Alcimus and his insistence on controlling the top priestly office fanned the still smoldering fires of revolt. The struggle blazed up; Alcimus was forced to flee the Holy City. Quickly Syrian forces appeared, and, although Judas Maccabaeus defeated them at Adasa just north of Jerusalem, he realized that outside aid was essential. His people were too few in number to withstand continuously the might of the far larger kingdom of the Seleucids. But to whom should the Jews apply?

His choice was clear. The Romans for some years now had not missed an opportunity to do what they could to enfeeble and cripple the Syrian rulers. Surely they would lend a sympathetic ear. So two envoys, Eupolemos and Jason, were chosen and started on their way to Rome in search of an alliance. They received a cordial reception, and the Senate acknowledged the independence of Judaea with the idea of making it a buffer state to separate the Syrian and Egyptian realms.

While the Judaean envoys were busy in Rome, the Syrians were not idle at home. Demetrius gathered an army and hurled it at the rebellious little land to the south. Judas Maccabaeus hastily rallied his forces and met this surprise invasion, but was defeated and slain at Elasa, north of Jerusalem, in 160 B.C.

When Alcimus had fled Jerusalem, the

The Maccabees

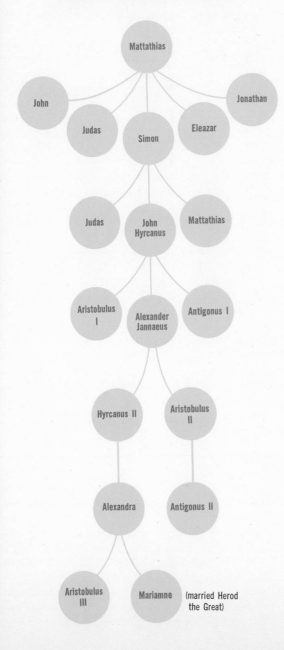

youngest of old Mattathias' sons, Jonathan, had taken over the High Priesthood. Now that Judas had been killed, he took over command of the army as well. This latter responsibility was, in a sense, thrust upon him. John, the eldest of the five brothers, had been taken prisoner a short time before and killed. At about the same time Eleazar, the next to the youngest, had been crushed to death by an elephant which he had wounded in battle.

Happily for the Jews, Syria now became embroiled in civil war. This gave Judaea a much needed period of peace, and with Rome's backing it now began to gain importance. Sparta signed a treaty of alliance with it. When the civil war in Syria ended, the new Syrian king, Demetrius II, named Judaea's High Priest and leader, Jonathan Maccabaeus, as its official civil and military governor.

Rome, which had been heavily involved in wars in the West, had at last completely vanquished an old and powerful foe, Carthage, the great city on the Mediterranean coast of northern Africa which had been founded by the far-trading Phoenicians some six hundred fifty years before. Rome also had made vassals of the Greeks and Macedonians and was now sufficiently secure to give more direct attention to matters in the East. Jonathan Maccabaeus, a sagacious statesman, thought he saw an opportunity for enlisting further Roman aid and dispatched envoys to the capital city on the Tiber. Nothing came of this because affairs in Syria, unstable as ever, proved to be his undoing. Another pretender to the Syrian throne, Tryphon, basely murdered the able Jewish leader at Ptolemaïs. In 142 B.C. Simon, the one remaining son of the old priest Mattathias, took over the leadership of Judaean affairs.

Under his wise guidance the little land knew continuing peace and a considerable measure of prosperity. During his eight years as ruler what had been no more than a religious community once again became a nation, and a remarkable event took place. In return for Simon's assistance in resisting the pretender Tryphon, King Demetrius II renounced all claim to tribute and granted the Jews their independence. The delighted people, at a solemn assembly called for the purpose, rewarded Simon Maccabaeus by proclaiming him and his descendants High Priests and ethnarchs (provincial governors) "until a faithful prophet should arise" (1 Machabees 14:41).

PALESTINE UNDER THE MACCABEES
166 TO 63 B.C.

Copyright by C. S. HAMMOND & CO., N.Y.

Scale of Miles

0   5   10   20   30   40

Perennial Rivers ~~~~~~
Seasonal Rivers & Streams ~~~~~~
Capitals ....◊

GROWTH OF MACCABEAN JUDAEA

Judaea at the start of the revolt, 166 B.C.
Acquisitions under Jonathan, 160-142 B.C.
Acquisitions under Simon, 142-134 B.C.
Acquisitions under John Hyrcanus, 134-104 B.C.
Acquisitions under Aristobulus I, 104-103 B.C.
Acquisitions under Alexander Jannaeus, 103-76 B.C.
Maximum extent of Maccabean dominions

The Maccabean revolt arose from the attempt of the Seleucid monarch Antiochus IV (Epiphanes) to force the Jews to give up their God and worship Zeus.

Site of Tryphon's treacherous seizure of Jonathan.

Besieged and razed by John Hyrcanus.

John Hyrcanus destroyed the Samaritan temple on Mt. Gerizim.

Original home of the Maccabees or Hasmonaeans.

Death place of Alexander Jannaeus.

In 63 B.C. Jerusalem fell before the forces of Pompey and Judaea came under Roman control.

Feast of Hanukkah is celebrated by the Jews in memory of the cleansing of the Temple by Judas Maccabaeus.

SELEUCID EMPIRE

The Great Sea (Mediterranean Sea)

PHOENICIA
COELE SYRIA
MOUNT LEBANON
Mt. Hermon
ITURAEA
SYRIA
GALILEE
SAMARIA
JUDAEA
IDUMAEA
PHILISTIA
GILEAD
GAULANITIS
DECAPOLIS
HOUSE OF TOBIAH
AMMON
MOABITIS
PERAEA
ACRABATHANE

Plain of Sharon
Plain of Esdraelon
Mt. Carmel
Mt. Tabor
Mt. Gerizim
Mt. Azotus

Sea of Galilee
Salt Sea (Dead Sea)

Leontes R.
Yarmuk R.
Jordan River
Jabbok R.
Arnon R.
Brook Zered

Sidon
Damascus
Tyre
Paneas
Cades (Kedesh)
Hazor
Mageth
Raphon
Carnaim
Bosor
Ptolemaïs (Accho)
Magdala
Arbela
Hippos
Gamala
Dion
Philoteria
Abila
Gadara
Edrei
Ephron
Dora (Dor)
Scythopolis (Beth-shan)
Pella
Strato's Tower
Samaria
Asophon
Gerasa
Apollonia
Capharsaba
Sichem
Amathus
Ragaba
Pharathon
Alexandrium
Joppa
Ramathaim
Gedor
Jazer
Beth-dagon
Adida (Hadid)
Gophna
Ephraim
Tyrus
Philadelphia (Rabbath-ammon)
Lydda (Lod)
Modin
Beeroth
Elasa
Bethel
Dok
Michmash
Jericho
Gazara (Gezer)
Jamnia (Jabneh)
Ekron
Beth-horon
Mizpah?
Adasa
Heshbon
Samaga
Cedron
Emmaus (Nicopolis)
Capharsalama
Jerusalem
Khirbet Qumrān
Medeba
Azotus (Ashdod)
Bethlehem
Timnah
Beth-zacharias
Ascalon (Ashkelon)
Free City State
Adullam
Bethsura
Tekoa
Machaerus
Anthedon
Marisa (Mareshah)
Adora
Hebron
Dibon
Gaza
En-gedi
Raphia
Arad
Masada
Kir-moab
Zoara

The Wilderness of Judaea, west of the Salt Sea, to which the rebel-
ling Jews fled, and from which they attacked their oppressors

In spite of this generous act, Simon considered it a more prudent course to trust the Romans rather than the Syrians, and he was much gratified when the Romans issued a decree, circulated to the peoples of the East, proclaiming a league of friendship with the Jews. However, this gesture, which cost Rome nothing, had to be dearly paid for by little Judaea. In another of the frequent changes of Syrian kings, Antiochus VII took the throne in 138 B.C. and laid a heavy hand upon this former subject people.

Rights and privileges were promptly withdrawn, and a Syrian army appeared in Judaea to collect back tribute. It was luckily defeated by two of Simon's sons, John Hyrcanus and Judas; Simon was now too old to take the field himself. His days were numbered; his son-in-law, Ptolemy, plotting to obtain power, slew this the last of old Mattathias' five sons.

Ptolemy's plot was unsuccessful, and in 134 B.C. Simon's son John Hyrcanus came to full power. He had already commanded the Judaean army for seven years. His experience proved of little benefit, for he had no more than disposed of his ambitious brother-in-law, Ptolemy, when the determined Antiochus led

yet another Syrian army into Judaea and the Maccabean found himself in an indefensible position. The only thing he could do was to take refuge within Jerusalem's walls. Even then hunger soon forced the besieged to sue for peace on any terms. The terms proved to be unusually harsh, including heavy tribute and the leveling of the city's fortifications.

Burdened with these serious problems, Hyrcanus, although still determined, dared make no moves until conditions eased. His opportunity finally came with the death of Antiochus in 129 B.C., and he promptly sent three ambassadors to Rome begging for aid. The Romans made their customary resounding promises; it was as usual the disorder in the Syrian court that gave the Jews their opportunity.

While his uncle and his father had not shrunk from being vassals of Syria, Hyrcanus was far more resolute, and fully determined to stand alone. So he set about perfecting the means by which he might do just that, building up a striking force which deserved the name of an army. His simple shepherds, fighting for their homes and pastures, did remarkably well in their native hills, but they were no match for

Jewish nationalist coin of the first century. Left, with the cup of manna; right, with pomegranates, Jewish symbol of fertility

well-armed and well-trained troops on a battlefield. Actually his "men from the hills" looked primitive in contrast to the professional soldiers of neighboring monarchs who had horses and chariots, shields, spears and fine swords. What could Hyrcanus do? He finally decided upon very much the same course King David had taken centuries before; he hired soldiers, paying them a fixed wage, and built up an honor guard, the prince's own, which would be responsible to him alone.

This move tended to be unpopular in itself, and the means Hyrcanus took to finance it were sufficient to tip the scales against him: he burrowed into the tomb of David and extracted treasures sufficient for his needs! The Maccabees had enjoyed wide popularity before this, but from that time, about 129 B.C., general approval of what had become the reigning house of Judaea tended to diminish.

Undaunted by criticism, Hyrcanus continued to raise Judaea's military power while that of Syria was decaying. A good soldier, he used his new fighting force effectively and began to extend his dominions. He conquered Samaria to the north, and destroyed the temple the Samaritans built upon Mount Gerizim after they had been refused a share in Zerubbabel's Temple in Jerusalem. He also conquered Idumaea to the south, where lived the descendants of the Edomites who had figured so prominently in early Bible times.

These conquests naturally provoked a contest with the Syrians. But that kingdom was rapidly slipping from power and its armies were permanently recalled from Palestine. Judaea had known more than a half century of conflict with Syria, but Syria's internal troubles, plus Roman intervention, had turned the tables and the "holy warriors" of the

house of the Maccabees had at last won out.

During the latter part of Hyrcanus' thirty-year reign, Judaea knew better days than any which had been experienced since the Golden Age in the time of Solomon. When this grandson of Mattathias died in 104 B.C., full of years and accomplishments, he was able to leave his son Judas Aristobulus a considerable kingdom.

This young man, who seems to have been the first of the Hasmonaean dynasty founded by the Maccabees to assume the title of king, held the throne for only about a year. His youngest brother, Alexander Jannaeus, succeeded him. While Jannaeus bore a Grecian name and is believed to have had strong Grecian interests, he was a fighter like his Maccabean forebears. Much of his twenty-seven-year reign was given to warfare directed against neighboring cities and kings. He pushed his conquests east of the River Jordan, and at his death in 76 B.C. the Promised Land had been restored to almost its original size.

However, during much of his time upon the throne, that land was racked by civil war of a religious character. There was a struggle between the Sadducees and the Pharisees, two opposing religious parties, or sects, which had come into being during the days of the old priest Mattathias and his five sons. The Sadducees believed in reason and compromise, while the Pharisees insisted upon the very strictest observance of religious laws, adding many new laws of their own.

The civil war came about because the Pharisees, who were trying to make over the people of the kingdom in their own image, became filled with intense hatred for the ruling house. During Hyrcanus' reign he had for a time favored them, but when he later shunned them they turned upon both him and his sons with unremitting hostility.

Jannaeus' military adventures had not all terminated in success. In the year 90 B.C. he suffered a severe defeat east of the Jordan at the hands of those nomadic descendants of Ishmael known as Arabs, and was forced to flee to Jerusalem. This military reverse provided the Pharisees with the opportunity they needed, and for the next six years they gave their ruler no peace. At one point Jannaeus decided to compromise with them and asked them exactly what it was they wished. To his amazement they promptly informed him that what they wished for most was his death.

The Pharisees even went to the nation's longtime enemy, Syria, and sought the intervention of one of the last monarchs of that dying kingdom, Demetrius III. A brief rebellion followed, in which Jannaeus came out the victor. His own hatred could be violent, and also calculated, if we can believe the story which follows, told by the ancient historian Josephus. By way of celebrating his victory over the Pharisees and their friends, he organized a revel involving his many concubines. In the midst of it, and in their presence, some eight hundred crosses were erected. To them were nailed an equal number of captive rebels, while the dying men's wives and children were slaughtered before their pain-numbed eyes. This account is questioned by scholars, as crucifixion was a Persian and Roman punishment and never used by Jews, who put people to death by stoning.

Upon the death of Jannaeus the reins of government passed into the hands of his wife, Salome Alexandra. She appointed one of her sons, Hyrcanus II, as High Priest, and seems to have turned over the government itself to the Pharisees, for they now had full control and allowed Salome little beyond the title of queen.

When Salome died in 67 B.C., there was a contest for the throne between Hyrcanus II and his brother, Aristobulus II. Hyrcanus managed to occupy the throne for three troubled months, but Aristobulus eventually won out. Surprisingly enough, the defeated Hyrcanus was not slain; he was soon intriguing with the Nabataean Arabs, to whom he made promises in return for their support in gaining the throne. The go-between in this plot deserves a trifle more than casual mention, for he and his descendants were to play a role in the affairs of the next two centuries. His name was Antipater; he was an Idumaean, who would become not only an important Roman puppet but also the father of that warped and ruthless monarch Herod the Great.

The contest for the throne between Hyrcanus and Aristobulus was only a family affair and of little consequence in contrast to happenings at that moment elsewhere. Rome, which had kept an interested and perhaps covetous eye for a century and a half on the area east of the Mediterranean, was now prepared to take a decisive part. In the year 66 B.C. Pompey, the great Roman general, conquered Pontus, a country on the shore of the Black Sea, and drove its king into exile in the Caucasus. Then, turning his legions toward the south, he finished off the Syrian kingdom founded by Seleucus Nicator two hundred fifty years before.

This conquering Roman hero had a legate, one Scaurus, working ahead of him, and when Scaurus arrived at Damascus he was told of the senseless war between the Judaean brothers which was still in progress at that very moment in Jerusalem. Hurrying to that city, Scaurus was gratified to find that both sides were prepared to offer him sizable tribute for aid from his master, Pompey. The matter was carefully reviewed, and it was decided that the more likely of the two aspirants was the younger, Aristobulus. When the Arabs heard that Rome would support Aristobulus, they withdrew their aid from Hyrcanus and departed for the desert.

As Hyrcanus still would not give up hope, the two warring sons of Jannaeus and Salome Alexandra presented their respective claims to Pompey himself, who had arrived in Damascus to see the sights. While the great man was making up his mind, a move on the part of Aristobulus encouraged the Roman commander to order the occupation of the Jewish capital. When resistance developed there, the city was quickly put under siege. Thus, in the fall of 63 B.C., Jerusalem was subdued and the Maccabean period came to an end. Judaea now became a vassal principality of Rome, with all the non-Jewish portions of its territory stripped away. Hyrcanus II was allowed to continue as High Priest and Aristobulus was taken as a prisoner to Rome.

From then until the close of Bible times, the Holy Land would be firmly under the heel of men from the city on the Tiber, far away across the Mediterranean to the northwest.

13. Rome and Herod the Great

Who were the Romans who were to play such a dominant role during the remainder of Bible times and during the early days of the Christian Church? Their beginnings are clouded by a haze of interesting but hardly trustworthy legends. One legend describes them as descendants of Aeneas and a small group of men and women who had escaped from Troy when that great city fell to the Greeks under Agamemnon. Another legend portrays them as descendants of Romulus and Remus, those twin sons of Mars. We first hear of them historically as one of several native tribes living in that broad plain in west central Italy through which flows the Tiber River. The area to the southeast of this stream was known as Latium, and, at a point about twenty miles from where the Tiber empties into the Tyrrhenian Sea, tradition says the city of Rome was founded in 753 B.C.

The site selected was a group of seven low, easily defended hills. The little settlement had to protect itself against some very aggressive neighbors: the Umbrians and Etruscans to the north, and to the south the mountain tribes known as Samnites.

Sometime during the sixth century B.C. the Etruscans managed to capture Rome. They did not hold it long; in 509 B.C. the Roman nobles rebelled and drove them out. The Etruscan king, Tarquin, sought to regain the throne with the help of the Etruscan army. This attempt was successfully withstood; the kingdom was done away with and the Romans set up a republic.

In place of a hereditary monarch, the grow-ing city was from then on governed by two consuls, each of whom was elected to hold office for but a single year. So effective was this form of government that it was retained for nearly five centuries.

The various cities of Latium eventually formed a league to promote trade, peace and intermarriage. Slowly Rome became the chief city in this confederation, much to the envy and ill will of the others. They were so jealous of her increasing power that when the Gauls, a people from far to the north, attacked Rome in 390 B.C. the neighboring cities refused to aid in its defense.

In spite of this, the Romans defeated the Gauls. Then, gaining still more strength, they began to dominate the affairs of the Latin League. In fact, Rome was soon important enough to make an alliance with Carthage, the powerful Phoenician trading city across the Mediterranean in northern Africa. At this time, too, she began building the first of her famous military roads and constructing fortresses at various points of military importance.

During the early period of growth, Rome suffered a sharp setback at the hands of the Samnites; those belligerent mountain people to the south forced a whole Roman army to surrender. Although the victors then joined with the Etruscans and the Umbrians in an attempt to break the mounting power of Rome, the city on the Tiber managed to prevail.

The war against the Samnites had drawn Roman troops far south, to the borders of Magna Graecia, that portion of lower Italy which had many Greek settlements. Chief

THE ROMAN WORLD
IN THE TIME OF CAESAR
60 TO 44 B.C.

Copyright by C. S. HAMMOND & CO., N.Y.

Scale of Miles

0 100 200 400 600

Roman territory at the beginning of the 1st Triumvirate–60 B.C.

Dependencies and client kingdoms

Limits of Roman control at the death of Caesar–44 B.C.

Territory acquired under the Triumvirate and Caesar

Major battles fought by Caesar ... ⚔

Capitals .... ⊕

Caesar raided Britain in 55 and 54 B.C.

Caesar conquered Gaul in 58–51 B.C.

In 49 B.C. Caesar crossed the Rubicon, the boundary of his province of Cisalpine Gaul, precipitating civil war.

Caesar defeated Pompey at Pharsalus in 48 B.C.

Pompey was assassinated at Alexandria in 48 B.C. Caesar defeated the Egyptians and placed Cleopatra on the throne in 47 B.C.

Caesar "came, saw and conquered" Pharnaces II at Zela in 47 B.C.

Crassus killed by Parthians at Carrhae in 53 B.C.

Under Caesar the Jews enjoyed semi-independent rule with religious freedom.

Map labels

Caspian Sea (Mare Hyrcanium)

Red Sea (Sinus Arabicus)

Black Sea

Aegean Sea

Adriatic Sea

Tyrrhenian Sea

Mediterranean Sea (Mare Internum)

Atlantic Ocean

English Channel

PARTHIAN EMPIRE

ARMENIA

MESOPOTAMIA

SYRIA

JUDAEA

EGYPT

Arabia

Nabataeans

CAPPADOCIA

PONTUS

GALATIA

BITHYNIA & PONTUS

PAPHLAGONIA

LYCAONIA

PAMPHYLIA

LYCIA

CARIA

MYSIA

ASIA

CILICIA

COMMAGENE

SOPHENE

CORDUENE

IBERIA

ALBANIA

COLCHIS

Caucasus Mts.

Sarmatia

Amadoci

Alani

Siraces

BOSPORUS KINGDOM

ROXOLANI

Bastarnae

Dacia

CARPATHIAN MTS.

Carpi

Moesi

THRACE

MACEDONIA

ACHAIA

Epirus

ILLYRICUM

NORICUM

RAETIA

CISALPINE GAUL

ITALIA

Etruria

SICILY

SARDINIA

CORSICA

BALEARIC IS.

NARBONENSIS

GALLIA

AQUITANIA

BELGICA

Armorica

Britain

Hibernia

Germania

Lombards

Goths

Rugians

Lemovii

Lugii

Semnones

Chauci

Frisians

Batavi

Treveri

Chatti

Hermunduri

Marcomanni

Quadi

SPAIN

HITHER SPAIN

FARTHER SPAIN

LUSITANIA

Cantabri

Astures

Vaccaei

Celtiberi

Turdetani

PYRENEES

AFRICA

NUMIDIA

MAURETANIA

CYRENAICA

Marmarica

Libya

Gaetulia

SAHARA

ATLAS MTS.

Syrtus Major

Syrtus Minor

Cities

Ctesiphon, Babylon, Seleucia, Palmyra, Petra, Jerusalem, Gaza, Samaria, Tyre, Damascus, Antioch, Salamis, CYPRUS, Tarsus, Edessa, Carrhae, Nicephorium, Artaxata, Tigranocerta, Trapezus, Sinope, Zela, Mazaca, Iconium, Laodicea, Ephesus, Magnesia, Pergamum, RHODES, CRETE, Sparta, Athens, Corinth, Pharsalus, Actium, Apollonia, Pella, Thessalonica, Philippi, Byzantium, Nicomedia, Ancyra, Zela, Apollonia, Tomi, Olbia, Tyras, Chersonesus, Panticapaeum, Palus Maeotis, Borysthenes R. (Dnieper), Tyras R., Ister R. (Danube), Tanais R., Rha R. (Volga), Don R., Vistula R., Albis R. (Elbe), Rhine R., Danube R., Euphrates R., Tigris R., Nile, Axes R., Cyrus R., Araxes R.

Alexandria, Naucratis, Memphis, Heliopolis, Pelusium, Thebes, Berenice

Cyrene, Barca

Leptis Magna, Sabratha, Thapsus, Hadrumetum, Carthage, Utica, Hippo Regius, Cirta, Icosium, Tingis, Lixus, Gades, Malaca, Corduba, Munda, Carthago Nova, Valentia, Toletum, Ilerda, Tarraco, Brigantium, Gallaecia, Burdigala, Dictones, Veneti, Lutetia, Cenabum, Avaricum, Alesia, Gergovia, Bibracte, Uxellodunum, Vesontio, Lugdunum, Massilia, Narbo, Volsae, Genua, Ravenna, Aquileia, Norela, Ancona, Luca, Corfinium, Brundisium, Tarentum, Croton, Capua, Neapolis, Messana, Syracuse, Rome, Rubicon R., Verulamium, Remi, Nervii

Dyrrhachium, Scodra, Narona, Durius R., Tagus R., Anas R., Ebro R., Rhone R., Loire R. (Liger R.), Seine R. (Sequana)

among these Greek colonies was a place called Tarentum, and there was soon the promise of a contest between that city and Rome. Seeking to gain the initiative, the people of Tarentum made an alliance with Pyrrhus, king of Epirus, a city-state in northwestern Greece. This vigorous sovereign, determined to be another Alexander the Great, landed his forces, including many war elephants, upon the Italian boot. He attacked the Romans with such vigor that they lost several battles to him in southeastern Italy.

Nonetheless, they were "Pyrrhic victories" indeed, for the king's losses were so great that in order to save himself and his army he had to sail home and abandon the cause of the Greek colonists. Promptly Rome seized their cities, and by 270 B.C. she was in control of all southern Italy.

This rapid increase in power now brought opposition from another quarter—Carthage. It proved to be the most demanding challenge Rome had yet encountered, resulting in a long, costly struggle and a fight to the death. Finally, in 146 B.C., the powerful African trading city was completely destroyed. During this time Rome had also increased her hold on Greece. When in that same year Corinth rebelled, a Roman army seized the city and reduced it to ashes.

The Eternal City was now mistress of most of the Mediterranean. She had gained wealth and strength sufficient to start her on the road to a great overseas empire, yet conditions within her walls became so unstable over the years as to preclude any major conquests. Trouble stemmed from the very unequal distribution of wealth, which resulted in threats by the Roman mob, a situation which the brothers Tiberius and Gaius Gracchus sought to correct. Both were murdered for their pains, and, during the unsettled period which followed, the Roman army seized power. Two generals now became consuls. The first was Marius, and the second a brutal yet very capable man called Sulla.

Sulla had a lieutenant who defeated the king of Pontus in Asia Minor and went on to extend the domain of Rome in the eastern Mediterranean area. He was none other than Pompey, who had captured Jerusalem by taking advantage of the quarrel between the two brothers Hyrcanus II and Aristobulus II. His great successes in the East made him for a time the most powerful man in the Roman world. But he was soon forced to bow to another ambitious Roman commander, Julius Caesar, whose fortunes were to be oddly linked to Syria and the Holy Land.

While Pompey had been busy in the East annexing territory that had previously belonged to the Ptolemies and the Seleucids, Caesar had been conquering a huge domain north of the Alps. He remained in Gaul and Britain for several years following an agreement to share the rule of Rome with Pompey and another general named Crassus. This Triumvirate, established in 60 B.C., was doomed to failure because each of its three members had a consuming ambition to rule alone.

Crassus met defeat and death in Mesopotamia. Such bonds as there were between the very dissimilar Pompey and Caesar snapped following the death of Pompey's wife, Julia, daughter of Caesar. When the Senate under pressure from Pompey voted to have Caesar removed from his army command, the break was complete.

Following his celebrated remark, "The die is cast," Caesar crossed the Rubicon with his army and was in command of all Italy in only sixty days without shedding a drop of blood. In forty days more, he had subdued Spain, Pompey's stronghold. Then, setting sail with his legions for Greece, Caesar defeated Pompey there at Pharsalus (48 B.C.).

Badly beaten, Pompey fled to Egypt, where he was promptly assassinated by orders of the king of that land. Caesar was now ruler of Rome in all but name.

Sailing from Greece in pursuit of Pompey, who he did not know was already dead, Caesar landed at Alexandria in Egypt at the head of a relatively small force and blundered into one of the most critical moments of his brilliant military career. A large Egyptian army, aided by a mob of citizens, fell upon him, and he was in desperate circumstances by the time his somewhat motley reinforcements from Syria came to his rescue. The most effective contingent was the 3000 troops commanded by Antipater, that enterprising Idumaean who had served as a go-between for Hyrcanus and his Arab allies. He now saved Caesar from serious embarrassment, if not from actual death, and did himself much good through his timely appearance.

Antipater had come into the spotlight prior

Julius Caesar, who was saved in battle by Antipater, appointed him and his sons (including Herod) to high offices in Palestine.

Two sides of a coin with the head of Julius Caesar

to the arrival of the Romans in Palestine. He was the son of Antipas, who had been governor of Idumaea under Alexander Jannaeus, and he had himself held that same office. During the struggle between the quarreling brothers, Hyrcanus and Aristobulus, he had not only aided Hyrcanus but had actually become the authority behind Hyrcanus' actions. Now Antipater was about to exert his influence in a wider sphere. His talent for being at the right place at the right time and giving assistance to the right people continued to stand him in good stead.

As soon as resistance had ended in Jerusalem, the deposed Aristobulus and his family had been shipped off to Rome in 61 B.C. to take their place among the conquered in Pompey's triumphal procession. Judaean affairs had been placed under the direction of the Roman governor of Syria. Although the Jews were permitted a measure of freedom within their own domain, they were restrained from attempting to expand through conquest of neighboring lands.

The results of Caesar's clash with Pompey were promptly felt in Judaea. Aristobulus was quickly released from his confinement in Rome and hurried off to Syria, there to take command of two legions and employ them to the benefit of Caesar. His efforts, however, met with no success, for he was soon poisoned by some of Pompey's supporters. At about this same time, Aristobulus' son Alexander was beheaded by Scipio, another of Pompey's friends; while a younger son, Antigonus II, hoping to revive the family fortunes, hurried before Caesar with a plea for his favor.

But Antipater seems to have had great influence abroad and was able to encourage the grateful Caesar to recognize Hyrcanus officially as hereditary High Priest and confirm him as the ethnarch, or regent, of Judaea. At the same time Antipater also received Roman citizenship, personal immunity from taxes, and the position of administrator of Judaea! While Hyrcanus, the dim-witted son of Alexander Jannaeus, continued as the nominal head of the little land, it was actually Antipater who wielded the power. He gave prompt evidence of this fact in 47 B.C. by appointing his eldest son, Phasael, governor, or tetrarch, of Judaea, while another son, twenty-five-year-old Herod, became tetrarch of Galilee and almost at once started his march to fame.

Antipater knew how to achieve fame and fortune for himself and his sons, yet he did not forget the people. This ambitious Idumaean also induced Caesar to grant arrangements to the Jews more favorable than those enjoyed by any other vassal community. The little land was freed from tribute, Roman garrisons were withdrawn, religious liberty was assured; its people were able to live according to their own laws and subject only to their own tribunals. Permission was also granted the Jews to rebuild the walls of Jerusalem which had been leveled by Pompey, and Joppa was added to Judaea, giving it a port on the Mediterranean.

The situation began to look more promising, and Antipater did his best to make the Jews content with their reasonably favorable position as a self-governing people within the vast Roman dominions. But the Jewish aristocrats did their utmost to bring his efforts to naught.

Typical of their strategy was the attempt to attack the father through his son Herod. The young man had done an excellent job in ridding all of north Palestine of the robber bands which had long been a scourge of that section. In so doing, he had executed Hezekiah, the bandit chief, and a number of his outlaw band. Now it happened that the power to inflict capital punishment was limited to the Jewish ecclesiastic and judicial council, the Sanhedrin, which was very jealous of its rights and privileges. So Herod was peremptorily summoned before this aristocratic body, which had decided to use this occasion to remove him from office and have him banished.

But Herod, who was bold and determined, had contempt for the highest Jewish tribunal and had no intention of submitting to their will. He was soon at Damascus, where he entered the Roman army and had himself appointed military governor of lower Syria. In this important Roman office he was in a position to make real trouble for his erstwhile antagonists and to strengthen greatly his father's hand.

The biggest news of this era came from Rome itself. Caesar, before leaving Egypt, had established the beauteous Cleopatra upon the throne and bound that country to him. Next followed victories in Africa against the remnants of Pompey's supporters led by Scipio and Cato. By then Caesar, the master of Roman might, was prepared to return to Rome to be received in hard-won triumph.

But his glory was short-lived. Certain men, needlessly fearing that he wanted to do away with the republican form of government and proclaim himself king, plotted against him. On the Ides of March, the fifteenth of March, 44 B.C., he was assassinated in the Senate. Once more the Roman world, soon to be an empire in name as well as in form, was thrown into turmoil.

ALONG WITH the news of Caesar's assassination, a new proconsul appeared in Syria. He was one of the murderers, and his name was Cassius. Every political underling from the mountains of Turkey to the mouth of the Nile quickly made his way to him. Like most power-hungry Romans, Cassius needed money badly, and he used these people to obtain it. To the eager Antipater was handed the onerous task of raising no less than seven hundred talents of silver, or the equivalent of nearly a million and a half dollars, from the people of Judaea.

Antipater sagaciously involved everyone he could in the task of extracting this huge sum from the reluctant people. Some of those who failed in their task were either executed or sold into slavery by the greedy Cassius. One among these, whom Antipater helped to have pardoned, nevertheless remained his enemy. His name was Malichus, and he especially resented the fact that Antipater's son Herod had raised his allotment of one hundred talents so promptly that he became favored by the Romans.

Malichus now decided to do away with Antipater and plotted to this end with the Jews and Arabs east of the Jordan. To Antipater's face he remained all friendliness and seems to have completely deceived the normally shrewd man. Suddenly a much easier means than war of achieving his purpose presented itself. The High Priest Hyrcanus' manservant, it was discovered, could be bribed. Through him, Malichus disposed of Antipater with a lethal dose of poison administered during a feast at Hyrcanus' home.

Hardly was Antipater, the administrator of Judaea, dead, when Malichus marched troops he had managed to raise into Jerusalem. This move was, of course, a serious threat to the murdered man's sons, Phasael and Herod. Their unsettled circumstances were further deranged by an upheaval at that moment in

Cleopatra and Ptolemy XVI, her son by Julius Caesar, shown on a wall relief of the Temple of Hathor at Dendera, worshipping gods and goddesses

Roman affairs. Mark Antony, one of Caesar's lieutenants and devoted friends, was determined to avenge his late commander by doing away with Cassius and all the other conspirators. So he and Octavian, a nephew and the heir of the mighty Caesar, drew Cassius into battle on the plains of Philippi in Macedonia, where, facing defeat, Cassius committed suicide. The Roman world now was at the disposal of these two brash young men.

In Judaea, Antigonus, younger son of the pretender Aristobulus, decided that this would be a favorable time to attempt to wrest the country from the control of his uncle, the High Priest Hyrcanus. To aid him in the enterprise he called upon the Parthians, a warlike people from a land near the Caspian Sea. Many of the Jews who disliked Herod and Phasael joined with Antigonus as he made his way toward Jerusalem. Phasael and Hyrcanus were made prisoners. Phasael committed suicide, while Hyrcanus had his ears cut off, a mutilation which disqualified him for his priestly office. He was then carried off by the Parthians to captivity in Babylon.

With his brother Phasael dead and the High Priest a captive, Herod, although he had a substantial number of loyal followers, felt his best chance lay in flight.

As a very young man Herod had been married to a member of a prominent Idumaean family; this, according to Jewish law of the time, was no deterrent to another marriage. Through his second choice he intended to strengthen his position materially, for the lady was Mariamne, granddaughter of Hyrcanus II. By marrying her he would become a member of the Judaean royal house.

Flight was now imminent. Under cover of night he took his first wife, his prospective second wife, her mother, Alexandra, his own mother and younger brother, together with his household and troops, and set out for the south. His first objective was the impregnable fortress Masada, which stood on an isolated hill on the west coast of the Salt Sea. There he left family and troops under the charge of his brother Joseph, while he hurried on to Egypt and from there to Rome. The year was 40 B.C.

It was a very astute move, for the thirty-two-year-old Herod was received with every mark of reliance and support, as son of the man who had aided Caesar in Egypt. The two men of the hour, Octavian and Antony, promised their aid, and by a decree of the Senate Herod was named king of Judaea.

Back in Palestine during his absence, many things had happened. Antigonus had risen to be both High Priest and king in Jerusalem, but he had failed to make his position secure. He had spent too much time and effort trying to capture distant Masada from Joseph. That castle, which could be reached only by two crooked, hard-to-climb paths, had defied his best efforts, and he was still heavily involved there when Herod returned. And since the Parthians, whom Antigonus had brought into the land, had plundered the people, he had become most unpopular. Consequently Herod was hardly ashore when the dissatisfied began joining his forces.

The siege of Masada was quickly relieved, whereupon the new king, Herod, set out for Jerusalem. His supporters were far too few in number at the moment to lay siege to its stout fortifications. He was forced to bide his time and await assistance from the Romans. Finally, in 39 B.C., Antony came in person to Asia Minor to take supreme command of military affairs in the East. Caius Sosius was made legate of Syria and given the task of seeing that Antony's friend Herod was at once placed upon the throne. As soon as spring arrived, Sosius, at the head of a considerable army, marched down through Phoenicia and fell upon Jerusalem. But so heroic was its defense that it was five long months before the city fell — and then on the most sacred day of the year, the Day of Atonement. Its defenders, it seems, had stoutly refused to fight on this holy day. The year was 37 B.C.

Antigonus, who had fomented all the trou-

Pleading his case before the Roman Senate, Herod was named king of Judaea by decree. So began the infamous dynasty of persecutors of the early Christians.

Left: Silver coin with head of Antony, minted at Antioch; the obverse side (damaged) is stamped with the head of Cleopatra. Right: Head of Cleopatra from coin of Alexandria.

ble, was seized and hauled away to Antioch, where he was beheaded. The Roman soldiers, maddened by Jerusalem's long resistance, cruelly slaughtered many of the inhabitants. This bloodbath was, in a way, a fitting prelude to the forthcoming marriage of King Herod and the princess Mariamne, a union which would one day come to a most bloody end.

This son of the late Antipater was in many ways as able a ruler as his ambitious father. But although surnamed "The Great," he had extreme weaknesses which brought him notoriety of quite another sort. From the start it was clear that he was dominated by but one consideration — to further his own ends at all cost. He was not exceptional — in those times ruthless ways were commonly used to preserve power. However, he was possessed of an unusually suspicious and jealous nature, and many of his acts, especially in his later life, indicate that he was extremely neurotic.

His flint-hard attitude first became apparent when he ordered the slaughter of forty-five Sadducees, members of the Sanhedrin which had opposed his entrance into the Holy City. His suspicions and jealousies very soon also involved him in family troubles. After he had made Aristobulus III, the seventeen-year-old brother of Mariamne, High Priest, the young man's growing popularity worried him so much that he had him drowned during water games held at a feast in Jericho in 36 B.C. The murdered Aristobulus' mother, who was of course Herod's mother-in-law, not deceived about the

true nature of her son's death, turned to Cleopatra of Egypt for help. Herod was ordered to appear immediately before Antony, whom Cleopatra held firmly enmeshed in her wiles.

Antony had taken a bad drubbing at the hands of the Parthians and was in such dire need of Herod's unquestioned allegiance that he refused to hear the case against him. With all charges dropped, Herod set off for home at once; to appease Cleopatra, Antony gave her lower Syria.

Herod's marriage to the exquisite Mariamne had been far more than one of convenience, for on Herod's part it had stemmed from a devouring love. She, on the other hand, appears to have been as cold and unresponsive to him as she was enticing. When she learned that Herod had given explicit orders that she was to be slain if he did not return, lest she come into the possession of some other man, she turned completely against him. Most certainly she sided with her mother in respect to the murder of her brother, Aristobulus. And so, fully realizing her subtle fascination for her husband, she played a part, resisting him and slowly driving him insane with jealousy by way of revenge.

However, she antagonized Herod's sister, Salome, who was fully as unscrupulous as her brother. During Herod's absence at Antony's headquarters, Mariamne had been forced because of circumstances to see much of Joseph, who was both Herod's uncle and Salome's husband, and who was serving as regent. Salome spitefully and untruthfully hinted at an affair between her husband and Queen Mariamne. The result was that Joseph was executed and Mariamne, Herod's beloved wife, was forgiven.

About this same time Cleopatra, who hated Herod, attempted to gain possession of Idumaea and remove it from Herod's rule. Once again Mark Antony came to his rescue and upheld him. Once again a sop was probably tossed by the Roman to his enticing lady. The records are not too clear in this matter, but the cities of Gaza and Joppa were not, in 30 B.C., any longer parts of the Judaean kingdom.

The Egyptian queen's unfriendliness toward Herod caused her, unwittingly, to serve him rather well. When the break came between Antony and Octavian, Caesar's heir, the king of Judaea hastened to offer his support to Antony, his patron. Cleopatra would not allow

Octavian, who made Herod king of the Jews in 40 B.C., became emperor as Augustus Caesar in 27 B.C.

Antony to accept Herod's help. As a result he had no active part in the fateful battle of Actium on September 2, 31 B.C., which made Octavian — a few years later to be named Augustus Caesar — the complete master of the evolving Roman Empire.

An incident which now took place showed once more Herod's excessive suspicion. Old Hyrcanus, whose mutilation had debarred him from his former sacred office, was now in his dotage and had been allowed to return to spend his remaining days in Jerusalem. However, as he was one of the last male members of the Hasmonaean dynasty, Herod saw in him a possible rival and had him executed.

The time had come when it was necessary for Herod to solidify his position with his new lord and master, Octavian. Putting Mariamne and her mother under guard in one fortress and the other members of the family in another, the much troubled king set off to the island of Rhodes for his rendezvous. There he readily proved he could be quite as useful to Octavian as he had formerly been to Antony. And having been reconfirmed as king of Judaea, he hurried back home to make preparations for the entertainment of his newest patron, who was about to march into Egypt.

The reception was held at Ptolemaïs (the modern port of Acre), along the coastal highway in Phoenician Syria. There the Roman forces were given ample provisions, and a token consisting of eight hundred talents was presented to the commander Octavian. To make Octavian's way safer and easier, Herod had also provided that water be supplied for him and his troops all the way to Egypt.

After the suicides of Antony and Cleopatra at Alexandria in 30 B.C., Herod hastened down to Egypt to congratulate Octavian and was bountifully rewarded for his pains. Cleopatra's bodyguard of four hundred picked Galatians was presented to him, and much of the territory that had been taken from his domain was restored. Once again he began to feel secure.

Herod was not home very long before Mariamne's treatment of him brought to full flower his torturing jealousy. How many times had he thought to put an end to it all! Now his sister, Salome, reported that his lovely but distant wife was plotting against him. She bribed Herod's cupbearer to report that Mariamne had given him a very suspicious

THE DOMINIONS OF HEROD THE GREAT
37 to 4 B.C.

Copyright by C. S. HAMMOND & CO., N.Y.

Scale of Miles

0   5   10   20   30   40

Perennial Rivers ....

Seasonal Rivers & Streams .....

Capitals ....

Cities of the Decapolis ☐

Kingdom of Herod the Great – 4 B.C.

Decapolis

Autonomous city-state of Ascalon

Roman province of Syria

Tetrarchy of Lysanias

Ulatha and Panias were placed under Herod's control in 20 B.C.

Herod's first territory was Galilee, given to him by his father, Antipater.

Hippos and Gadara were cities of the Decapolis given to Herod by Augustus.

The Decapolis was a league of neighboring city districts united for mutual protection against marauding tribes. It was not a compact geographical or political unit with definite boundaries.

City and port were built by Herod.

Herod rebuilt Samaria, giving it the new name of Sebaste.

Cleopatra for several years held many towns including Jericho and much of the coast.

Herod gained control of Jerusalem in 37 B.C., defeating Antigonus, and began to rule Judaea as king.

ABILENE

Abila

Damascus

Abana R.

Sidon

MOUNT LEBANON

Leontes R.

ITURAEA

MT. HERMON

Pharpar R.

PHOENICIA

Tyre

PANIAS

Paneas

ULATHA

TRACHONITIS

The Great (Mediterranean Sea) Sea

Ecdippa

Cadasa

Gischala

Lake Semechonitis

GAULANITIS

BATANAEA

Raphana

Ptolemaïs

Jordan

GALILEE

Tarichaea (Magdala)

Arbela

Sea of Galilee

Gamala

Hippos

Dion

Kanatha

AURANITIS

Sepphoris

Gaba

Nazareth

Philoteria

Yarmuk R.

Abila

Gadara

Edrei

MT. CARMEL

Plain of Esdraelon

Dora

Caesarea (Strato's Tower)

SAMARIA

Scythopolis

Pella

Bostra (Bosora)

DECAPOLIS

Gerasa

NABATAEA

Plain of Sharon

Sebaste (Samaria)

Sychem

Mt. Gerizim

Amathus

Jabbok R.

Apollonia

Antipatris

Alexandrium

River Jordan

Philadelphia

Joppa

Thamna

Phasaelis

Lydda

Gophna

Modin

Bethel

Bethennabris

AMMON

Jamnia

Ekron

Gazara

Emmaus

Beth-horon

Jericho

Livias (Beth-haran)

Essebon

Azotus

Jerusalem

Mt. of Olives

Khirbet Qumran

PERAEA

Ascalon

Hyrcanium

Bethlehem

Herodium

Callirhoë

Dibon

JUDAEA

Beth-gubrin

Marisa

Bethsura

Machaerus

Hebron

En-gedi

Salt Sea (Dead Sea)

IDUMAEA

Masada

Bersabee

MOABITIS

Arnon R.

Elusa

Kir-moab

NABATAEANS

Brook Zered

"love potion" to administer to his master — perhaps poison. The investigations, though inconclusive on this point, roused Herod's emotions still more, and he resolved that Mariamne must die. She was tried, and in 29 B.C. he signed her death warrant. Of all the countless other ghosts to haunt him none filled him with remorse like the recollection of this proud, disdainful creature whose love and respect he had been totally unable to command.

Though there would be other victims along Herod's bloody trail, he had certain accomplishments which, in all fairness, deserve mention. Herod was a great builder. He rebuilt the fortress of Baris, standing hard by the Lord's House dominating Jerusalem, and renamed it Antonia in honor of his former patron. For his own residence he constructed a combination home and fort — the Upper Palace — which was also capable of fully controlling the city. Following this, in 20 B.C., he started to restore and enlarge Zerubbabel's Temple, which was very dilapidated. Work on the Holy of Holies was completed within two years and work on the outer Temple at the end of six more years, but the work of restoration was still going on forty years later at the time of the Crucifixion. What resulted was a far larger and more beautiful edifice than that which Zerubbabel had been able to erect.

These were not Herod's only building projects. On the site of the ancient port of Strato's Tower, twenty miles south of Mount Carmel, he built the seaport of Caesarea, complete with a huge breakwater, and a temple with a colossal statue of Augustus Caesar. Herod did an admirable job, too, of rebuilding the city of Samaria, renaming it Sebaste, the Greek equivalent of the name Augusta. He also beautified and improved several other cities in his domain with gymnasia, temples, theaters and marketplaces. His projects were, in fact, so extensive that by the year 10 B.C. funds were running uncomfortably low, and once again David's tomb was opened and ransacked for treasure.

Herod's sons by the beloved Mariamne, Alexander and Aristobulus, who had been educated in Rome, were now grown to manhood. So too were several more young men, the children of his other wives. Among them the firstborn was Antipater. Herod does not seem to have been partial to him, favoring Alexander and Aristobulus instead. They were handsome,

polished youths, tremendously popular with the Jewish people, and Herod treated them for a time as his principal heirs. The elder had been married to Glaphyra, daughter of the king of Cappadocia, while Aristobulus, in an attempt to weld the family more closely together, had been wed to his own first cousin, Bernice, the daughter of Herod's sister, Salome.

The great attention paid these younger sons by Herod naturally bred a lively jealousy on Antipater's part. As he apparently had some of the persuasive powers of the grandfather for whom he was named, he began to put them to work. He poured into his father's ear tales of the many defects of his two half brothers. Antipater also had followers in the court circle, and with the help of this clique he did an extraordinary job of further poisoning his father's mind. A few missteps on the part of Alexander and Aristobulus, and Herod called for their heads. His onetime favored sons were put to death and Antipater was appointed his successor, with another son, Herod, second in line.

Very much encouraged by this success,

The land of Galilee, of devout Jews who yearly journeyed to Jerusalem for the Passover

Crown Prince Antipater was now ready for further intrigue. This time his intended victims were none other than Salome, his father's sister, and two more of his half brothers, Archelaus and Antipas, then in Rome being educated. He accused this trio of plotting to dispose of Herod. This accusation did not stick, but was promptly turned upon Antipater himself. The once hopeful prince was cast into prison.

Uneasy indeed lies the head that wears a crown, and this was particularly true in Herod's case. Whom could he trust? Surely not Antipater, so he was at last executed. For a time his son Antipas stood foremost in the aging king's mind. Then he was demoted in favor of his brother Archelaus. Archelaus was to become king of Judaea while Antipas was made tetrarch of Galilee, and of Peraea, as the lands east of the Jordan were now called. Another of Herod's sons, Herod Philip II, was to rule over three other sections of the kingdom. This proved to be the final disposition of Herod's affairs as confirmed at his death, except that the emperor Augustus designated Archelaus as ethnarch, rather than as king, of Judaea.

One of the most sublime of all events, the birth of Jesus Christ, occurred very near the close of this active, bloody and in many respects revolting life. Herod was perhaps already in the grip of a terrible, fatal disease — some believe it to have been cancer — when, in 5 or 4 B.C., dismaying news was brought to him. A son born of the line of David would succeed to his throne! The dynasty that he had founded was to be thrust aside. So bitter was this prophecy to the dying king that he ordered the legendary slaughter of the innocents, the slaying of the infants of Bethlehem — a command of which this ruthless man was quite capable.

Even after his death, his opponents were not to live, if he could help it. So Herod ordered his sister, Salome, and her new husband, Alexas, to fulfill one final hideous duty. They were to have all the leading Jews of Judaea confined in the circus at Jericho, the city where he lay dying. Then, at his death, all these unfortunates were to be slaughtered. This monster was determined that there would be mourning at the time of his death — even though that mourning would not be for him.

14. The Youth of Jesus

The Roman Empire demanded of all its subject peoples both taxes and military service when necessary. The taxes were of two kinds. First there was an impost, levied upon goods or property, the collection of which was farmed out to publicans, or collectors, whom the taxpayers of the Holy Land looked upon with the utmost contempt. These men collected taxes on many things, not only on land but also on fruit trees, vegetables, grapes in the vineyards, grain, flocks and herds and even fish from the sea. Working for the hated Romans, they were extortioners, hard men who grew rich through manipulation. They were regarded as sinners (Luke 19:2, 7). There was also a head or poll tax assessed against each male. This tax, plus the need for draft records, required frequent taking of the census. The method employed for this was similar to that used by the Hebrews as early as Moses' time (Exodus 30:12-13; Numbers 1:18).

Such a numbering of the people was called for in the latter days of the reign of Herod the Great. It meant that many families had to journey to their hometowns to be registered. This duty fell upon a carpenter then living in the peaceful little village of Nazareth in Galilee. He had to make a three-day journey to Bethlehem of Judaea, far to the south, for this man, Joseph, belonged to the house and family of the great king David. It would be a most trying journey, for his wife, Mary, was expecting a baby very shortly. But go he must, and she could not be left behind.

It was there in Bethlehem that the Child was born. The ancient little town, which had been the home of Ruth and Naomi and which David had known so well as a child and youth, was filled with people who had also come to register. And so the little family had to be content to find shelter in a stable set in a cave in the hillside. There was perhaps a house, used as an inn, standing before this grotto, an arrangement such as may be found in Bethlehem even to this day.

It was a poor and simple place, but the Child born there was a very special child indeed — the promised King. The night was filled with a chorus of heavenly voices, and shepherds tending their flocks of fat-tailed sheep on the neighboring hillsides came during the dark hours to pay Him humble homage. There was also a heavenly phenomenon in the night sky, known today as the Star of Bethlehem, and it was this star which brought the Wise Men from the far-off land of Media in search of the Child whose birth it heralded.

The three kings stopped at Jerusalem to ask directions at Herod's court. St. Matthew relates that their inquiry aroused Herod's suspicions, touching off the order for the slaying of the innocents. But Joseph, forewarned by the Angel of the Lord in a dream, took Mary and the tiny Jesus away to Egypt.

We can only guess at the route they took. Fleeing from Bethlehem they probably followed the east-west trail which ran from Jerusalem to the coast, joining the great Damascus-to-Egypt caravan route a little above Gaza.

Where did they go in Egypt? While the Bible does not say, the traditions of the Egyptian Coptic Church offer a perplexing choice of localities. Chief among them is a little garden at the edge of ancient Heliopolis, six miles outside modern Cairo. There an Egyptian sycamore, noble but lacking even one quarter of the necessary age, is pointed out as the "Virgin's Tree." This spot has been venerated for centuries.

The stay in Egypt could not have been for long, as Herod died at Jericho in 4 B.C. According to Matthew 2:19-20, the Angel of the Lord appeared once more to Joseph in a dream saying that he should take the Child and His mother back into the land of Israel, for they were dead who sought His life.

Bethlehem, the city near Jerusalem to which Ruth had come and where her descendant David was raised. Here another descendant, Joseph, who had migrated to Nazareth, returned with Mary, also of the house of David.

A brief explanation of the date of Herod's death, 4 B.C., is perhaps in order. The calendar which most of Christendom observes is known as the Gregorian calendar; it was established by Pope Gregory XIII in 1582 and adopted in England and her American colonies in 1752. Its initial date, 1 A.D., is supposed to be the year in which Jesus was born. The Gregorian calendar is based on one worked out by the good Roman abbot Dionysius Exiguus during the sixth Christian century. He used the fragmentary knowledge of his time and therefore erred by four to six years.

The first attempt to establish the correct date for the birth of Jesus had been made about two hundred years before. A fourth-century analyst had declared, "The Lord Jesus Christ was born on December 25th — a Friday — the fifteenth day of the New Moon." This would make his birthday fall upon the final day of the depraved Saturnalia carnival celebrated by the pagan Romans.

We know that Herod was made king by the Senate in the Roman year 714, and that his death came in 750, or earlier, in 749, which would be 4 or 5 B.C. according to our reckoning. It therefore follows that, if Jesus was born before Herod's death, and if He actually was born in December, His natal year must have been at least 5 B.C. But it was very likely earlier than the month of December.

When Herod died, and the time came for all the important Jews of Judaea to be herded into the stadium at Jericho and killed, as the pain-crazed man had ordered, their mass slaughter proved too revolting for even the callous Salome. Before news of Herod's death was made public, she and her husband dismissed the pitiful prisoners.

Herod was buried at the fortress of Herodium, to the southeast of Bethlehem. There were few mourners indeed.

The new king, Herod's son Archelaus, whose reign was to end in disaster ten years later, had difficulty from the very start. The people of his realm broke out in open revolt and demanded that he make amends for the many heinous crimes which had been committed by his father. They also demanded that he remove the High Priest appointed by Herod, and when he refused to do so a vast crowd gathered in the Temple courtyard. To quell this disturbance Archelaus called out his troops, and all three thousand assembled in that sacred precinct were slaughtered.

Joseph, so some think, had planned to make his home in Bethlehem when he returned from Egypt, but the disturbances were then going on in nearby Jerusalem. Directed by the Angel of the Lord, he took his little family back to Nazareth.

What route did Joseph and Mary and the Child follow on their return? Assuming that they passed through Bethlehem after returning from Egypt, as pious Jews they would not have taken the highland trail up through the city of Samaria. The Samaritans, descendants of those Babylonians, Syrians and other eastern peoples whom Sargon II had settled around that ancient city after he had led the Ten Tribes off into bondage, were looked down upon by the Jews, always to be avoided. The Holy Family undoubtedly followed the Joppa road west to Lydda, the point where that road was intersected by the ancient caravan route which ran from the East through Damascus and then south to Egypt. From Lydda they would have headed north, the well-traveled route leading them homeward first across the Plain of Sharon and then across the Plain of Esdraelon (Jezreel). Not far below the village of Nain, they would have left the great caravan route and taken a local trail which climbed to the north, for Nazareth lay in the hills.

Nazareth was about midway between the international caravan route which the returning travelers had just left and Sepphoris, the capital of Galilee. Despite this, Nazareth was somewhat a place apart in that Hellenized land, which was much more populous and bustling in those days than it is today. There is evidence that the little village lay in a quiet backwater off a surging sea of business and trade. By contrast with its surroundings, which were probably heavily Gentile, Nazareth was almost completely Jewish and given to the most orthodox customs and beliefs. So strict a place was it, in fact, that the Apostle-to-be Nathanael quoted the derisive question often asked by its neighbors: "Can anything good come out of Nazareth?" (John 1:46).

But Nazareth did have some contact with the outer world. When Jesus was ten years old, the Romans destroyed the city of Sepphoris and crucified two thousand of its inhabitants. Their crosses lined both sides of the road for several miles to the north and south. The Romans committed this brutality as a punishment to the Jews of that section for joining a revolt led by a man called Judas the Gaulanite.

At what season of the year did Joseph, Mary and the Child arrive in Nazareth? One of the most violent outbursts to occur in Jerusalem following the death of Herod came as the Passover was approaching, in early April. If this disturbance was the cause for the change in Joseph's plans, then the Holy Family would have reached the northern hill country when it was at its loveliest. By the time the latter rains had ceased in early April, the growing grain would have painted the sear, lifeless winter fields a brilliant green. In those days, as now, there was a wealth of flowers. The first among them to bloom in the spring were the crocuses, followed by cyclamens, anemones, the blooming flax and other "lilies of the field" (Matthew 6:28-30).

The grain grew rapidly from then on, for both wheat and barley were ready for harvest in the highlands by late May. Along with the grain and the wild flowers, the fig tree — an important Jewish symbol — would deck itself out in pale leaves and tiny fruit, while the pomegranate blossoms contributed flashes of vivid scarlet, and the apricot and other fruit trees added their own colorful touches. Here

PALESTINE IN THE TIME OF CHRIST

Copyright by C. S. HAMMOND & CO., N.Y.

Scale of Miles

0 5 10 20 30 40

Perennial Rivers ....
Seasonal Rivers & Streams ....
Capitals ....
Roads & Trade Routes ....

Tetrarchy of Lysanias
Tetrarchy of Philip
Tetrarchy of Herod Antipas
Territory under Roman procurator
Areas tributary to Salome
Decapolis *
Independent *
Roman province of Syria

Cities of the Decapolis ....□

*The Decapolis and Ascalon retained their independence under the Roman governor of the province of Syria.

Archelaus, upon Herod's death, became ruler of Judaea, Samaria and northern Idumaea. His reign lasted until 6 A.D. when he was removed and exiled. His territory then was placed under a Roman procurator.

Salome, Herod's sister, was given Jamnia, Azotus, Phasaelis and Archelaïs. They in turn passed to Livia, wife of Augustus, and then to the emperor Tiberius.

The Great Sea

(Mediterranean Sea)

Caesarea
Residence of Roman procurators.

ABILENE
Abila
Damascus

Sidon

Sarepta

PHOENICIA
MOUNT LEBANON
Leontes R.
MT. HERMON

Tyre

PANIAS
Dan   Caesarea Philippi
ULATHA
Lake Semechonitis

Cadasa

Gischala

Seleucia
Raphana

TURAEA

TRACHONITIS

GAULANITIS   BATANAEA

Chorazin
Bethsaida Julias
Capernaum
Gergesa?
Gamala
Dion

AURANITIS
Edrei

Ptolemaïs

Jotapata
Cana
Sephoris
Nazareth

Tabigha
Magdala
Horns of Hattin
Sea of Galilee
Tiberias
Philoteria

GALILEE

Hippos
Yarmuk R.
Abila
Gadara
Capitolias

MT. CARMEL
Kishon R.
Mt. Tabor

Plain of Esdraelon
Nain

Dora

Ginaea
Scythopolis
Pella
DECAPOLIS

Salim?

SAMARIA

Sebaste (Samaria)
Sychem (Sychar?)
Mt. Ebal
Mt. Gerizim
Jacob's Well
Salim?

Alexandrium

Apollonia
Antipatris

Arimathaea?

Joppa

Lydda (Diospolis)
Gophna
Bethel
Ramah

Gerasa

Amathus
Jabbok R.

Phasaelis

Archelaïs

Ephraim

PERAEA

Jericho

Bethennabris

Philadelphia

Jamnia
Ekron
Gazara
Nicopolis (Emmaus)
Emmaus
Bethlehem
Azotus
Ascalon

Marisa
Bethsura
Hebron

Juttah

Gaza

Raphia

Bersabee

Elusa

JUDAEA

Jerusalem
Bethany
Mt. of Olives
Khirbet Qumrân
Herodium

Wilderness of Judaea

Masada

IDUMAEA

Julias (Livias, Beth-haran)   Essebon

Ruins of Essene community found here; also Dead Sea Scrolls in caves nearby.

Callirhoe
Machaerus
Dibon

Salt or Dead Sea (L. Asphaltitis)

Arnon R.

MOABITIS
Kir-moab

Brook Zered

AMMONITAE

GILEAD

River Jordan

NABATAEANS   ARABIA

was the rousing annual promise that all may have life and, out of God's great bounty, have it more abundantly (John 10:10).

The hillsides around Nazareth are generally a little too steep for easy cultivation, but they do furnish pasture for many small flocks of sheep and goats. And in those ancient days, as today, the herdsman usually had his creatures well trained. If they began to stray they returned when they heard him calling (John 10:2-5), so he spent the long hours watching over them from the pleasant shade of a tree or jutting rock. At such times one might hear the notes from his pipe rippling over the warming air or see him with a tapering spindle, a baked clay whorl and a heap of combed wool, twisting and spinning it into yarn from which his wife would then weave the family's clothing. By the time Jesus was born, life was much changed and perhaps far less severe than it had been when the tribes fought their way into the Promised Land after bondage in Egypt. But among the common people one still had to work hard if one expected to eat.

What languages were spoken locally? In Nazareth, as elsewhere in the Holy Land, many languages were used and so one had to be quite a linguist. At the time of the Chaldean Empire a Semitic tongue known as Aramaic came into general and widespread use. Laban had employed it in Haran even in the early days (Genesis 31:47), and after the return from the Babylonian Captivity it became the common tongue of Palestine as well as Syria. Hebrew was still understood by the Jews, of course, for it continued to be their sacred language, yet it was Aramaic that was spoken in the homes. Roman domination also had its influence; it brought with it some use of Latin, while the great trade routes which ran through the Holy Land, north and south, resounded with numerous other dialects and lesser tongues. In the streets and marketplaces, conversation was generally carried on in Greek. This was not the classical Greek of the Golden Age in Athens, but Koine, or common Greek, which had become the commercial tongue of Syria, Palestine and Egypt. It was in this language that the great bulk of the New Testament was first written. The differences between it and classical Greek were not well known or appreciated until the 1890s. As soon as scholars had a better understanding of them, there was an expanding interest in new and revised translations of that part of the Bible.

What was commerce like? The trade routes of Palestine were alive with traffic. After the days of Solomon, international exchange, except perhaps with Phoenicia, had lessened, but with the return from the Captivity commerce flourished once more. Freedom from local wars during the years of domination by the Seleucids and then the Romans served as an encouragement to trade. After Rome conquered Palestine, manufacturing increased by leaps and bounds in some sections of Italy; these finished goods were traded with the Holy Land for grain and other foodstuffs, of which Rome seemed always to be in need. Even today the remains of iron tools, utensils and horse-

134

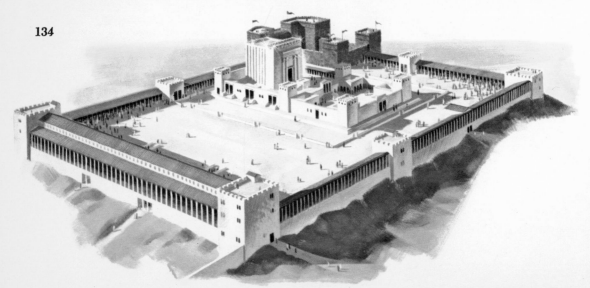

Herod's dazzling Temple, ornamented with gold, was begun in 20 B.C., but the great double walls and outer courts were not completed until 62 or 64 A.D.

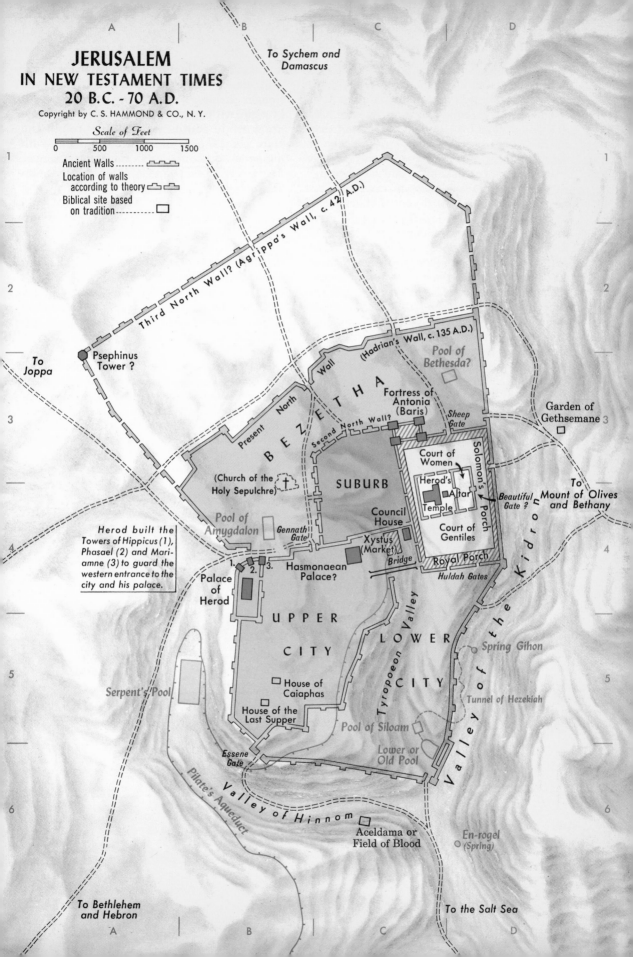

JERUSALEM
IN NEW TESTAMENT TIMES
20 B.C. - 70 A.D.
Copyright by C. S. HAMMOND & CO., N.Y.

Scale of Feet

0   500   1000   1500

Ancient Walls
Location of walls according to theory
Biblical site based on tradition

To Sychem and Damascus

Third North Wall? (Agrippa's Wall, c. 42 A.D.)

To Joppa

Psephinus Tower ?

Present North Wall

(Hadrian's Wall, c. 135 A.D.)

Pool of Bethesda?

B E Z E T H A

Fortress of Antonia (Baris)

Sheep Gate

Garden of Gethsemane

Second North Wall?

(Church of the Holy Sepulchre)

SUBURB

Court of Women

Herod's Temple

Altar

Solomon's Porch

Beautiful Gate ?

To Mount of Olives and Bethany

Pool of Amygdalon

Gennath Gate

Council House

Court of Gentiles

Herod built the Towers of Hippicus (1), Phasael (2) and Mari- amne (3) to guard the western entrance to the city and his palace.

Xystus (Market)

Hasmonaean Palace?

Bridge

Royal Porch

Huldah Gates

1. 2. 3.

Palace of Herod

U P P E R

C I T Y

Tyropoeon Valley

L O W E R

C I T Y

Spring Gihon

Serpent's Pool

House of Caiaphas

Tunnel of Hezekiah

House of the Last Supper

Pool of Siloam

Valley of the Kidron

Essene Gate

Lower or Old Pool

Pilate's Aqueduct

Valley of Hinnom

Aceldama or Field of Blood

En-rogel (Spring)

To Bethlehem and Hebron

To the Salt Sea

shoes bearing names of makers located in the Campania south of Rome are unearthed in Palestine, while a Roman manufacturer named Fortis seems to have flooded that land with his oil-burning lamps molded from clay. Goods — and people — were on the move, but the increased tempo of the times probably affected staid little towns like Nazareth very little.

What were the homes like in Nazareth? Most of them had but a single room. There were four limestone walls — with perhaps only one small window — covered over by a flat roof, with poles as rafters, strewn with a thick coating of branches and then straw and weeds, and topped off with some eight inches of clay. This had to be tamped and kept rolled; ancient roof rollers are still frequently discovered. The floor was usually given over to the animals, while the family's living quarters were on a *rowyeh*, or raised platform across the rear, which was reached by a flight of very narrow stone steps. There, in the poorer homes, a mat was spread on the floor, and on it the family ate the evening meal. There too, as the light began to fail, other reed pallets were laid out side by side, so that coverings could be shared for the night's sleep.

Home training long had been and still continued to be the principal schooling for all Jewish children; some group instruction was given in the synagogues which sprang up in every village, town and city of the land after the return from Babylon. There the children sat on mats upon the stone or tile floors, and in unison recited quotations from the Law. Much time spent in expounding and explaining these Scripture passages helped to develop reasoning power. It is probable that the children had to learn to read from the sacred rolls, and possibly to write as well. Some of the more able scholars whose parents could afford to provide for them were taken into the great religious school connected with the Temple at Jerusalem.

Jesus, however, seemed destined to spend His life on earth mostly among the common people, and, as was the case with any and all Jewish boys, He was undoubtedly taught a trade. He probably served an apprenticeship with His own father, going to work when very young. While it is customary today to think of the carpenter as the builder of houses and other structures, his tasks twenty centuries ago were more varied. Palestine was then a land

of farming and herding, and many of the tools and utensils for carrying on such activities were wooden, made by the village carpenter. Since it was before the days of lumberyards, the carpenter's work began in the woods, felling trees, or at least working their trunks and branches and roots into timber and boards from which to shape and work out many needed objects.

When Jesus was ten or eleven years old, Archelaus, who had become as great a tyrant as his father, Herod the Great, was summoned to Rome to answer charges of misrule and cruelty made against him by his brothers and his subjects. These charges were proven to Augustus Caesar's satisfaction, and so the last king of Judaea was banished to Gaul, where ultimately he died. The ethnarchy which Augustus Caesar had bestowed upon Archelaus was abolished, and in 6 A.D. Judaea became a Roman province. To the Jews generally, losing their rights as a nation and becoming merely another Roman province with a Roman procurator as their ruler was a shattering blow. The land which had been promised to their fathers, and for which their ancestors, especially the Maccabees, had fought so heroically, was now in the hands of Gentiles. As a consequence the pious Jews from all parts of the land were most careful to visit their Holy City for as many of the sacred feasts as possible.

Jesus was first brought to the Temple by His parents when little more than a month old to be presented to God, as was the religious

custom. And it was at that time that He was hailed as the Christ by Simeon and the aged Anna the Prophetess, who spent her days and nights there praying and fasting (Luke 2:22-38). According to Luke, Joseph and Mary made the pilgrimage from Nazareth to Jerusalem each year for the celebration of the Passover, and so we can safely say that Jesus accompanied them although only one such childhood trip is actually recorded in the Four Gospels. This journey was made in April, by which time the latter rains were over and the trail along the Jordan was again passable. It was the preferred course for the pilgrims living about the Sea of Galilee and to the north, and may have been used by the large party with which Joseph and Mary and their Son, now twelve years old, chose to travel in the interest of safety. On the other hand they may have gone from Nazareth south to the Joppa road, and then on to Jerusalem. His parents lost Him in the city on this occasion, and discovered Him confounding the elders. We can assume that Jesus visited the Temple on later occasions before His ministry, because a young Jew at the completion of his thirteenth year became a "son of the Law" and was subject to all its requirements, including at least three yearly visits to the Temple.

During all the days of Jesus' youth, and for many years after He had grown to manhood, the Temple was still being rebuilt. Damage

which it had suffered during the riots in the early days of Archelaus' reign was also being repaired. The edifice itself, which was very impressive, stood in a complex of courts twice the size of that surrounding Zerubbabel's Temple, and closed in by a wall forty-three feet high. This was pierced by nine huge gates, four on the north side, four on the south and one on the east. Beyond the consecrated area there was a ritual wall past which it was a capital offense for anyone who was not a Jew to go. Signs in Greek, carved in the stone at its various gateways, warned: "Let no alien pass through the barrier about the sanctuary.

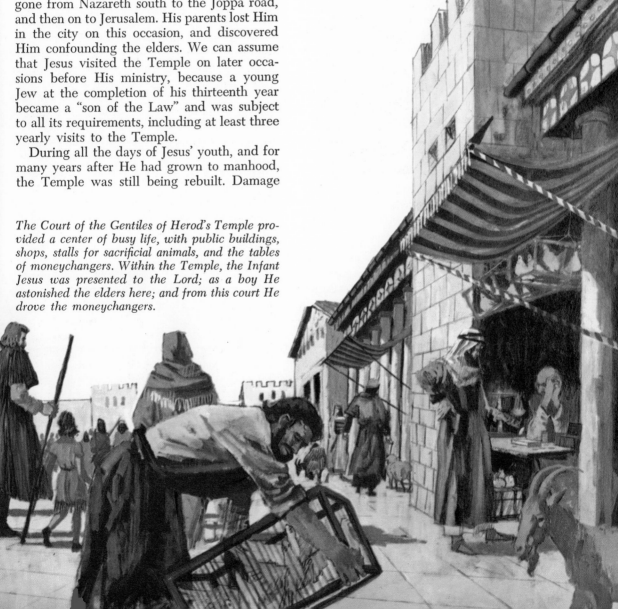

The Court of the Gentiles of Herod's Temple provided a center of busy life, with public buildings, shops, stalls for sacrificial animals, and the tables of moneychangers. Within the Temple, the Infant Jesus was presented to the Lord; as a boy He astonished the elders here; and from this court He drove the moneychangers.

The Wailing Wall, part of the fine masonry, standing seventy-five feet high, with which Herod surrounded the sanctuary area

Anyone so trespassing will pay with his life."

This House of God was under the control of the High Priest, who was also the presiding officer of the seventy-man Sanhedrin, the superior council for the whole province in temporal matters and the supreme court in religious affairs for all Jews. The Sanhedrin, except on the Sabbath and other holy days, could pass a sentence of death. After Judaea became a Roman province any such sentence had to be confirmed by the procurator before being carried out. The Sanhedrin also heard charges of blasphemy and the transgressing of the Law, and even Roman citizens accused of profaning the Temple were obliged to appear before this august body. It maintained its own police force (Matthew 26:47), and in matters where Roman interests were not primarily involved it had

wide and effective power. Where the affairs of the empire were at stake, the procurator was all-powerful; he could even remove the High Priest and appoint another in his place. This Jewish council met in a building to the west of the Temple near the xystus, or market, and close by the innermost city wall.

Members of the Sanhedrin were men of prominence — priests, scribes and elders, some belonging to the Pharisee party and some to the Sadducees. During Jesus' childhood, after the revolt at Sepphoris, another party was formed, the Zealots. These people, returning to the concept held before the days of King Saul, believed God to be the sole ruler of Israel, and maintained that tribute was due to Him alone. Whether they were represented on the Sanhedrin is not quite certain. However, it is known that they provided further reason for the Romans to believe that the Jews were not capable of governing themselves.

After Judaea had been made into a province following the banishment of Archelaus, there began a long procession of procurators. In other lands the duties of Roman procurators were chiefly the collection of tribute and the sitting in judgment in tax matters. In Judaea, since there was no legate to serve as their superior officer, their duties were much broader. They were responsible for running the government and were in direct charge of military and judicial affairs. The procurator of Judaea usually lived in the Roman city of Caesarea on the coast and was in Jerusalem only at the time of the feasts, when he customarily brought with him a strong armed force.

The fifth among these procurators of Judaea was appointed in the year 27 A.D. and managed to last out a ten-year term. His name was Pontius Pilate. He was appointed by Tiberius, who had become emperor on the death of Augustus thirteen years before. Almost at once he was at loggerheads with his Jewish subjects. First he marched troops into the Holy City bearing standards on which were graven images of the emperor. He took money from the Temple treasury to build an aqueduct to carry water from the highlands to the south into the city. There were frequent misunderstandings mixed with outright tyrannical offenses. He made it very evident that his idea of justice was whatever worked to his particular benefit, and for his Jewish subjects he had nothing but the most thoroughgoing disdain.

15. His Ministries

At the time that Pontius Pilate arrived in Judaea to take up his new post, a young preacher began to attract great crowds in the Jordan Valley. There, at Bethabara, or Bethany, on the east bank of the stream, he was making ready "the way of the Lord," urging the need for immediate and sincere repentance. After the penitents confessed, they were baptized by this preacher in the waters of the river as a token of their having been cleansed from sin.

His name was John the Baptist, and some believe that he was a member of the Essenes, a sect that had arisen, like the Pharisees and Sadducees, during the days of the Maccabees. While not mentioned in the Bible, this group seems to have had about four thousand members in the time of Christ. It was a monastic order, living a simple, plain and highly disciplined life, with monasteries in the barren Wilderness of Judaea.

Suddenly, several years ago, some of their religious writings burst upon the world; scrolls came to light that had been prepared by their scribes in the centuries immediately before Christ. They are the now famous Dead Sea Scrolls, found in caves about Khirbet Qumrân

At right: Aerial view of Qumrân cave where the Essenes hid a large part of their library of scrolls as they fled the Romans in 68 A.D. Below: A Dead Sea Scroll, commentary on the biblical book of Habakkuk (Habacuc).

139

on the northwest shores of the Dead Sea. While much scholarship has already been expended upon these unique documents, some of them only fragments, it is still too early to establish their proper relation to the Bible story.

The year that John the Baptist began preaching in the Jordan Valley was evidently a Sabbatical year, when the fields were left to rest, and many laborers had the leisure to attend his exhortations. In fact, their numbers were great enough to concern the Temple authorities in Jerusalem. They sent men to spy upon this preacher, who was acting without their sanction, and who announced a new dispensation — the advent of the Kingdom of God and the baptism of the Holy Spirit (Matthew 3:2-11).

Either very late in the same year, or early in the year following, a certain young man, a relative actually, called upon John the Baptist there by the Jordan. He was, of course, Jesus, and He asked to be baptized. When John hesitated, He persisted in His request, until He too had received this wondrous cleansing rite which marked the beginning of His glorious ministry.

The Four Gospels record that, during His approximately thirty-three years upon earth, Jesus made some fifty journeys. Some were very short, while others extended many miles and were of several weeks' or even months' duration. In a few cases His route is fairly well indicated, while in others there is no clear suggestion of either His path or the towns and cities He visited. Unfortunately, too, there are places mentioned by name whose location it is impossible to determine.

The spot where John the Baptist baptized Jesus is a case in point. It is spoken of in the Bible as Bethany Beyond Jordan; two centuries after the close of Bible times a famous early Christian writer called it Bethabara. Neither name helps in locating it. It would seem natural for John to have preached near a main travel route, so that a fair audience would be assured for his sermons.

Jesus probably used one of the Jordan Valley routes to reach John the Baptist and receive His

Capernaum, the busy seaport on the Sea of Galilee which Jesus made the center of His early ministry

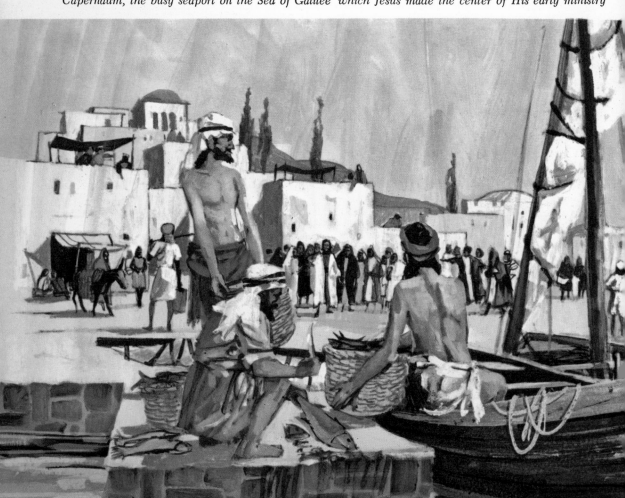

baptism. He could have forded the river near Adamah and continued along the well-traveled road which paralleled it on the eastern side.

Following His baptism, Jesus journeyed south the full length of the Jordan and entered the barren Wilderness of Judaea just west of the Salt Sea. It was there that He spent forty days and experienced His Temptation.

Emerging from the Wilderness of Judaea, Jesus then entered upon the early phases of His ministry. He returned to Bethabara, where He enrolled His first disciples, four men who had come there to listen to John the Baptist. They were Philip, Bartholomew (Nathanael), and two fishermen — the brothers Andrew and Simon Peter.

Jesus now returned to Galilee, where He attended a wedding feast at Cana, a little village two hours' walk north of Nazareth. Here, in the presence of His mother, He performed His first miracle, turning water into wine.

Leaving Cana, Jesus and His mother and His disciples went to Capernaum, a city which lay

141

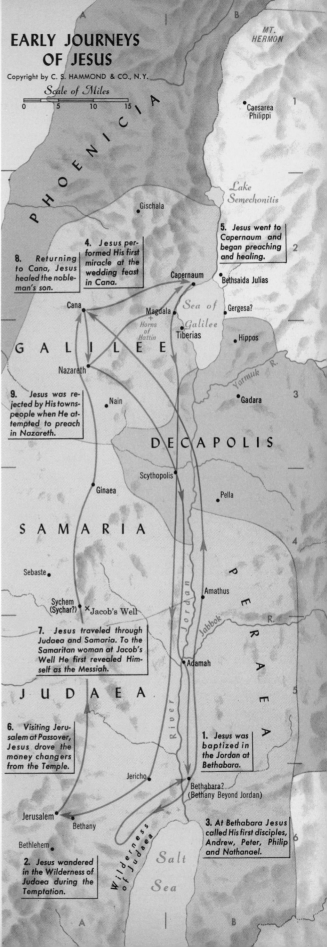

EARLY JOURNEYS
OF JESUS

Copyright by C. S. HAMMOND & CO., N.Y.

Scale of Miles

0   5   10   15

MT. HERMON

PHOENICIA

Caesarea Philippi

Lake Semechonitis

Gischala

4. Jesus performed His first miracle at the wedding feast in Cana.

5. Jesus went to Capernaum and began preaching and healing.

8. Returning to Cana, Jesus healed the nobleman's son.

Capernaum

Bethsaida Julias

Cana

Magdala

Sea of Galilee

Gergesa?

Horns of Hattin

Tiberias

Hippos

GALILEE

Nazareth

Yarmuk R.

9. Jesus was rejected by His townspeople when He attempted to preach in Nazareth.

Nain

Gadara

DECAPOLIS

Scythopolis

Pella

Ginaea

SAMARIA

Sebaste

Sychem (Sychar?)   × Jacob's Well

Amathus

P
E
R
A
E
A

Jordan River

Jabbok R.

7. Jesus traveled through Judaea and Samaria. To the Samaritan woman at Jacob's Well He first revealed Himself as the Messiah.

JUDAEA

Adamah

6. Visiting Jerusalem at Passover, Jesus drove the money changers from the Temple.

1. Jesus was baptized in the Jordan at Bethabara.

Jericho

Bethabara?.. (Bethany Beyond Jordan)

Jerusalem

Bethany

3. At Bethabara Jesus called His first disciples, Andrew, Peter, Philip and Nathanael.

Bethlehem

2. Jesus wandered in the Wilderness of Judaea during the Temptation.

Wilderness of Judaea

Salt Sea

upon the northwest curve of the Sea of Galilee and which was to be the headquarters of His early ministry. This was the metropolis of the region—a trading and manufacturing center and fishing port all in one. Its remains have been uncovered at Tell Hùm, which stands a little more than two miles from where the Jordan enters the lake.

From this bustling little city originated many recorded journeys, and quite likely others not described. First among them was one to Jerusalem for the Passover of 27 A.D. This was undoubtedly made down the west side of the Jordan, and then up the long fifteen-mile climb from Jericho. And it was during this visit that one of the most stirring events of His ministry took place: the first cleansing of the Temple. Taking a whip of ropes, Jesus drove the sacrificial animals, the sheep and the oxen, from the courtyard. Then, overturning the tables of the moneychangers, He cried out that they should take these things hence and not make His Father's House into a house of merchandise (John 2:13-16).

Next came a journey through the Judaean countryside. It must have been quite an extensive one, for not much else is told about Him during the balance of that year. The places visited are completely unknown to us today. However, we know that at this time Jesus and His disciples traversed the customarily avoided Samaritan country. Here the celebrated meeting with the Samaritan woman took place. Wearied from His long walk, Jesus rested at Jacob's Well on the outskirts of the village of Sychar, close by ancient Shechem, while His disciples went in search of food. It was to a Samaritan woman, one of that despised people, who came to draw water at the well, that Jesus first revealed Himself as the Messiah (John 4:25-26).

Completing this journey, Jesus, now in His thirtieth year, returned to Cana in Galilee, where He performed a second miracle, healing a nobleman's son who was sick unto death (John 4:46-54). Then, going to His home in Nazareth, He preached in the synagogue. But being rejected by His townsmen, He left the beautiful little village and took the path which led over the shoulders of the mountain called the Horns of Hattin, toward Tiberias on the shore of the lake. This latter town, built by Herod Antipas and named for the reigning Caesar, was strongly Gentile in population and spirit and so was carefully avoided by Jesus. It is very evident that He applied His efforts almost without exception to centers of Jewish life, and that He had little or nothing to do with areas which were chiefly Hellenistic, or Grecian, in population and outlook.

Turning north toward Capernaum, Jesus now made a brief visit to towns of eastern Galilee. Great crowds gathered to hear Him speak, and many followed after Him. It was at this time that He healed a leper and a paralytic and also enlisted three more disciples. Jesus first saw James and John, the sons of Zebedee, mending their nets on the shores of Galilee. Near Capernaum He came upon a tax collector named Matthew and called to him, "Follow me."

It was now spring. Jesus and His followers started south for Jerusalem to keep the Passover. This trip was marked by the healing of the cripple at the Pool of Bethesda on the outskirts of Jerusalem.

Returning to Capernaum, Jesus found that His followers there had now grown to a multitude. Seeking a few days of quiet, He retreated from the confusion of that busy metropolis to the seclusion of the hills. He took with Him

GALILEAN MINISTRY
Copyright by C. S. HAMMOND & CO., N.Y.

3. Jesus retreated from Capernaum into the hills where He preached the Sermon on the Mount (at the Horns of Hattin?).

6. After Jesus' second rejection at Nazareth, He sent out His disciples to preach while He toured central Galilee alone.

7. Jesus sought retirement near Bethsaida Julias. Followed by the multitude, He fed them from five loaves and two fishes.

5. After crossing the Sea of Galilee, Jesus healed the demoniac at Gergesa.

1. Jesus toured eastern Galilee performing miracles, and returned to Capernaum.

4. Jesus led His disciples through southern Galilee, preaching and performing miracles. At Nain He raised the widow's son to life.

2. During Jesus' yearly visit to Jerusalem for Passover, He healed the cripple at the Pool of Bethesda.

Chorazin
Capernaum
Bethsaida Julias
Tabigha
Sea of Galilee
Magdala
Gergesa?
Cana
Horns of Hattin
Tiberias
Sepphoris
GALILEE
Nazareth
Mt. Tabor
Yarmuk R.
Nain
DECAPOLIS
Gadara
Scythopolis

Scale of Miles
0 2 4 6 8 10

only a small group of disciples, and on this occasion He appointed His Twelve Apostles: those already mentioned as well as Thomas, James the Less, Simon the Zealot, Judas (Jude) the brother of James, and Judas Iscariot.

The multitudes from Capernaum now sought Him out. They were joined by people from all parts of Judaea and from the seacoast and Tyre and Sidon. The message of the Kingdom of Heaven which He had been preaching was known far and wide and had stirred their souls. They found Him on the slopes of the Horns of Hattin and there He delivered the Sermon on the Mount. It is there that He spoke those undying words which begin, "Blessed are the poor in spirit: for theirs is the Kingdom of Heaven. . . ."

Jesus now traveled about Galilee with His disciples, preaching and healing the sick. Few details have come down to us, except those of the spiritual change which came over Mary Magdalene and the dramatic raising of the widow's son at the gate of Nain. This was a small city five miles southeast of Nazareth.

After this circuit of Galilee, Jesus sailed across the lake into an area bearing a wide variety of names in the Gospels: the country of the Gergesines, Gerasines or Gardarenes. Gergesa seems most probable as the original place, and its approximate location is now set near the Arab village of Kursī. There Jesus drove the evil spirits out of a possessed man into a herd of swine, which then plunged into the sea. When He returned from this phase of His ministry, Jesus was probably moving into His thirty-second year.

This was about the time of His second return to Nazareth. He preached again in the synagogue and was scoffed at and denied by His townsmen. They were filled with doubts concerning Him and asked each other, "Is not this the carpenter's son?" Jesus answered their lack of belief by leaving Nazareth and saying, "A prophet is not without honor, save in his own country, and in his own house."

To add weight to this sad rebuke, messengers now arrived and announced to Jesus that John the Baptist had been beheaded by Herod Antipas. The evil Herodias had demanded John's death, and her beautiful daughter Salome had beguiled Antipas into ordering this vile deed.

Jesus instructed His Twelve Apostles and sent them forth to preach the Gospel of the

The Pool of Siloam at Jerusalem. Here the man blind from birth received sight through Jesus (John 9).

Kingdom of Heaven. When they returned, He led them to the quiet of a desert area northeast of the Sea of Galilee near Bethsaida Julias. But the multitudes followed, and there then took place the miraculous feeding of the five thousand. Raising His eyes toward heaven, Jesus blessed the five loaves and two fishes which were sufficient only for Him and His Apostles, and they thereupon multiplied into enough to feed all the great throng which had gathered about Him.

THE LATTER part of Jesus' ministry began with a tour of that rural area of Phoenicia which lay close to the pagan cities of Tyre and Sidon (see map on page 145). Moved by the deep faith displayed by a certain woman, He healed her deranged daughter.

From Phoenicia, Jesus then traveled across the hills and fields of Galilee which He knew so well, and crossed the Jordan just below the great lake in order to enter a region dominated by a number of Grecian cities and known as the Decapolis. The people of this region, hearing that He was in their midst, came from all parts, bringing their lame, blind, sick, dumb and maimed. He denied none and performed many

Mount Hermon (seen from the Sea of Galilee) is a traditional site of the Transfiguration.

miracles while teaching and explaining the message of the Kingdom to come. This journey ended with a crossing from east to west of the northern portion of the lake, and a landing at the town Dalmanutha. Some scholars believe Magdala is meant, but the evidence is incomplete and the location is still a mystery.

Sailing from Dalmanutha across to Bethsaida Julias, Jesus and His Apostles made their way north to visit certain Jewish communities near the idolatrous city enlarged and beautified by Philip the tetrarch and named Caesarea Philippi ("the Caesar of Philip") in honor of the emperor Tiberius. As the city stood beside a main source of the Jordan at the foot of Mount Hermon, this gigantic eminence has been accepted as the site of the Transfiguration, that moving moment when the divinity of Christ

was revealed to His three trusted Apostles, Peter, James and John. However, tradition has also shown strong partiality for Mount Tabor, far to the south near Nain and Nazareth. In fact, there have been three commemorative churches on this lofty hill.

There was a return to Capernaum once again. And as the autumn of the final year advanced, Jesus left Galilee for the last time and started south toward Jerusalem, His purpose being to attend the Feast of Tabernacles, which customarily fell in the latter part of October. The early rains were then due and had perhaps begun, rendering the trail west of the Jordan impassable south of Scythopolis, which was the ancient Beth-shan. At least the Master this time passed again through the heart of the Samaritan country, where He was not welcomed because all could tell that He was a pilgrim on His way to the Temple. This rejection by the Samaritans did not, however, turn Jesus' heart against these people, for soon after this experience He told His famous parable of the Good Samaritan who befriended a Jew who had been stripped and beaten and left half dead by robbers.

Jesus spent about two months in or about Jerusalem, staying much of the time with Lazarus at Bethany, which was located on the road from the city that first swings up over the Mount of Olives and then drops sharply down to Jericho. Toward the year's end, He took this very road down into the Jordan Valley to carry His ministry into Peraea, the area east of the river.

There in Peraea, during the early months of His thirty-fourth year, Jesus received the urgent message from Martha and Mary begging Him to return at once to Bethany. Their beloved brother, Lazarus, was dying and they sought His help. When Jesus arrived at their home Lazarus had already been dead three days, but, going to the tomb, He ordered that the stone be removed. Then, crying out in a loud voice, "Lazarus, come forth," He performed the miracle of miracles, bringing His friend back to life.

Jesus now returned once more to Peraea. The path He took on this occasion seems to have been different from the one on His previous visit. He stopped at a village called Ephraim, as mentioned in John 11:54. Its exact location is unknown, but it would certainly have been somewhere north of Jerusalem and west of the Jordan, so that He would on this trip have forded the river quite a distance upstream from its mouth.

For some time past the Pharisees and others in Jerusalem who believed in the strictest observance of the Law had frowned upon the teachings of Jesus. They felt that He was assuming power and misleading the people, and they were concerned by the great multitudes that followed Him, fearing that their Roman masters might object. They now began to voice open opposition to Jesus; tensions began to mount. Jesus was warned of all this by His friends, who begged Him henceforth to avoid Jerusalem. Firm in His faith and purpose, He brushed their warnings aside. As He came back up the long grade which led from the Jordan Valley to Bethany in the closing days of March,

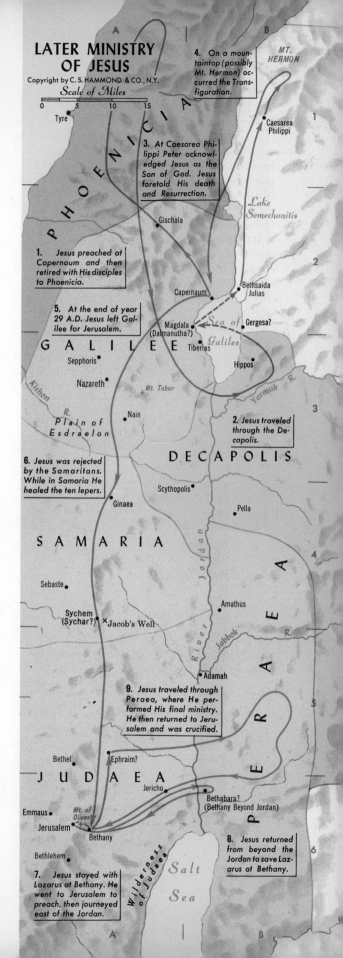

LATER MINISTRY OF JESUS

Copyright by C. S. HAMMOND & CO., N.Y.

Scale of Miles

0   5   10   15

1. Jesus preached at Capernaum and then retired with His disciples to Phoenicia.

2. Jesus traveled through the Decapolis.

3. At Caesarea Philippi Peter acknowledged Jesus as the Son of God. Jesus foretold His death and Resurrection.

4. On a mountaintop (possibly Mt. Hermon) occurred the Transfiguration.

5. At the end of year 29 A.D. Jesus left Galilee for Jerusalem.

6. Jesus was rejected by the Samaritans. While in Samaria He healed the ten lepers.

7. Jesus stayed with Lazarus at Bethany. He went to Jerusalem to preach, then journeyed east of the Jordan.

8. Jesus returned from beyond the Jordan to save Lazarus at Bethany.

9. Jesus traveled through Peraea, where He performed His final ministry. He then returned to Jerusalem and was crucified.

MT. HERMON

PHOENICIA

Tyre

Caesarea Philippi

Gischala

Lake Semechonitis

Capernaum

Bethsaida Julias

Magdala (Dalmanutha?)

Sea of Galilee

Gergesa?

GALILEE

Tiberias

Hippos

Sepphoris

Nazareth

Mt. Tabor

Kishon R.

Plain of Esdraelon

Nain

Yarmuk R.

DECAPOLIS

Scythopolis

Pella

Ginaea

SAMARIA

Jordan River

Sebaste

Amathus

Sychem (Sychar?)

×Jacob's Well

Jabbok R.

Adamah

PERAEA

Bethel

Ephraim?

JUDAEA

Jericho

Bethabara? (Bethany Beyond Jordan)

Emmaus

Mt. of Olives

Jerusalem

Bethany

Bethlehem

Wilderness of Judaea

Salt Sea

His travels on this earth were virtually over.

He arrived at Bethany six days before the last Passover He would ever celebrate. He attended a feast at the home of Lazarus, during which Mary anointed His feet with precious oils. During the next six days Jesus remained in Bethany, making short trips back and forth to Jerusalem from that little town on the Mount of Olives. From there He made His triumphant entry into Jerusalem amid the waving of palm fronds and the joyous cries of His followers.

But His trips between Jerusalem and Bethany were filled with peril; on the Thursday evening following the Last Supper He was on His way to Bethany when He was seized by the Temple guard in the olive grove at Gethsemane, where He had gone to pray.

We do not know the exact place where He stood trial before the Roman procurator, Pontius Pilate — a trial more famous than any other. We are not absolutely certain even where Calvary, "the Skull Place," actually was. Tradition places it at the site of the Church of the Holy Sepulcher.

ONLY about fifteen localities of the many which Jesus must have visited on His journeys through Galilee are mentioned in the Bible, but there is little doubt of the meaning and import of what He taught there. Though the precise spot on which the Crucifixion took place cannot be pointed out, there is little doubt in the minds of well over half a billion Christians concerning the full significance of all that lies behind that sublime death upon the Cross.

How many miles were involved in these journeys of Jesus? Not too many, as distances are measured today. But what other travels in all history have so greatly influenced so many down the long corridor of the ages? What other journeys, since the world began, have had greater significance?

The Garden of Gethsemane, on the Mount of Olives, where Jesus was seized. The trees standing on this spot are of great age, and are believed to be shoots of those under which Jesus prayed.

The home of Mary, mother of John Mark, in Jerusalem. This was the meeting place of the first Christian groups, and a typical home of the time. At the door, a mezuzah, a scroll in a container, served to bless the departures.

16. The First Missionaries

On that hazy spring morning when the risen Lord met and ate with His disciples by the lakeside in Galilee, He gave them very specific instructions. They were to return to Jerusalem and remain there until they had received power by having the Holy Spirit bestowed upon them. They were to be witnesses to their departed Master, not only in the Holy City itself, but throughout Judaea and Samaria and to the very ends of the earth (Luke 24:49 and Acts 1:8).

The Holy Spirit descended upon the Apostles during the celebration of the ancient harvest festival of Pentecost, which apparently came at the very beginning of June in that year of 30 A.D. Immediately following this, the Church began to take visible form. Obeying the instructions which Jesus had so carefully set, the Apostles spent their earliest efforts in carrying the Gospel to the Jews of Jerusalem and the rest of Judaea. Peter and John went to the Temple and preached in the courtyard while the other Apostles and certain disciples whom they had appointed as missionaries preached in synagogues in the city and in neighboring towns and villages.

Before long there were so many converts to the new faith that they began to hold religious meetings which were independent of the Temple and of the synagogues. Jerusalem was neither so large nor so important as other cities in Palestine and Syria. From the first there was a tendency to reach out to the Jewish communities in those parts and spread the Gospel which was rapidly developing within the *ekklēsia*— the assembly, or church — which the Apostles had organized. So it was that the missionary efforts, which have made the Church of Christ a most potent force in world affairs, began almost immediately following the Resurrection.

The Apostles and missionaries traveled into many lands, from Syria to Macedonia and Greece and as far as Italy. Some of their journeys were short, while others covered great distances. The report of their remarkable works is contained in The Acts of the Apostles, one of the most fascinating books in the Bible.

PHILIP: The first Christian missionary seems to have been Philip, not the Philip who was among the original followers of Jesus, but a new convert, designated "the Evangelist." He had been chosen as a deacon to look after the welfare of the members in Jerusalem, but when they scattered following the stoning of Stephen, the first Christian martyr, he also left the city (Acts 11:19).

He traveled up into Samaria, where he preached, performed many miracles and made numerous converts, including the archsorcerer Simon the Great (Acts 8:4-25). On another trip west of Jerusalem into the coastal plain once held by the ancient Philistines, he encountered and baptized the Ethiopian eunuch, whom many believe to have been the first Gentile convert to Christianity. He then carried his work to the city of Azotus, and then up the coast as far as the city of Caesarea, where he probably lived and worked for the remainder of his days (Acts 8:26-40; 21:8).

PETER: More effective were the efforts of the foremost among Jesus' early followers and the leading light of the first church at Jerusalem, the Apostle Peter. His first missionary work beyond the city and its environs took him north into Samaria, accompanied by the Apostle John, who had been so beloved by the Master.

Preaching in many Samaritan communities, they brought word of the Holy Spirit, and confirmed believers in Christ.

It was probably during the following year that Peter, presumably alone this time, set out down the road toward Joppa, stopping in all the villages along the way. At Lydda, west of Jerusalem, he healed a case of palsy and converted many. At Joppa he brought the disciple Tabitha, or Dorcas, back to life.

Here Peter experienced a most revealing vision. In it God made clear that His Kingdom was to know no boundaries, and that the Church of Christ was to be taken to the Gentiles as well as to the Jews.

Obeying this command, Peter went to Caesarea, where he baptized Cornelius, the resident Roman centurion, together with his whole family, thus officially recognizing these Gentiles as believers in Christ. His bold step seems to have created a great stir among the faithful at Jerusalem, and it was evidently several years before this act, which had required Peter's abundant courage, became approved practice (Acts 11:2-18).

This formerly gruff, impulsive fisherman, who had acquired deep humility, now seems to have journeyed up the coast to Syrian Antioch. This was the city where the followers of Christ were first known as Christians, and there the propriety of accepting Gentiles into the new faith was also seriously questioned. Peter defended his stand, as he also did later most resolutely and effectively, at a council meeting in Jerusalem (Acts 15:7-12).

Peter now seems to have visited Corinth in distant Greece and may have traveled widely in other lands, accompanied by his wife (1 Corinthians 9:5). If he was not actually at Babylon (1 Peter 5:13), then he was at the mystic Babylon which is Rome. And it was there that he glorified God through a martyr's death (John 21:19). Beyond this the Scriptures tell us nothing, yet tradition is rich with accounts of his other labors, fortunes and ministry.

BARNABAS: Many feel that the Church began its material existence in the home of Mary, the mother of the John Mark to whom the writing of the second Gospel is attributed (Acts 12:12). She is reported to have had a nephew named Joses, or Joseph, who had come from the island of Cyprus and had served for a time as a Levite, probably at the Temple. An early convert, he

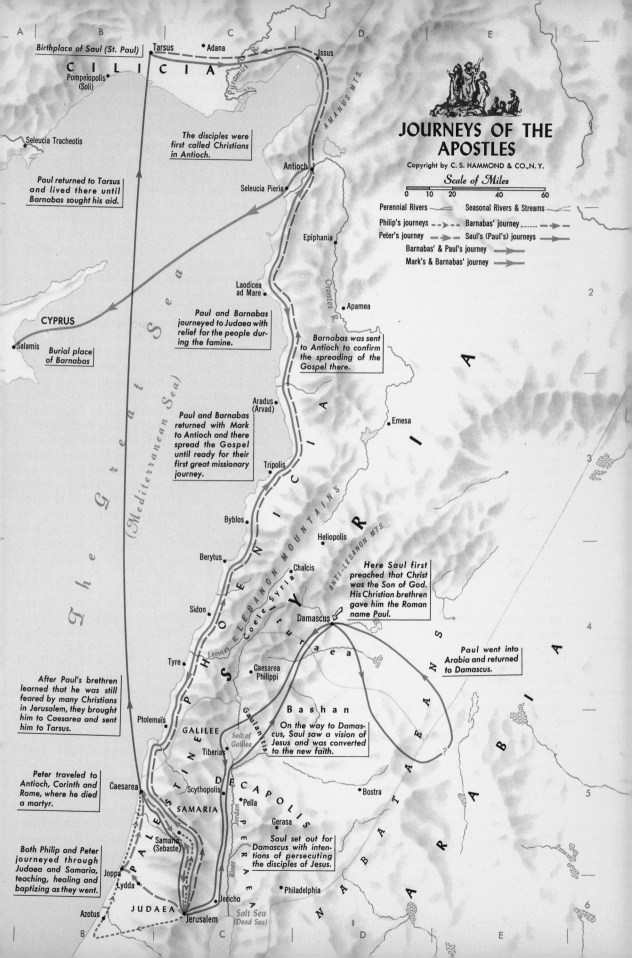

JOURNEYS OF THE APOSTLES

Copyright by C. S. HAMMOND & CO., N.Y.

Scale of Miles

0 10 20 40 60

Perennial Rivers	Seasonal Rivers & Streams
Philip's journeys	Barnabas' journey
Peter's journey	Saul's (Paul's) journeys
Barnabas' & Paul's journey	
Mark's & Barnabas' journey	

Birthplace of Saul (St. Paul)

C I L I C I A

Pompeiopolis (Soli)

Tarsus
Adana
Issus

Seleucia Tracheotis

The disciples were first called Christians in Antioch.

Paul returned to Tarsus and lived there until Barnabas sought his aid.

Antioch

Seleucia Pieria

Epiphania

Apamea

Paul and Barnabas journeyed to Judaea with relief for the people during the famine.

Barnabas was sent to Antioch to confirm the spreading of the Gospel there.

Laodicea ad Mare

CYPRUS

Salamis

Burial place of Barnabas

Paul and Barnabas returned with Mark to Antioch and there spread the Gospel until ready for their first great missionary journey.

Aradus (Arvad)

Emesa

Tripolis

Byblos

Heliopolis

Berytus

Chalcis

Here Saul first preached that Christ was the Son of God. His Christian brethren gave him the Roman name Paul.

Sidon

Damascus

Paul went into Arabia and returned to Damascus.

Tyre

Caesarea Philippi

B a s h a n

After Paul's brethren learned that he was still feared by many Christians in Jerusalem, they brought him to Caesarea and sent him to Tarsus.

Ptolemaïs

GALILEE

Sea of Galilee

Tiberias

On the way to Damascus, Saul saw a vision of Jesus and was converted to the new faith.

Peter traveled to Antioch, Corinth and Rome, where he died a martyr.

Caesarea

Scythopolis

D E C A P O L I S

Pella

Bostra

SAMARIA

Gerasa

Both Philip and Peter journeyed through Judaea and Samaria, teaching, healing and baptizing as they went.

Samaria (Sebaste)

Saul set out for Damascus with intentions of persecuting the disciples of Jesus.

Joppa

Lydda

Azotus

Philadelphia

JUDAEA

Jericho

Jerusalem

Salt Sea (Dead Sea)

The Great Sea

(Mediterranean Sea)

P H O E N I C I A

S Y R I A

N A B A T A E A

A R A B I A

LEBANON MOUNTAINS

Coele Syria

ANTI-LEBANON MTS.

AMANUS MTS.

Orontes R.

Leontes

Jordan River

PALESTINE

PERAEA

Ituraea

Gaulanitis

had turned his wealth over to the Apostles, who had given him the new surname of Barnabas (Acts 4:36-37).

The next mention of Barnabas in the Scriptures is his defense of Saul, better known as Paul, he who had viciously persecuted the early followers of Christ, had taken part in the stoning of Stephen, and had then become a convert himself (Acts 9:27). Several years later Barnabas was sent to Antioch to aid in the work of the young church there among both Jews and Gentiles. Recalling Paul's ability to preach, Barnabas went north to Tarsus and persuaded this former persecutor of the Christians to return with him and aid in this missionary labor. They worked together in Antioch for a whole year (Acts 11:26).

At the end of that time, they set off for Jerusalem bearing a contribution from the Christians of Antioch to their poor brethren in Judaea. Returning shortly with Mark, they then set out on what is generally considered to be the first of the Apostle Paul's missionary journeys, which will be covered in the next chapter (see also map of Paul's first and second journeys on page 154). Paul and Barnabas had a falling out over whether young Mark, the latter's cousin, should accompany them. At a later date Barnabas took Mark with him to Cyprus.

These two missionary journeys are perhaps the only ones Barnabas ever made. At least no others are recorded, and tradition has it that he was ultimately buried on the island of Cyprus which had been his early home.

SAUL (PAUL): Saul, the man destined to serve as the great Apostle to the Gentiles, was born in Tarsus in Cilicia on the mainland north of Cyprus. He was of a pious Jewish family, and was sent to Jerusalem when fairly young to attend the famous school conducted by the celebrated rabbi Gamaliel. Thus his journeys began some years before his missionary efforts in behalf of the Church.

While living in Jerusalem as a student, Saul, who was named for Israel's first king, became inflamed against the early followers of Christ and persecuted them in a most horrible manner, seeking them out and turning them over to the authorities. He was, in fact, so determined to eradicate them that he undertook a journey to Damascus to search for Christ's followers and bring them back bound to Jerusalem for trial. It was at this time, on the road to Damascus, that he was suddenly enveloped in a brilliant light, fell to the ground and heard the voice of Jesus.

Saul's conversion was complete, and he immediately began to preach his newfound faith in Damascus, where he lived on a street called Straight. He preached with conviction and energy, but the Jews of Damascus, knowing how he had persecuted Christians in Jerusalem, mistrusted him and plotted to kill him. He was finally forced to escape in a basket which his friends lowered over the city wall (Acts 9:3-8, 20-25).

Saul, or Paul, the Roman version of Saul by which he was now called, took refuge for a time somewhere in Nabataean Arabia, meditating upon the great change which had come over him. He went back once again, perhaps only briefly, to Damascus, finally returning after an absence of three years to Jerusalem. The Christians there were still afraid of him because of the part he had played in their persecution, so he was sent home to Tarsus to see what he might accomplish for the church in that area. It was here, after about six years of which there is no record, that Barnabas found him, probably following his trade of tentmaker, and drew his tremendous abilities back into the mainstream of Christian activities. It is easy to see how Paul had been well prepared through his past travels for those far greater ones which will be described in the following chapter (see also maps on pages 154 and 158).

JOHN MARK: John Mark, who caused the disruption between Paul and Barnabas on Paul's first missionary journey, is thought to have been a convert of Peter's. Fortunately the dissension with Paul was short-lived, and Mark remained active in early Church affairs. It is possible that he spent the next ten years in Jerusalem, or even in Cyprus with Barnabas. At the end of that time he went to Rome, adding his salutations to those of Paul and Luke in the Epistles to the Colossians and to Philemon (Colossians 4:10; Philemon 24).

From the former reference, it appears that he planned soon to go to Asia Minor. It is even possible that he met Peter in the East (1 Peter 5:13), but it is presumed that it was at Rome that he wrote the second Gospel. He certainly contributed his share to the spread of the new

The silver chalice of Antioch, discovered in 1910, long believed to have held the Holy Grail, the cup of Jesus at the Last Supper. Now dated third to sixth century A.D.

faith by traveling great distances; he may have continued missionary activities even after Peter was martyred, for the time of his death is uncertain.

JOHN: The Apostle John, who was associated with Peter in and about the Holy City immediately following the Resurrection and Pentecost, and who traveled up into Samaria with him in the early days, seems then to have returned and stayed at Jerusalem for some time. He was surely a pillar of strength there during the long series of persecutions that beset the infant Church. And he was one of the Apostles and elders who extended the warm handclasp of fellowship to Paul when he came to Jerusalem after his first full-scale missionary journey (Acts 15:6; Galatians 2:9).

Later in life, after the spadework had been done by Paul, and very likely after Paul's martyrdom, John appears to have taken charge of the churches of Asia. Tradition makes him a bishop, with his see centered at Ephesus. From there he is supposed to have been exiled to the island of Patmos in the Aegean Sea. This is said to have occurred during the persecution of the early Christians under Domitian, and some believe that while on Patmos he wrote the Book of Revelation — the Apocalypse — in 95 A.D. Freed soon after the accession of the emperor Nerva the following year, John is supposed to have returned to his diocese in Ephesus and to have died there during the reign of Trajan (98-117 A.D.).

John was perhaps the last of the twelve original followers of the Lord to die, and, while not an extensive traveler, he was certainly a most faithful servant. Three of the more prominent of the Apostolic fathers — Polycarp, Papias and Ignatius — were his pupils.

LUKE: Luke, a physician, probably a Greek of Antioch, is thought to have been first a convert to Judaism, and then, through Paul's ministrations, to Christianity. Though he has long been considered the author of both the third Gospel and the book of The Acts, he himself is mentioned but three times in Bible text (Colossians 4:14; Philemon 24; 2 Timothy 4:11). This might give the impression that he had only a very minor part in the early missionary effort.

However, in the above references Paul indicates that Luke was with him in Rome, and speaks of him as a fellow worker. Consequently it has been assumed that, at those points in Luke's descriptions of Paul's missionary journeys where the words "we" and "us" are used, he means that he was with Paul (Acts 16:10-17; 20:5–21:18; and 27:1–28:16).

Hence it seems that on Paul's second journey they went together from Troas as far as Philippi (see next chapter and map on page 154). They came together again at this same city on Paul's third trip, and Luke seems to have stood by in Jerusalem during the two years Paul was imprisoned at Caesarea (see next chapter and map on page 158). From there Luke accompanied Paul to Rome, where he probably remained with him until his martyrdom. The time and manner of Luke's death are not known.

TIMOTHY, TITUS, SILAS and APOLLOS: The book of The Acts could be as long as the New Testament itself and still not answer half the questions which might readily be asked about the men who carried Christianity into large sections of Asia and Europe during that first critical century. How many long miles did the beloved Timothy, Paul's close companion and secretary, walk after setting forth from his home at Lystra in Lycaonia with the Apostle? As the latter's apostolic deputy, how often did he range back and forth between Rome and Ephesus, relieving the older man of much enervating travel?

Titus, a Gentile convert of Paul's, journeyed with the Apostle from Antioch to Jerusalem, to the council where Paul argued against the necessity of circumcision for Gentiles. He was also for a time Paul's deputy, and his appearances in such widely scattered places as Ephesus, Corinth, Macedonia, Crete and Dalmatia reveal the countless hours he spent making his way, staff in hand, over the Roman roads or, depending upon fitful winds, sailing from port to port.

There was also Silas, a member of the Jerusalem church, sent first to Antioch and later taken by Paul, in place of Mark, on that second memorable journey. Paul and Silas were in prison in Philippi and worked together in many other cities. At a later time, under the name Silvanus, he seems to have served as scribe to Peter, recording Peter's First Epistle. Some also believe that it was Silas who delivered this letter to its destination.

There is still another traveler, whose activities are not too thoroughly detailed. He was the Alexandrian Jew Apollos, eloquent and zealous, who in very early days passed through Asia Minor and Greece converting many. At Ephesus he met and worked with a dedicated couple, the tentmaker Aquila and his good wife, Priscilla. Paul had great confidence in Apollos, and some scholars believe that Apollos is the author of the stirring Epistle to the Hebrews.

It took much traveling under the most difficult circumstances and much dedicated preaching to introduce the newborn Christian faith to what constituted the civilized world in the years immediately following Christ's death on Calvary. Happily this admirable effort was not in vain. Today we owe a great debt of gratitude to these first true missionaries.

17. The Journeys of Paul

Barnabas was a good and zealous disciple of Jesus Christ and filled with the Holy Spirit. Yet he was but one man in the bustling city of Antioch, where the missionary church he was helping to conduct was growing by leaps and bounds. He needed help and especially from one who could expound the fine points of this new faith to the full satisfaction of varied minds, both Jewish and Grecian. What should he do?

Less than one hundred fifty miles away in the next province, Cilicia, in the city of Tarsus at the end of an arm of the Mediterranean, was the man he needed. His name was Paul, and he was full of fire and thunderings since his startling conversion in a noonday vision on the road to Damascus. Paul was still feared in Jerusalem because of his former brutal persecution of Jesus' followers, but here at Antioch he could be most helpful. So Barnabas temporarily abandoned his flock and started northward. In what was then no doubt a comfortable and attractive city at the foot of the Taurus Mountains, he found the brilliant Benjamite he sought, probably busy at his trade of tentmaking.

During the six years Paul had been in Tarsus since his return from Jerusalem, he had presumably converted only an occasional individual, for Tarsus was a university center

The Appian Way, most famous of all Roman roads, over which Paul passed on his way into Rome (Acts 28:15)

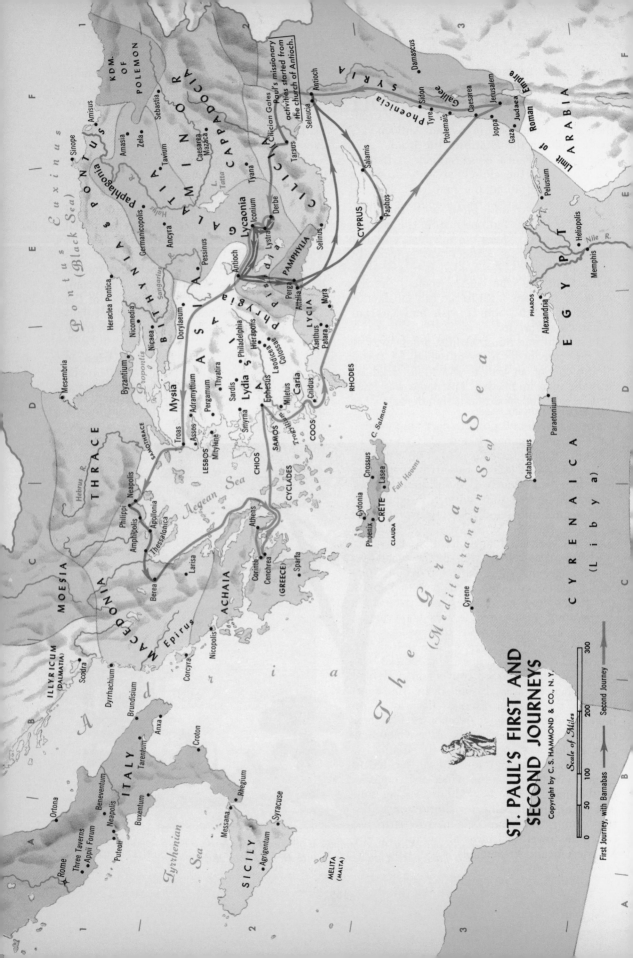

ST. PAUL'S FIRST AND SECOND JOURNEYS

Copyright by C. S. HAMMOND & CO., N.Y.

Scale of Miles

0 50 100 200 300

First Journey, with Barnabas ⟶
Second Journey ⟶

Paul's missionary
activities started from
the church of Antioch.

much given to Stoic philosophy. Whether Barnabas' persuasive powers were particularly compelling, or whether Paul longed for more fertile ground is not certain, but in any event they were both soon in Syrian Antioch, actively building the House of the Lord.

A year of Paul's effort added to that of Barnabas, and the church at Antioch was a thriving organization; the new faith had indeed found one of its truly dominant figures. The thirty-six-year-old Jew now began to make plans for a series of the most remarkable missionary activities ever recorded. When the time was right, under the direction of the Holy Spirit, he undertook the first of the trips in the company of Barnabas and Barnabas' young cousin, John Mark.

Leaving Antioch, they took the road which passed through that city from the East, and followed it sixteen miles to the port of Seleucia, which lay five miles north of the mouth of the Orontes River, away from the mud banks deposited by that stream as it entered the Mediterranean.

There they found passage on a ship headed for the mountainous island of Cyprus, the eastern tip of which lay about eighty miles to the southwest. Across this strip of the brilliant blue, sun-drenched Mediterranean their little open-decked ship, with its brightly colored square sail, would have crept cautiously; it would then have followed the southern shore of Cyprus to their destination at Salamis.

They preached for a time in the synagogue of this important town, assisted by young John Mark. Next they made their way to Paphos, the Roman capital of the island, which lay at the southwest corner of this very rugged block of land, preaching as they went.

At Paphos they were called before the proconsul, Sergius Paulus. This official was almost on the point of conversion and baptism, when he was dissuaded by the court habitué, the sorcerer Elymas. By way of rebuke, Paul called down temporary blindness upon the meddling deceiver, after which Sergius Paulus was converted to the Faith.

Paul, Barnabas and John Mark decided to go next into the Roman province of Pamphylia on the mainland of Asia Minor. Taking ship at Paphos, the three headed northwest to the tiny country made up of a narrow strip between the towering Taurus Mountains and the Mediterranean. Presumably they landed at

Attalia and then moved inland about ten miles to Perga, famous for its nearby shrine to the Asian fertility goddess Artemis, who was known as the queen of Perga. There, for some unexplained reason, John Mark parted from them and headed back to Jerusalem.

Paul and Barnabas now set off north over the mountains to Pisidian Antioch, chief city of the Roman province of Galatia. Paul preached the first sermon of which we have a record (Acts 13:16-41). It touched off such violent opposition, however, that the two missionaries were expelled from the town.

Paul and Barnabas now journeyed east to Iconium, where their many conversions resulted in further persecution. They then turned south through Lycaonia, visiting Lystra and Derbe. At Lystra the miraculous cure of a cripple made the heathen populace attempt to worship the two missionaries as if they were the Roman gods Jupiter and Mercury. There also the very estimable Timothy was converted (Acts 16:1-3). But feeling flared up there too, and Paul was stoned and left for dead by the mob (Acts 14:19).

He recovered, however, and after working

The Orontes River at Syrian Antioch. Paul set out from here to the port of Seleucia on his first journey with Barnabas and John Mark.

155

at Derbe he and Barnabas retraced their steps through the very same cities where they had been so roughly used. They visited each town all the way back to Perga and strengthened the churches they had founded. Then, sailing from Attalia, they returned to Syrian Antioch.

The first of the three missionary journeys of Paul, the great Apostle to the Gentiles, had been completed. He and Barnabas had in no sense been wayfaring, for their steps had been under the direction of the Holy Spirit, and so arranged that they might carry the Word to areas directly to the west of those lands in which the Gospel had previously been preached. Churches had now been founded at some of the larger cities in the south-central part of Asia Minor, from which points their influence would spread. Paul, who headed this missionary activity, was trained and steeped in Judaism, though born, reared and widely experienced in the Gentile world. His outlook was thus very broad, and the future seemed most promising.

Then came a threatened schism in this burgeoning faith. Certain converted Pharisees, who still remained strict in their beliefs, were demanding that the Gentiles accept circumcision, despite the Lord's having revealed to Peter that the non-Jewish converts were not to be bound by the full burden of the Mosaic Law. So great was the disturbance at Antioch, where there were many converted Gentiles, that the church there decided to send Paul, Barnabas and others to reach an understanding on this question with the Apostles and elders in Jerusalem.

It was a serious threat, but fortunately the crisis was safely passed. Paul won his point, laying down the principle of universal salvation. Though hatred and hostility would continue to be directed against him from certain quarters, the way was now opened for carrying the Gospel of Christ to all peoples. The time of this important meeting of Paul and the other Apostles in Jerusalem was 49 A.D.

It was perhaps in this same year that Paul proposed to Barnabas a second missionary journey, only to break with his staunch companion over whether or not to take John Mark with them. Choosing Silas instead, he set off overland to the north, first visiting churches in Syria and then swinging west through Cilicia to his home city, Tarsus. From there, by way of the famous defile in the Taurus Mountains, the Cilician Gates, they went on to Derbe. Paul was now once again in Lycaonia, where his life had been sought on the previous visit. But, unafraid, he moved on to Lystra, where they were joined by Timothy. The three then seem to have gone as far as Iconium and Pisidian Antioch. The further course of their journey is open to question.

It is reported that Paul was prohibited by the Spirit from preaching in the Roman province, called Asia, which lay just to the west of Pisidian Antioch. It is also said that he was forbidden to enter Bithynia, which lay just below the Black Sea. And so he, Silas and Timothy seem to have made no stops until they came to one of the chief seaports of Mysia, the city of Troas. It was there that the Spirit in a vision directed that their missionary efforts now be carried into Europe. Luke joined them.

Paul and his three companions now boarded

The Cilician Gates, famous pass in the mountains north of Tarsus, through which Paul traveled on his second and third journeys. For four thousand years invaders from the north entered through this defile.

Preaching to the populace at the synagogue and along the famous "Straight Way," Paul won converts among the worldly Gentiles of Corinth.

a ship and crossed the upper end of the Aegean Sea to Neapolis in Macedonia. They then moved inland by road ten miles to Philippi, the most important city in that district, where a strange and miraculous event took place. Paul and Silas were brought before the magistrate by the angry populace. They were whipped and thrown into prison and their legs were put into stocks. But during the night, while they were praying and singing praises to the Lord, a great earthquake shook the prison, opening all the doors and loosening the stocks. The prisonkeeper fell to his knees before them, begging to be baptized together with all his family, and the magistrate ordered that they be freed. As a result of this amazing occurrence Paul and his friends were able

to live for a while in Philippi enjoying peace. It was there that he established the first church in Europe, the church which continued to be most dear to him to the end of his days.

Luke remained behind, while Paul, Silas and Timothy moved on to the seaport of Thessalonica. Paul labored valiantly there, preaching three days in the synagogue and winning many converts, including Greeks. However, persecution finally forced him on to the southwest another fifty miles to Berea. There he met with considerable success.

Leaving Silas and Timothy in Berea, Paul then continued on his way to Athens. He was perhaps disappointed by his indifferent success in that sophisticated city, and soon moved on to Corinth, the great commercial port

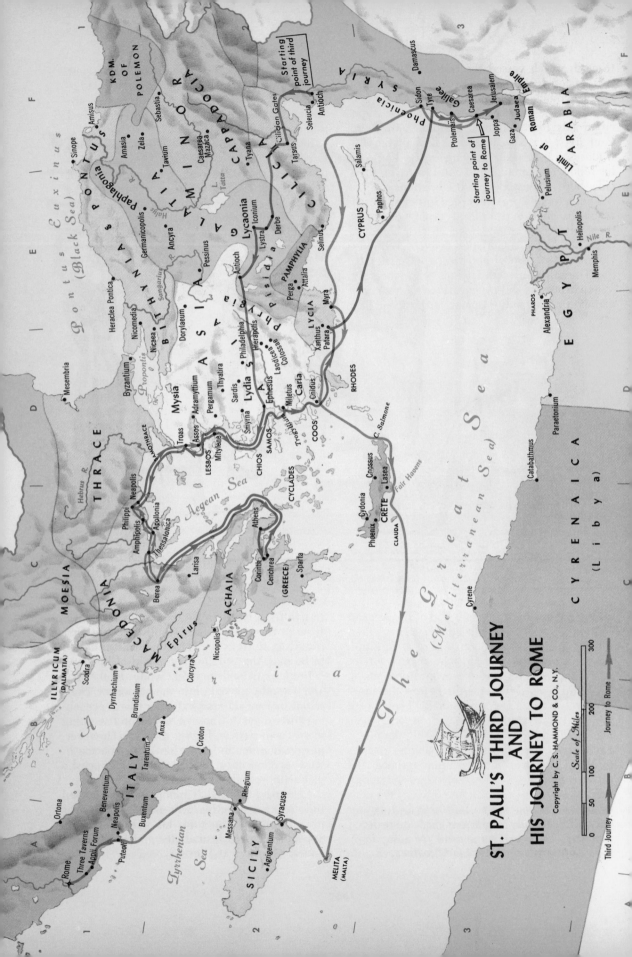

ST. PAUL'S THIRD JOURNEY
AND
HIS JOURNEY TO ROME

Copyright by C. S. HAMMOND & CO., N.Y.

Scale of Miles

0   50   100   200   300

━━━ Third Journey   ━━━ Journey to Rome

Starting point of third journey

Starting point of journey to Rome

through which passed the traffic between the two major sections of Greece. Corinth also handled much of the booming trade between Asia and the West. It was one of the main crossroads in the Roman Empire, and there Paul lived for a year and a half plying his trade as a tentmaker, staying in the home of his fellow craftsman Aquila and his wife, Priscilla, both dedicated Jewish Christians.

There, too, he preached the Gospel of Christ regularly, first in the local synagogue, and then, after opposition arose, in the home of one Titus Justus, a Christian convert. While in Corinth, Paul also wrote the two Epistles to the Thessalonians. Local Jews who sincerely felt that he was destroying Mosaic Law complained of Paul to the Roman authorities. The

Emperor Tiberius, who rebuilt Ephesus after an earthquake, not long before Paul's visits. At Ephesus Paul converted a great following to Christianity during his third journey.

new proconsul, Gallio, who arrived at his post about midsummer of 51 A.D., refused to judge the dispute and permitted Paul to go unhampered; the result was that he established a church in the city.

Realizing at length that there was much territory yet to be covered, the Apostle decided to turn again to the east. Taking Aquila and Priscilla as his traveling companions, he boarded a ship sailing to Ephesus, some two hundred fifty miles directly east across the Aegean Sea. There they met the ardent Apollos, preaching fervently but somewhat faultily, and hurriedly instructed him in acceptable Christian doctrine.

Paul preached in the synagogue for a short time until he felt pressed to report to the elders at Jerusalem. Promising faithfully to return to Ephesus, he left the church in charge of Aquila and Priscilla and set out by ship for Caesarea. From there he evidently made a hasty trip to the Holy City and, having acquainted the authorities with his accomplishments in Europe, he returned once again to Syrian Antioch, thus completing his second great missionary journey.

Paul spent about a year in Antioch before entering upon his third missionary undertaking, which seems to have begun in the year 54 A.D. He was concerned about the churches that he had helped to found in Asia Minor, so he set out overland, presumably retracing the steps he had taken during the early part of his previous tour. Having completed his task of "strengthening all the disciples" in these parts, he then went on west from Pisidian Antioch to Ephesus.

As this most influential city was the capital of the province of Asia, Paul now established himself there. It would appear that the Holy Spirit had removed the ban which had prevented Paul from preaching the Gospel within that province during his second missionary journey five years earlier.

For three years Ephesus would be the center of Paul's ardent labors, and he therefore must have come to know well this place of surpassing splendor. It had been built anew by the emperor Tiberius following the devastating earthquake in 29 A.D. Besides a large stadium, a fine theater, baths and an excellent public library, it also contained a magnificent temple of Diana, or Artemis, the popular Asiatic goddess of nature and fertility.

The temple of Fortuna at Ephesus, capital of the Roman province of Asia, where Christianity triumphed over the worship of Diana

For three months Paul preached in the synagogue at Ephesus and for the next two years in a lecture hall belonging to one Tyrannus, also within the city. He made many converts, especially among the Gentiles, and had many friends among the leading people, but he also acquired his usual quota of fervid enemies. On one occasion he was threatened by a mob which had been inflamed by the silversmiths who made small statues of the goddess Diana. They sold these statues to pilgrims coming to the temple and felt that Paul's work was damaging to their business.

It is probable that Paul wrote his famous Epistle to the Galatians here, to answer certain men in the cities of Derbe, Lystra, Iconium and Pisidian Antioch who were denouncing his Apostolic claims.

Questions of the new faith were posed, too, by the church in faraway Corinth, and to it went one of his famous letters, which has unfortunately not come down to us. Since more serious dissension continued to prevail there, Paul finally found it necessary to write the missive known to us as First Corinthians. There are some scholars who believe he even made a hurried trip to that city to bring harmony out of discord (2 Corinthians 12:14; 13:1). Others believe that the journey was made by Titus, for Titus did go there at one time as Paul's deputy.

After the upsetting experience with the

mobs roused by the silversmiths, Paul's position in Ephesus was most uncertain. He sent Timothy and another disciple, Erastus, on into Macedonia while he moved up the coast to Troas, where he had arranged to meet Titus, who was supposed to bring him word of how affairs stood in Corinth. Titus was not there when Paul arrived. After a reasonable wait, the Apostle pushed on into Europe, making his first call at the church at Philippi.

Somewhere along the way Titus caught up with him, bringing cheering news — the situation at Corinth had finally adjusted itself. Paul then sent a letter (Second Corinthians) ahead, and went on to Corinth himself after visiting the churches he had established on his second journey at Thessalonica and Berea.

He passed a part of the winter of 57-58 A.D. in Corinth, during which time he produced a document of profound value to the Christian Church — the important Epistle to the Romans. This, probably the greatest of his instructive messages, forcefully presents the doctrinal way of salvation, and shows decisively the Gospel power of God for the saving of all who believe.

Since it has been indicated that many of the great Apostle's activities were carried out through the guidance of the Holy Spirit, Paul may have known that his labors would culminate in Rome. The church already founded in that city by close friends and former associates was even then calling to him, and he had a great desire to visit it. But a most charitable duty first demanded his attention.

He had induced the Gentile churches of Macedonia, Greece and Galatia to make offerings for the relief of the poor Christians of Judaea, and he now proposed to take these funds to the Mother Church in Jerusalem as a clear indication of the good intent of the congregations he had added to the fold. As he was setting out to sail to Syria, a plot hatched by some of his enemies to kill him on this journey forced him to change his plans and return to Macedonia.

Several disciples traveled with him to Philippi in Macedonia, where he met Luke. Sending the disciples on ahead, he and the evangelist lingered with the Philippians until after the Passover. Then, sailing across to Troas, they rejoined the disciples and stayed with them in that city for a week. It was there that Eutychus, often called "the church sleeper," fell from the third floor of a building during Paul's lengthy evening discourse, was picked up dead and was miraculously restored to life by the Apostle (Acts 20:9-10).

Paul and his party now made their way down the island-studded coast of the province of Asia, stopping at Assos, Mitylene and Samos and finally coming to Miletus, which was about thirty-six miles south of Ephesus. Since he hesitated to visit the latter city in person because of the riot instigated against him some months before by the silversmiths, Paul asked the elders of the church to meet with him at the little seaport of Miletus. There, in stirring words, he took most affectionate leave of them (Acts 20:18-35). Later, from captivity in Rome, he would send them his Epistle to the Ephesians, which he desired to have circulated among the churches of Asia Minor.

Paul now set off again toward the south, the vessel making stops at the islands of Coos (Cos) and Rhodes.

From Rhodes Paul and his party swung east to Patara, on the coast of Lycia, where a change in ships was made. The Phoenician craft they now boarded sailed west of Cyprus and landed them at Tyre. There they were well received. But the members of the church warned Paul that trouble was awaiting him in Jerusalem and were loath to let him leave.

After a week's stay, the ship continued to Ptolemaïs, and then to Caesarea. There Paul and his companions were entertained by Philip the Evangelist, and it was at his home that the prophet Agabus made a most distressing forecast. Binding his own hands and feet with Paul's girdle, Agabus foretold that the Jews at Jerusalem would similarly bind the zealous missionary and hand him over to the Roman authorities. Here was a second unmistakable warning, but Paul could not be dissuaded. With his arrival in the Holy City, he completed his third missionary journey.

His reception by the Mother Church was most warm, and, after having heard the report of his ministry among the Jews and Gentiles of Asia Minor, Macedonia and Greece, the whole council praised God. As many of the Jewish Christians were still opposed to him, he was asked to demonstrate his own continuing fidelity to Judaic customs by taking part with certain others in a Nazarite vow at the Temple. During the ceremony various Jews from the province of Asia raised a great tumult. They accused him of bringing Gentiles into

*The island of Rhodes, on the busy sea-lane between Syria and Greece. Paul's
ship probably anchored briefly in the harbor of Lindos (left) on his third journey.*

the sacred precincts, and would have slain him had he not most fortunately fallen into the hands of the Romans. As he was a Roman citizen, the commander of the garrison at Jerusalem, Claudius Lysias, sent him under strong guard to Caesarea, along with a letter to the procurator, Felix, turning the whole matter over to him. Here Paul remained a prisoner for the next two years.

Despite violent allegations, Felix refused to prefer any charges against Paul and gave him a reasonable amount of freedom, allowing friends to call upon him in Herod's castle, where he was detained. While the procurator trembled at the Apostle's vehement preaching, he hoped that Paul or his friends would produce a sizable bribe with which to purchase his liberty. Since it was not forthcoming, the Apostle was still imprisoned when a new procurator, Porcius Festus, arrived in Judaea.

This high Roman official, hoping to please the Jews of his territory, sought to persuade Paul to go to Jerusalem to be tried. Knowing that would certainly mean his death, Paul asserted his rights as a Roman citizen and appealed his case to Caesar.

Before he could start on his way to stand trial in Rome, Paul was forced to appear before a visiting dignitary, Herod Agrippa II, great-grandson of the founder of the Herodian dynasty. Agrippa was the ruler of two tetrarchies in Palestine. And although the original Greek text merely hints at it, this king had a real contempt for all such disturbers of the peace. But even Agrippa admitted that the prisoner brought before him had committed no crime and therefore could have been set free had he not already appealed to Caesar.

It was apparently early in the fall of 60 A.D. that Paul started on his fateful voyage to the city on the Tiber. Along with other prisoners, he was placed aboard a ship with Luke and a Thessalonian named Aristarchus. This first vessel, a coasting ship of Adramyttium, took them only as far as Myra in Lycia, after having made a single stop at Sidon.

There they shifted over to an Alexandrian merchantman, bound for Italy, a large open-decked ship, built of heavy timbers with a high bow and stern, and rigged with a great square sail. The season was already well advanced, and the winds proved unfavorable.

Following the coast to the north and west past the island of Rhodes to Cnidus, they then sailed south to Crete, rounding the Cape of Salmone with the greatest difficulty. Working their way gingerly along that island's southern shore, they finally found anchorage in the sheltered bay called Fair Havens. It was by now mid-October, the end of the safe sailing season, and Paul advised remaining where they were. But the ship's owner wished to push on to Phoenix, further along the coast, where there was a safer harbor.

They were hardly around the headland beyond Fair Havens when violent winds from the northeast struck them and sent them scudding to the westward, where they feared they might run aground on the small island of Clauda. Escaping this danger, they were then seized by a tempest which held them at its mercy for two full weeks, forcing them on and on to the westward. All aboard began to give up hope except Paul, whom the Lord's Angel had assured that not a single soul among them would suffer death.

Eventually, on the fourteenth night, the sounding lead began to show shallower water — they were evidently approaching land. So they cast over all four of their anchors as darkness settled down, and with great patience and fear prepared to wait out the dark hours.

When at last daylight came, they could make out a small bay with a strip of beach not far ahead of them. So the anchors were quickly cast off, the sail was hoisted, and they headed in toward the strip of sand. The ship ran aground in the breakers, and under their crushing force began to fall apart. There was nothing left to do but leap overboard. Some could swim; others clung to the wreckage, but, as Paul had forecast, all reached the shore safely.

Where were they? It developed they had been shipwrecked upon the island of Melita, or Malta, as it is known today, which is just under sixty miles south of the far larger island of Sicily. There on Melita they were forced to stay for the next three months. Fortunately the people of the island, although spoken of as "barbarians" in the original Greek text of The Acts since they were neither Greeks nor Romans, proved to be most kindly and hospitable. And Paul, by many miraculous deeds of healing their sick, gained special honor among them.

Finally, when the season became more favorable again, a ship of Alexandria that had wintered in the harbor took the castaways aboard and headed north for Italy. It made a stop at Syracuse on the island of Sicily, another at Rhegium at the toe of the Italian boot, and then moved up across the Tyrrhenian Sea to Puteoli, a few miles west of the modern city of Naples. This was the chief port for vessels coming to the Italian peninsula from north Africa, Egypt and the East. There Paul found a group of Christians, with whom his guard allowed him to remain for a week.

In the meantime, some of the ship's company apparently moved on ahead, so word reached the Christian community in Rome that the great Apostle was approaching. Consequently Paul had gone but part of the distance up the famous Appian Way to Rome when he met the first of two welcoming committees at the Appii Forum (Market of Appius), forty-odd miles below his destination. About ten miles farther on, at the Three Taverns, the second group anxiously awaited him. There was no doubt that Christ's followers were exceedingly happy to have Paul with them at the Roman capital.

What happened next, and just how Paul reached the city, and into whose custody he was delivered are matters of speculation. This much, however, is certain: he was soon placed in some degree of military confinement and chained to a soldier for safekeeping.

Appeals were no doubt promptly made to the emperor in his behalf. Yet if one had no friends in high places and lacked money to bribe officials, the hearing of one's case by the exalted ruler of the empire was a slow business.

Since his imprisonment promised to last for a long time, the Apostle Paul seems to have hired a house in which to live with his Roman guard. The last sentence of Luke's account tells that he continued in this manner for two whole years, and also emphasizes the fact that he pursued his missionary activities in Rome unhampered.

There is an ancient legend that after two years Paul was released from his imprisonment, traveled extensively throughout the Mediterranean world, was imprisoned again and executed in Rome at a later date. But on these matters the Bible is silent. If Paul did make further journeys we do not have sufficient evidence to trace them on the map.

18. The Later Herods

Herod
and His Descendants

Son of Antipater, Caesar's savior, husband of a Maccabean princess, ruled Judaea under Rome

Herod the Great

Married his niece Herodias; sent Jesus to Pontius Pilate

Antipas

Aristobulus

Herod Philip

Herod Philip II

Married his niece Herodias, fathered infamous Salome

Married niece Bernice

Plotted the death of John the Baptist

Herod Chalcis

Agrippa I

Herodias

Bernice

Agrippa II

Drusilla

Salome

Judged Paul the Apostle at Caesarea

Married great-uncle Herod Philip II; danced before Antipas for John the Baptist's head

Married - - - - - - -

Four generations of Herods are mentioned in the New Testament. The first by that name is Herod the Great, the founder of the dynasty, who died about the time Jesus was born. The second is his son, Herod Antipas. Then there are his grandson, Herod Agrippa I, and his great-grandson, Herod Agrippa II.

Herod Antipas, better known to Bible readers as "Herod the tetrarch," was of course the easily swayed ruler who permitted the cruel beheading of John the Baptist. During his student days in Rome, he had fallen madly in love with his niece, Herodias, who was also the wife of one of his half brothers. Having divorced a Nabataean Arab princess, he now wed this Herodias, an unprincipled, designing woman, who saw in her new husband greater promise of riches and fame than his somewhat older half brother had offered.

Herodias proved to be a masculine, headstrong creature, who dominated the weak, peace-loving Antipas as completely and as unfortunately as Jezebel had prevailed over Ahab. She it was who craftily brought about the death of John the Baptist, because he had questioned her morality. Her daughter Salome was the legendary dancer who demanded John's head. Herodias would, a few years later, cause her husband almost to lose his own head because of her consuming jealousy.

Herod Antipas had come to prominence largely because one of his half brothers, Aristobulus, had been executed by their suspicious, irascible father. Aristobulus had left five children behind him, among whom were Herodias and a son called Agrippa, the young man who was to cause Herod Antipas much trouble and bring about his downfall. Agrippa's widowed mother, another strong-willed woman named Bernice, of whom he stood in some awe, managed to send him to Rome for an education and keep him amply supplied with spending money. He consequently became quite a wastrel, yet he craftily employed his funds — when he had them — in making himself highly popular with influential people.

Through his mother and his aunt, a woman called Salome who lived in Rome, Agrippa became known in the emperor's family, while the brilliant Antonia, daughter of Mark Antony and mother of the emperor Nero, was his patroness and defender. He was especially friendly with Drusus, the ruling Tiberius' elder son, and also well acquainted with the younger, Claudius, whose hesitancy in speech and whose retiring ways had earned for him the reputation of being a backward boy.

With Drusus' death in 23 A.D., Rome lost its appeal for Agrippa. When his mother's death stopped his income, he headed for home, leaving behind him a host of angry creditors.

For a time Agrippa lived in Idumaea, where he found life excessively hard, and would, it is claimed, have attempted suicide had it not been for his resolute wife. He would also have been in desperate financial straits had not his uncle Herod Antipas the tetrarch come to his aid. This weak but kindly ruler appointed Agrippa to a government post and provided him with a small income, but at the same time made his life uncomfortable by telling all who would listen of his own generosity in providing for this spendthrift.

Agrippa finally broke with his uncle, and in 36 A.D., about six years after Jesus' Crucifixion, he set off for Rome again, his purpose being to bring charges against the man who had befriended him. He cleverly worked his way back into the good graces of the emperor Tiberius and became a favorite of the popular young Roman Gaius. Then a foolish remark to the effect that the old emperor had lived too long landed him in prison, where he remained until Tiberius died a few months later.

A very strange happening, according to legend, took place at the prison camp. One day, as the unhappy Agrippa stood brooding beneath a tree, a large owl lighted on a branch directly above his head. A German prisoner quickly explained that this was a sign of good luck, for it meant the young man would soon be released and good fortune would come to him. "But," warned the prisoner, "beware! The next time such an owl appears, it means you will die within five days." Happy over the first part of this prophecy, the rash young Agrippa little realized in how few years the remainder of it would also come to pass.

Young Gaius, who now became Roman emperor under the name of Caligula, was encouraged not only to set Agrippa free but also to crown him king of a sizable area in Palestine, the tetrarchies of Herod Philip II and Lysanias. The new monarch appeared to be in no hurry to go home; he remained in Rome for another year and a half, making friends of important people who might later be helpful to him. When he finally did return to Palestine to take over his tetrarchies, he found that his sister Herodias was bitterly jealous of the turn of events which had changed him from a penniless vagabond into an important ruler.

She began almost at once to nag her aging husband, Herod Antipas, insisting that he go to Rome and demand a kingdom superior to the one recently given the scapegrace Agrippa. In the spring of 39 A.D. she finally succeeded.

When Agrippa discovered what was happening, he sent one of his own freedmen hurrying off to Rome, bearing an accusation against Antipas. This complaint reached the emperor first, and, when Herod Antipas appeared before his sovereign, he was quickly banished to faraway Gaul, and his tetrarchy of Galilee and Peraea was given to Agrippa. This fine present called for a quick trip to Rome on Agrippa's part, so that he might properly thank Caligula in person.

Returning from Rome to Palestine in the fall of 39 A.D., Agrippa stopped in Egypt, where the Alexandrian Jews, most unhappy about their treatment, asked his help in obtaining concessions from the emperor Caligula, with whom he seemed to be on such excellent terms. Their demands were but one of many indications of the tension that was then mounting. Caligula gave them some help, but Jewish unrest under the Romans increased from that time on, making the next thirty years of Palestinian history very bloody ones.

The trouble in Alexandria came to a head when certain Greeks living in that city broke into a local synagogue and erected an altar to the emperor Caligula. When the Jews removed it, the matter was referred to Rome as evidence of disrespect to the divinity of the emperor. His imperial highness was incensed over this indignity. He was determined

DOMINIONS OF HEROD AGRIPPA I
37 to 44 A.D.
Copyright by C. S. HAMMOND & CO., N.Y.

Scale of Miles

Perennial Rivers ....   Capitals ....
Seasonal Rivers & Streams .....   Cities of the Decapolis □

Kingdom of Herod Agrippa I -41 A.D.
Decapolis
Autonomous city state of Ascalon
Roman province of Syria

Agrippa received the tetrarchies of Philip and Lysanias in 37 A.D.

Agrippa received the tetrarchy of Antipas (Galilee and Peraea) in 39 A.D.

Agrippa died after a sudden and dramatic illness at Caesarea in 44 A.D.

Agrippa was given Judaea and Samaria by Claudius in 41 A.D.

The Great Sea (Mediterranean Sea)

PHOENICIA

ABILENE

ITURAEA

TRACHONITIS

BATANAEA

GAULANITIS

AURANITIS

DECAPOLIS

GALILEE

SAMARIA

JUDAEA

IDUMAEA

PERAEA

NABATAEANS

Salt Sea (Dead Sea)

MOUNT LEBANON

MT. HERMON

MT. CARMEL

Plain of Esdraelon

Plain of Sharon

Mt. Gerizim

Sea of Galilee

Lake Semechonitis

Place names
Chalcis
Abila
Damascus
Sidon
Sarepta
Tyre
Dan
Caesarea Philippi
PANIAS
Cadasa
Ecdippa
Gischala
Seleucia
Raphana
Ptolemaïs
Capernaum
Bethsaida Julias
Kanatha
Jotapata
Taricheae
Gergesa?
Hippos
Gamala
Dion
Sepphoris
Tiberias
Nazareth
Philoteria
Abila
Edrei
Dora
Gadara
Bostra
Caesarea
Ginaea
Scythopolis
Pella
Gerasa
Sebaste (Samaria)
Sychem
Apollonia
Antipatris
Thamna
Phasaelis
Joppa
Gophna
Archelaïs
Lydda
Bethel
Gazara
Beth-horon
Jericho
Essebon
Jamnia
Ekron
Emmaus
Julius (Livias)
Azotus
Jerusalem
Philadelphia
Ascalon
Bethlehem
Herodium
Beth-gubrin
Machaerus
Marisa
Bethsura
Hebron
Adora
Engaddi
Anthedon
Gaza
Masada
Ziklag
Kir-moab
Bersabee
Elusa

Kishon R.
Jordan
Leontes R.
Yarmuk R.
River Jordan
Jabbok R.
Arnon R.
Brook Zered

to teach these subject people a lesson, one they would understand no matter where they lived. An order was hurried off to the newly appointed legate of Syria, requiring him to procure and erect a statue of Gaius Caesar Caligula in the likeness of Jupiter in the Holy of Holies of the Temple of Jerusalem.

According to one account, when Agrippa learned of Caligula's order, he decided to go immediately to Rome. Another version states that he was en route and actually first heard of the emperor's order from his own lips. So great was the shock of this announcement that Agrippa promptly fainted, but he pulled himself together and with great courage and tact persuaded the monarch to put aside this profane enterprise which would have been an intolerable sacrilege to all Jews.

It was but a short time later that Caligula was set upon and assassinated. The date was January 24, 41 A.D., and Agrippa was still in Rome. A turmoil arose at once as to who should succeed the dead Caesar. It was finally settled when certain soldiers hunting through the palace came upon the late emperor's uncle, Claudius, son of Tiberius and brother of Drusus, whom Agrippa had known years before as the backward prince. Through the years, Claudius had been kept in seclusion and away from the public, yet to the group in power at the moment he seemed the logical nominee for the vacant throne. One of the last things Agrippa, as ruler of the Jews, expected was to be cast as a kingmaker, yet he soon found himself serving as the go-between in the case of Claudius versus the Roman Senate. He, probably more than anyone else, convinced the reluctant candidate that he should become the next emperor.

For this service Agrippa received a prompt reward; Judaea and Samaria were added to his domain. His holdings now rivaled those of his grandparent, Herod the Great. And at his request one of his brothers, another man named Herod, was made king of the tiny principality of Chalcis in Syria, thirty miles northwest of Damascus. The liberal treatment accorded Herod Agrippa I, as he was now known, had in part been founded on the emperor Claudius' hope that under a king of their own religious beliefs the freedom-loving Jews might be more tractable.

Agrippa hurried home to enjoy his increased power, but was soon to find that he was little

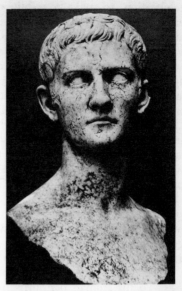

Caligula, friend of Herod Agrippa I in his youth, first to appoint Agrippa a ruler in Palestine

more than a Roman puppet. He began to build a wall around one of the newer districts of Jerusalem so that it too might be within the fortifications. Word came from Rome to stop the work. In Roman eyes the effort appeared to be nothing more than a step toward Jewish independence.

Agrippa may also have given his Roman supporters concern in other matters. During his student days he had adopted many Roman ways, but on his latest return from Rome he made many magnificent sacrifices at the Temple, and presented to that holy building a handsome golden chain which his friend the emperor Caligula had given him. He was now determined to be a sincere, pious Jew, even requiring that any and all Gentiles who married into the family of which he was the head be fully bound by every detail of the Law of Moses.

It was as the new champion of strict Jewish practices that Agrippa took his strong stand against the heretical sect centering in Jerusalem — the Nazarenes, or followers of one Jesus of Nazareth, whom a former procurator, Pontius Pilate, had put to death. To stamp out this persistent sect, Agrippa had one of its leaders, the Apostle James ben Zebedee, beheaded and another, the Apostle Peter, thrown into prison. He intended, after the Passover celebration, to make a public example of Peter before a great audience. To the amazement of all, Peter was mysteriously and miraculously freed from prison. As he lay sleeping between two soldiers to whom he was chained, the Angel of the Lord appeared and, touching him on the side, said: Arise up quickly. At this command Peter's chains fell off. Then the Angel led him past other soldiers who were guarding the door, out into the city streets and through the great iron gates in the city wall, which had opened of their own accord. Agrippa himself hurried away to Caesarea (Acts 12:1-19).

Herod Agrippa I became very popular with his Jewish subjects, though he allowed his own "graven image" to be stamped upon coins, had his statue set up in the Gentile sections of his realm and took part there in pagan festivities. To his Roman overlords he began to seem an ineffective ruler. Many of his actions seemed to the Romans to have at least a treasonable air and, since such instances were reported to Rome, his patron, the emperor Claudius, sent Agrippa a sharp reprimand. To add to his difficulties with Rome Agrippa also took an aggressive attitude toward his neighbors, making many moves without informing the Roman government. His ambitions, in fact, had he been able to continue to exercise them, might soon have made serious trouble for him. Instead his popular reign came to a sudden and rather dramatic end in the year 44 A.D.

He had gone to Caesarea to attend the Roman games, so that he might dazzle the crowd with his new robes heavily ornamented with silver thread. The Greeks and Romans there poured applause upon him, calling him a god, which was an act of blasphemy in the eyes of every reverent Jew.

Then came an appalling moment. Agrippa suddenly looked up and saw, perched on an awning rope not too far above his head, an ominous owl. His heart seemed to stop within him as he recognized this desolating omen. Falling to the ground, he was stricken with pains and was carried away to the palace. Five days later he died, the victim, as the Bible assures us, of his pride, which had kept him from giving honor at all times to God (Acts 12:20-23).

Thus passed away another Herod, a man as ambitious as his grandfather had been,

but far more amiable and without the older man's resolution and driving will. He had, for a time, restored Judaea and the other chief Jewish centers in Palestine to the status of a kingdom, and had sought, so far as he dared, to foster Jewish hopes and abide by Jewish beliefs. There was unfeigned grief and lamentation throughout his realm at his departure.

Herod Agrippa I left behind him a son, Marcus Julius Agrippa, who was to become Herod Agrippa II, and two notorious daughters, Bernice (Berenice) and Drusilla, all three of whom are found in Bible text. The quarter century between his passing in 44 A.D. and the fall of Jerusalem in 70 A.D. was destined to be perhaps the most violent period of similar length in all of Jewish history.

The emperor Claudius wished to place upon the Judaean throne Agrippa's seventeen-year-old son, who was then in Rome living in the imperial household. His advisers opposed the plan, and once more a procurator was sent out from Rome to rule Palestine. This tactical error could have been avoided by placing a Jew rather than a Roman in direct charge of these proud people. Nevertheless, the seeds of discord were ready to sprout and take root in any case.

Trouble thus awaited Caspius Fadus, the first of a new series of procurators, when he arrived in Palestine in 44 A.D. The Zealots, a sect long dedicated to opposing the Romans, were fomenting rebellion. To counteract their efforts and win Jewish approval, Fadus placed Herod, king of Chalcis and brother of the late king, in charge of all religious matters, including the nominating of the High Priest.

Though Fadus had prevented bloodshed and was beginning to restore goodwill, he unfortunately left the scene during his second year in office. He was succeeded by the carefully chosen Tiberius Alexander, nephew of the famous Jewish philosopher Philo. Within a year this prodigy proved to be a dismal failure. A Zealot revolt broke out, and by the time the replacement, Cumanus, arrived in 48 A.D. the situation was menacing. When Herod, king of Chalcis, died that same year, Claudius gave this little realm in Syria to young Agrippa in an attempt to stop further trouble. The dead king Herod's right to govern all religious matters in Jerusalem and nominate the High Priest of the Temple also passed to Agrippa.

Right: Oldest synagogue inscription in Palestine, dating from before 70 A.D. Below: Ruins of a synagogue of Capernaum, second or third century A.D., possibly built over the remains of the one in which Jesus taught.

The Emperor Nero, who expanded Agrippa's territory in Palestine and granted him the title Herod Agrippa II

The newly appointed king was still in Rome when Cumanus suddenly appeared there from Palestine to answer charges that he had been lax in permitting a savage outbreak between the Jews and the Samaritans. Young Agrippa was perhaps influential in having the procurator banished as a means of appeasing the Jews, while a Roman tribune who had also offended them was sent back to Jerusalem to be executed. Yet this did not appease the angry people.

In the year 52 A.D. another procurator, Antonius Felix (Acts 23:24), came to govern Judaea. The year before, the emperor Claudius had taken away the little kingdom of Chalcis and given Agrippa, in its place, a larger domain, the territory east of the Sea of Galilee and the Upper Jordan known as the lands of the Gaulanites, Trachonites and Batanaeans. Agrippa also retained religious authority in Jerusalem.

It was at about this time that Agrippa's too constant companionship with his sister Bernice began to create a scandal. The times were evil, and the land of Palestine was filling with robbers, brigands and assassins who would commit murder for hire. In 54 A.D. Claudius was slain, and a new emperor, the unsavory Nero, came to the throne. He soon granted additional territory to Agrippa — four Palestinian cities including the famous city of Tiberias on the west shore of the Sea of Galilee. The monarch, who was now called Herod Agrippa II, delighted as had his father before him in styling himself "the Great King, the friend of Caesar, the pious, the friend of Rome." Agrippa was decidedly Roman in his ways, considering himself a member of the Roman nobility, and used his full name of Marcus Julius Agrippa on his coins and inscriptions. He straddled the fence skillfully by appearing at the same time to be basically a Jew, and forcing those who entered his family by marriage to embrace the Jewish faith.

In Judaea, where the early Christian and Jewish events were centered, Agrippa remained an impassive observer of an unalterable flow of events. When Felix was succeeded by Porcius Festus in 60 A.D. Agrippa went to Caesarea, accompanied by his sister Bernice, to pay his respects. It was then that he tried, and failed, to convict the Apostle Paul of wrongdoing, and would have set him free had Paul not already appealed to Caesar.

Agrippa made it clear at all times that he had no intention of becoming embroiled in any disputes where he had no primary interest, and he devoted much of his time to his building operations, such as the enlargement of the palace in the Holy City and extensive new structures at Caesarea Philippi and Berytus (modern-day Beirut).

Judaean conditions were growing rapidly worse, despite the change in procurators every few years. The attitude of the Jews toward the Romans was exceedingly bitter; their synagogues became virtual schools of rebellion. Their own affairs were in a sorry state, too, for the Jews were breaking up into factions which extended through all levels, both social and economic, to the Temple hierarchy itself. Even appointments to the High Priesthood were sometimes accompanied by bloodshed. The country was entering the throes of revolution, and the cure for that, in Roman eyes, was to garrison the land with sufficient legions to crush it at the first sign of mass lawlessness.

When Festus died in office in 62 A.D., supreme power in Judaea rested briefly in the hands of the newly appointed High Priest Ananus. In a burst of misguided zeal he called the Sanhedrin into session without proper authority, and summoned before it James the Just, head of the church of Jerusalem, and other leading Christians. They were condemned to death and, without the sanction of the Roman procurator, the whole group were stoned to death. Although Ananus was immediately deposed as High Priest by Agrippa, his acts had turned Gentile sympathies away from the Jews.

At about this time the restoration of the Temple, begun by Herod the Great some eighty years before, was finally completed. About eighteen thousand men were suddenly out of work; this serious situation added to the general insecurity of the time. An appeal was made to Agrippa to tear down a portion of the Temple structure and rebuild it as a make-work project. He refused to do this, but he approved the use of Temple funds for repaving certain of Jerusalem's streets with marble. Suddenly a part of the Temple complex, faultily built, collapsed, and work was begun again, though the structure was destined never to be completed. Now utter catastrophe lay only a few years ahead.

Albinus, who finally arrived as procurator to succeed the deceased Festus, began his tour of duty with a show of vigor. The extremists among the Zealots, called the Sicarii because of the wicked curved knife which was their chief weapon, soon forced this Roman into a most unfavorable position by all sorts of excessive and criminal acts. In 64 A.D. he was succeeded by Gessius Florus.

This newcomer's approach was aggressive and soon became openly brutal. He was also unfortunate in that a decision made by Nero in Rome soon after Florus' arrival in Palestine set off serious riots in Caesarea. They were so severe that many Jews in that area fled from the land.

In the year 66 A.D. Florus sought to raid the Temple treasury to make up a deficit of some forty talents in tribute owed to Rome. The forthcoming Jewish war might very well have begun then had not Agrippa, returning from a trip to Egypt, made a strong, thought-provoking speech to the people of Jerusalem. He proved to them conclusively that continued resistance to their Roman masters might sound the death knell not only of the Jewish nation but also of the Jewish religion as they knew it. He even persuaded the people to offer voluntarily the deficit in the tribute, and personally led a cavalcade to the Temple to rebuild its damaged colonnades.

Then, feeling that he must continue on his way to his own kingdom, where conditions demanded his attention, King Agrippa II left the Holy City, which he was fated never to enter again.

19. The Fall of Jerusalem

Herod Agrippa II had calmed the mounting tensions in Jerusalem. As soon as he left, the revolutionary elements began to rise up again. This time, under the leadership of one Eleazar, commander of the Temple, their activities took on a decidedly treasonable form. He made a proposal that no sacrifices be offered in the sanctuary on behalf of any Gentiles. As the only such offering at that particular period was one for the happiness and well-being of the Roman emperor, the intention behind this proposal was to insult the volatile Nero.

The leading Jews realized what the results might be and tried desperately to prevent this foolish move. The Doctors of the Law pleaded with the people at a mass meeting in the Temple courts, begging them not to call down destruction upon their own heads — but to no avail. Tempers were fanned to white heat, and there were enough fanatics among the priests and Levites so that the sacrifice ceased. The ancient Jewish historian Josephus points to this as the beginning of open rebellion.

Records reveal that the Sanhedrin hurriedly sent requests to both the Roman procurator, Florus, and Herod Agrippa II for military aid. Their efforts, however, were insufficient, and it was soon apparent that effective help could come only from the Roman legate in Syria, Cestius Gallus.

It was late summer of 66 A.D. before Gallus was able to start south from Antioch with some 40,000 soldiers. It was September before he appeared at the walls of Jerusalem, having on the way quelled revolt in Galilee.

Gallus was astounded when he met with resistance rather than capitulation, and immediately attacked the well-fortified city. The siege was so valiantly withstood that he was forced to abandon it. Having failed to subdue the countryside around Jerusalem, he was soon in real trouble. His retreat rapidly turned into a rout — a headlong flight. By the time he reached Caesarea he had lost 6000 men, large quantities of war materials, and all hope of bringing Judaea to abject submission.

Reveling in their easy triumph, all the factions of the Jews now joined in promoting the cause of independence. Their hopes were to be short-lived.

Word of Gallus' sorry failure was hurried to Rome, where its seriousness was fully understood, and Nero picked his greatest general, Titus Flavius Vespasian, to put Palestine back in its proper place. By the spring of 67 A.D. some 50,000 troops had been massed at Ptolemaïs on the coast eighty miles north of Jerusalem. Galilee was again subjugated, and the Roman army went into winter quarters.

Anarchy now took hold of the Holy City, and a violent civil war weakened its powers of resistance. Hoping this internal strife would continue to his benefit, Vespasian spent his time the following spring in crushing such opposition as he could find in Samaria, Peraea and Idumaea. By summer he felt secure enough to lay siege to Jerusalem, and was about to start such operations when word arrived from Rome of the death of the emperor Nero (June 68 A.D.). This brought his activities to a halt; he awaited renewal of his orders from Rome.

For a time there was rebellion in the faraway Roman capital as well as in that of the

Jews. Three men in turn, Galba, Otho and Vitellius, were proclaimed emperor and promptly overthrown. Then the scene shifted to the East; it appeared that the army attacking Palestine was the most formidable power block within the whole empire. Suddenly the army decided upon its own commander as emperor, and placed Vespasian securely upon the throne. The Jewish War was abandoned for almost two years, but was not by any means forgotten. Finally, in the spring of 70 A.D., another sizable Roman army was organized, this time at Caesarea, and its command entrusted to the emperor's own son, Titus.

And what of the Jews during this lull in hostilities? Instead of preparing for the inevitable, they spent the time in internal strife. Not until the Roman forces swung down through Samaria and encamped before Jerusalem's walls did they stop fighting within. There were three stout rings of stone walls around the city and at least three massive towers guarding interior vantage points. They would now have to be defended with all the frenzied valor that could be summoned.

Titus gave the people of Jerusalem a chance to surrender, knowing that it would be refused. When the refusal came, the siege began.

It took only a few short weeks to breach the two outer walls and gain full possession of the lower portion of the city. But the tower of Antonia and the interior fortifications offered such resistance that Titus decided to throw up an earthen wall around the city and starve the inhabitants into yielding. When this failed, an assault on the Antonia was finally carried out, bringing it into Roman hands on July 5.

The attackers now concentrated upon the Temple and its surroundings. It was August 10 before it fell. With their revered shrine destroyed and starvation only a few days away, the defenders gave up. The Upper City finally was overrun, and by September 7 of the year 70 A.D. the siege was completed. According to Josephus, over one million Jews had perished.

Titus ordered that Jerusalem be completely leveled, and the work of demolition began at once. Only a few choice objects and a few prominent personages were saved to adorn the commander's march of triumph in Rome. The city was obliterated. Of the inhabitants who had survived, 100,000 are said to have been led away to work as slaves in Egyptian mines, while others were distributed to various Roman amphitheaters to be slaughtered in spectacles.

Jerusalem had fallen, but fighting dragged on in Judaea for three years, terminating with the capture of the remote fortress of Masada in the Wilderness of Judaea on the west shore of the Salt Sea. It was there that, years before, Herod the Great had left his family when he went to Rome in search of a crown. It was there that Eleazar, commander of the Temple and leader of the Sicarii, the Zealot extremists, now made a last desperate stand.

Rather than suffer death at the hands of the Romans, these proud and determined people decided upon mass suicide. After tearful and touching farewells the men killed their wives and children. They then drew lots and every man in ten killed nine until all 960 were dead — the last man plunging a sword into his own breast. When the Romans entered, they found not one living soul.

What of the last Jewish king, Herod Agrippa II? Having failed to dissuade the Jews from revolting against the Romans, he fought at the side of Vespasian and was wounded at the siege of Gamala, a city east of the Sea of Galilee. Following the fall of Jerusalem, he removed to Rome, where he died about 100 A.D.

The fanaticism and violence of the Zealots, especially the Sicarii, taught the Romans a lasting lesson. Titus, drawing upon the failure of those who had gone before him, now felt that the basic scheme of governing Judaea must be changed. Reverting to the manner of governing generally used throughout the Roman Empire, he decided that the Jews could not henceforth be allowed to administer their own internal affairs.

It was difficult for the secular-minded, matter-of-fact Roman to understand a people whose whole lives, thoughts and actions were governed by their spiritual beliefs. It was hard for the Roman to understand that the Jew, taught from childhood to believe that he was one of God's elect and a member of a Chosen People, looked upon all governments, except of his own choosing, as an insufferable yoke.

It had taken several generations of Roman overlords to realize fully just what unbridled Jewish zeal could do. Emperor Vespasian issued a decree to terminate the religion for all time. His edict was thus a most harsh one. All outward marks and tokens of the Jews as

*Masada, fortress bastion of Herod the Great, was the last strong-
hold of the Jews after the destruction of Jerusalem by Titus.*

a separate and distinct people were to be erased. Jerusalem, their Holy City, together with the Temple, the House of their God, was already in ruins. The High Priesthood was abolished. So, too, was the once potent Sanhedrin. And, lest the religious center be moved to Egypt and revived there, a Jewish temple which had been in use in that land for some time was closed. The Temple tax of a half shekel imposed upon every Israelite twenty years of age or older, irrespective of where he lived (Matthew 17:24), was now to be paid for the upkeep of the principal shrine of the Roman Jupiter on the Capitoline Hill in Rome. And in the manner set by the Assyrians after the capture of Samaria centuries before, a colony of Roman veterans and their families was settled in the vicinity of the demolished Jerusalem.

Other Jewish centers in Palestine were also reorganized, and great efforts were expended in Romanizing the province. As the Jewish population still predominated, a large force had to police the land, and Roman control continued to be neither certain nor successful.

Soon after the fall of Jerusalem, Titus turned military affairs in Palestine over to one of his lieutenants and devoted his attention to other matters. Two gory events which occupied much of his time were the celebrations, that autumn, on the birthdays of his father, Vespasian, and his brother, Domitian. Spectacles were held in the amphitheaters at both Caesarea and Berytus, at which thousands of Jewish captives perished in gladiatorial exhibits and in combat with lions and other wild beasts.

In quite another vein was Titus' love affair with the fascinating Bernice, daughter of Agrippa I. She was a woman of strong contrasts — exceeding beauty and charm, and very low morals. She had been married to her uncle, Herod, and left a widow by him. Her extreme and continued intimacy with her own brother, King Agrippa II, had led to a great scandal. To quiet it, she had married Polemon, king of Cilicia, but she soon abandoned him to live again quite openly with Agrippa. Then for a time she had been the mistress of Vespasian, and she now captivated his son, Titus.

Still she was faithful enough to her Jewish upbringing so that on one occasion at least she shaved her head and abstained from wine for a month as part of the fulfillment of a vow. Though it is possible that her religious zeal was not wholly sincere, she may have softened her powerful lover's attitude toward her people, particularly those Jews dispersed widely throughout the empire.

Titus had his share of enemies, and they began to spread the rumor that he was planning to supplant his father on the throne. To put an end to these stories he now hastened home to Rome and joined his father, Vespasian, in the combined triumph decreed them for their victory in Palestine. In the procession certain sacred vessels of the Temple, the golden seven-branched candlestick and the Scrolls of the Law, were exhibited. In it, too, marched seven hundred of the fairest and handsomest Jewish captives. As the huge parade made the traditional pause before the shrine of Jupiter Capitolinus, Simon bar Giora, a leader of the Zealots, chief among the enemy, was put to death.

Coins were struck to commemorate Vespasian's and Titus' victories, and a magnificent arch was later erected in the Forum to give further testimony to the downfall of Jewish nationalism. It is said that all the treasures from the Temple in Jerusalem were deposited in the Roman temple of peace, except the Scrolls of the Law and the curtain from the Holy of Holies, which were carefully kept in the imperial palace.

Titus was now appointed co-ruler with his father. Although Bernice was in Rome he did not make her his wife, as the Roman populace had particular hatred for women of the East. Disappointed, Bernice left Rome but appeared again in 79 A.D. at the time Titus became emperor following his father's death. This Herodian woman was one of the last of her family to play a conspicuous part in history. Even if she had achieved her desire, her marriage would have been short-lived, for Titus' reign ended two years later, in 81 A.D.

During his brief reign, Titus had become
176 exceedingly popular, which made the task of

his brother, Domitian, who succeeded him, more difficult.

During the early part of Domitian's rule, he governed astutely and well. But as he grew older he became ferocious to the point of barbarity. He made the lot of the Jews who had sought refuge in Rome unbearable. Some of them were reduced to begging; the more prosperous did their best to hide their origin so as to evade the special taxes heaped upon them. Because Domitian was ever short of money in the latter part of his reign, his tax collectors harried the Jews not only in Rome but throughout the empire. Insult and the utmost penalties were visited upon any Gentiles who befriended the Jews.

While there had been little or no persecution of the Christians under either Vespasian or Titus, Domitian's hostile and cruel nature reached out to his new sect, and he made an attempt to crush it. The Apostle John's exile to Patmos (Revelation [Apocalypse] 1:9) is believed to have taken place at this time, and some of Domitian's relatives with Christian leanings were banished or executed.

Even the emperor's wife could tolerate him no longer; at her instigation he was slain in his forty-fifth year. He was succeeded in 96 A.D. by the emperor Nerva, whose reign was characterized by justice and clemency. The Jews appear to have found life less harsh, and the Apostle John was permitted to return to Ephesus. He was one of the last of the Twelve Apostles and is supposed to have survived for

A triumphal procession for Titus and his father, Vespasian, marked the return of the Roman general from the Jew

a year or more after Trajan took the throne in 98 A.D.

This new emperor, Trajan, was the most famous general of his time, and during his nineteen-year reign the empire knew unsurpassed prosperity and reached its greatest extent in territory. He had many admirable qualities, and was equally competent as soldier, statesman and administrator. The Jews had little to fear from him and enjoyed some share in the good times.

By contrast it was now the Christians who began openly to resist the worship of heathen gods and the emperor. Two highly interesting letters, still extant, by the famous Roman writer Pliny the Younger describe the situation in Asia Minor. Appointed Roman governor of Bithynia and Pontus about 110 A.D., Pliny became aware that more and more members of this new sect were brought before him for judgment. Rather than take an arrogant stand, he did his best to learn what he could about these followers of Christ and then reported his findings, along with suggestions concerning them, to Trajan.

The emperor sent word back to Pliny commending his conduct in this matter and outlining certain rules to be followed in dealing with Christians. They were no longer to be hunted out. Anonymous indictments were to be disregarded, and those willing henceforth to worship the gods of the Romans were to go free. However, those who persisted in the new faith were to suffer death.

Shortly afterward Trajan had his first direct contact with Christianity. He conducted in person a war against the Parthians in the East and was for a time at Syrian Antioch. The church was still as active in that city as it had been two generations before, in Paul's time, and the number of communicants was large. It nettled the emperor, fresh from his victories, that this large group, imbued with what he considered a reprobate spirit, refused to honor the Roman gods from whom he believed his successes had come.

When Trajan indignantly threatened them with death, their bishop, Ignatius, begged the right to be heard. Trajan began to cross-examine this virile, fearless Christian leader, but Ignatius was not to be cowed. As a result of his intrepid defense, he was condemned to be taken to Rome, there "to be devoured by the beasts for the gratification of the people." So it was that Trajan turned against the Christians, and the venerable chief of that sect in Asia was brought into the Colosseum to make sport for the Roman mob.

The Parthian War and Christian religious resistance were only two of the difficulties which confronted Trajan at this period. In 116 A.D. the Jews again sought to revolt. This time the uprising was not limited to Palestine, but embraced Jewish communities in many lands. Perhaps the most determined revolt was in Mesopotamia, that ancient land between the Tigris and Euphrates rivers. While the trouble was being dealt with there, other Jewish

177

r Titus, who directed the siege of Jerusalem, utterly destroyed the Temple and carried its treasures back to Rome.

THE ROMAN EMPIRE
AT ITS GREATEST EXTENT
c. 117 A.D.

Copyright by C. S. HAMMOND & CO., N.Y.

Scale of Miles

0   100   200   400   600

━━━ Maximum extent of Roman control in the time of Trajan, 98-117 A.D.
⋯⋯⋯ Capital
━━━ Roman walls

The Germanic tribes exerted constant pressure on the Rhine-Danube frontier, placing the Empire on the defensive. The western provinces and Italy were overrun by Germanic invaders in the fifth century.

Trajan's conquests east of the Euphrates were abandoned by Hadrian in 118 A.D.

In 395 A.D. the Roman world was divided into separate eastern and western empires.

centers along the eastern Mediterranean shore blazed up in orgies of brutality. The Jews' purpose seems to have been to exterminate if possible all their Gentile fellow citizens; on the island of Cyprus alone it was reported that they slew the almost incredible number of 240,000. Nearly as many Greeks and Romans were slaughtered in the province of Cyrenaica to the west of Egypt on the African coast. When the Roman legate in the land of the pharaohs was threatened, retaliation was swift and equally brutal.

Death seized Trajan in 117 A.D. while he was en route to Rome from his campaigns in the East. Although the Jewish disturbances had seriously interfered with the Parthian War, the empire to which Hadrian succeeded was at its greatest, reaching from Britain to the cataracts of the Nile, and from the Atlantic Ocean to the Tigris River. It embraced the greatest variety of people: Britons, Gauls, Greeks, Egyptians, Germanic tribes and Semites, including Arabs and Jews. The new emperor would need all his versatility and breadth of view to understand his various subjects and weld them together. But Hadrian was a staunch adherent of paganism, and the Christians came to suffer even more grievously at his hands than they had under Trajan. Previously grouped with the Jews, this sect was now separately recognized and expressly condemned. They were compelled to denounce Christ and sacrifice to pagan gods. Those who refused were tortured, thrown into dungeons or put to death. The massacres formerly visited upon the Jews were turned upon the Christians. The situation finally reached such extremes that even the proconsuls protested. Hadrian was eventually forced to issue a decree forbidding further attacks upon the followers of Jesus.

During the latter part of Hadrian's reign, the Jews attempted another rebellion. An early edict of the former emperor Trajan prohibiting circumcision, the observance of the Sabbath and the reading of the Law had roused unquenchable hatred of the Romans. For nearly fifteen years it had festered in their spirits. When Roman forces began to refortify Jerusalem, the site of the Holy City, and to bar Jews from the area, their anger grew to fury. In their troubled state the Jews believed that it must surely be the moment when the promised Messiah (Jeremiah [Jeremias] 23:5-6) would come to deliver them.

The Colosseum at Rome. Passages through which gladiators and wild beasts entered the arena may be seen; originally they were covered by a wooden floor.

Suddenly, in 131 A.D., a pretender, one Bar Cocheba, or Bar Kokhba, appeared in Palestine. He was a man of courage and military capabilities, but whether he was an outright impostor or merely an excessive fanatic is hard to judge. However, he had the endorsement of a famous Doctor of the Law, Rabbi Akiba, and, taking command of the Jewish host, he was accepted as the long-hoped-for deliverer of Israel.

All the first moves in this desperate holy war were victories for Bar Cocheba. But the Romans soon brought in additional forces, and the revolt quickly turned into a war of extermination. The caves with which Judaea abounds were filled with poor frightened humans seeking refuge from Roman might.

Rome's intention was now to drive the children of Abraham from the Promised Land, and the efforts exerted to this end left an indelible imprint upon the Holy Land down into modern times. Even the term Judaea was discarded, and the area took the name of Syria Palaestina. Jews were prohibited on penalty of death from entering Jerusalem or coming to any point within sight of it. The city was rebuilt as one of the centers of Roman life in the East. The name Jerusalem was discarded, and it was now called Colonia Aelia Capitolina: Colonia to denote its Roman colonial status, Aelia for one of the personal names of the emperor, and Capitolina because it was dedicated to Jupiter Capitolinus.

179

The rebellion under Bar Cocheba was the last heroic attempt of the Jews to regain national independence until modern times. The dispersion which had begun under Trajan was now completed. The Jews were driven from their land to survive as best they could. Some made their way to far-off India and China. Others drifted into the Arabian peninsula, Egypt and Africa. Still others wended their way up into what we know today as Russia and Europe, when those areas were still vast dark forest lands inhabited only by barbarian tribes. Following this vast dispersion the Jews, the Children of Israel, lived among strangers. For almost two thousand years, until the founding of the modern state of Israel, these people were deprived of a homeland.

The Romans had succeeded in scattering the Jews into the most distant parts of the known world, but they did not succeed in eradicating their religion. Wherever the Jews went, they carried their ancient beliefs with them. Now that the Temple was no more, they worshiped God within their homes and in their synagogues just as they had during those remote days of the Babylonian Captivity.

That handful of Jews which remained in the Holy Land after the great dispersion made a desperate attempt to keep Palestine as the center of Judaism. With the greatest difficulty they opened rabbinical schools, and in about 200 A.D. certain of their most learned rabbis compiled their oral laws into a scroll known as the Mishnah. This was to serve as a complement to the written Law contained in the Old Testament and it was to be copied and distributed to Jewish communities everywhere. By 450 A.D. the Mishnah was greatly expanded with explanations and commentaries into what we now know as the Palestinian Talmud. This work was also done for the benefit of Jews who were living in distant lands.

When Constantine became emperor, he closed the rabbinical schools; so Babylon, where a large community of Jews had existed since the days of the Captivity, inherited the responsibility of serving as the principal center of Jewish thought and culture. It was there, in 500 A.D., that the famous Babylonian Talmud was compiled, a Talmud which superseded the Palestinian Talmud and which still serves today, together with the books of the Old Testament, as a most sacred writing of Judaism.

The temple of Jupiter at Baalbek (Heliopolis), magnificent Greek and Roman city between Damascus and Tyre. Six of the Temple's sixty-foot columns still stand.

The Arch of Titus, built in the Forum at Rome to commemorate the fall of Jerusalem. A frieze depicts the triumphal procession celebrating the Roman victory.

20. The Spread of Christianity

Caesar had dispersed the Jews; but Christ and His followers would in due time conquer Caesar.

The term "church" (Greek *ekklēsia*, assembly) makes its first appearance in Bible text in the words of Jesus: Thou art Peter, and upon this rock I will build my church (Matthew 16:18). There it is intended to convey the idea of an assembly or society of men and women united under God, acknowledging Jesus Christ as Lord and Master, and meeting regularly for religious instruction and worship.

Such a community came into existence during Christ's ministry; it was made up of the Twelve Apostles, disciples, and other followers of the Man of Galilee. It was drawn together more firmly by the horrors of the Crucifixion and the triumph of the Resurrection. But it was not finally welded together until the Holy Spirit descended upon the Apostles at Pentecost in June of the year 30 A.D. From that moment, the early Church began its forward march, adding many new members in and about Jerusalem.

At the outset, the Church was naturally considered an offshoot of Judaism; it continued to be closely allied with the older faith for fully a generation after its founding. But it proved to have overwhelming significance in its own right, quite apart from Judaism or the Law of Moses, and so it eventually gained its independence and began to spread.

Church history as recorded in the Bible terminates with the close of the book of The Acts. By then there were followers of Christ not only in the Holy Land but also in Asia Minor, Greece and Rome. Paul expressed the wish to carry his missionary efforts to Spain, and according to tradition he "reached the bounds of the west."

This rapid spread of the Gospel was due in large part to the ardor of that little group of dedicated men whose preaching carried the Word ever forward to new hearers. But their success might have been far less spectacular had it not been for the Roman Empire that provided good roads, relative freedom from brigands, and prosperity sufficient for such missionary effort to find contributions for its support. The common culture widely spread by the Greeks and preserved by the Romans proved to be fertile soil for the seeds of Christian teaching, while the Pax Romana, the maintenance of stable government over virtually the entire civilized world, permitted the peaceful spreading of the Gospel.

One other prevailing condition benefited this new faith. Philosophy had for several centuries placed increasing emphasis upon personality, bringing about a new attitude toward the human mind and heightening the value placed on individualism. Christianity, which was then only one among several new beliefs and religious systems, fitted in more closely with this changed way of thinking than any of the others and proved more satisfying to an ever increasing number of people.

The words of Jesus — Come unto me, all you who labor — may have registered first with the slaves and poor freedmen. His message was caught and acted upon also by many whose lot in life seemed on the surface to be relatively pleasant. A few at least of the individuals mentioned in the closing chapter of Paul's Epistle to the Romans are thought to have been people of considerable consequence.

It is hard to say how great a distinction between Jew and Christian existed in Rome during the years following Paul's residence and presumed martyrdom there. For another generation, or even longer, the two beliefs were often apparently confused. But it is probable that little attention was paid to either sect prior to one of the major decrees of the emperor Titus. During his two years on the throne he issued the historic edict claiming divinity for himself, his forebears, family and descendants, and ordering their worship as gods.

Domitian built up this theme of emperor worship to considerable heights, erecting a temple to the God Emperors and establishing a priestly college to encourage such worship. He even required that he be addressed as "Our Lord and God." Such adulation was of course contrary to both Jewish and Christian tenets, and, since members of both sects refused to worship these human deities, the two groups were marked for trouble.

Others than the Christians and Jews suffered from Domitian's fury, but it was probably the Christians who endured the brunt of his persecution, at least in Rome. Many were put to death, including Flavius Clemens, the emperor's first cousin, while his wife, Domitilla, also a relative of the emperor, was banished. This early Christian woman has long been of much interest to scholars. On land believed to have belonged to her are some of the most famous catacombs — the underground burial places in which early Christianity maintained its existence in Rome for several centuries.

In spite of persecution the Church continued to spread, and was soon firmly established throughout the empire. There were growing Christian colonies in virtually all the more important commercial centers, with outstanding churches at Antioch, Smyrna, Ephesus, Alexandria and Carthage. However, it was the church at Rome that moved into the ascendancy — it had surely borne the brunt of persecution, numbering among its martyrs Peter and Paul. By the latter half of the second century Irenaeus, who became bishop of Lyon in Gaul in 177 A.D., thought it best to warn all believers: "It is most necessary that each church should agree with this church [at Rome]." Some years later Cyprian, bishop of Carthage and one of the greatest early authors of Christian doctrine, wrote: "Who-

The catacombs of San Gennaro outside Rome. Most of these Christian burial places, used also as refuge from the Roman persecution, were constructed in the third and early fourth centuries.

ever separates himself from the Church is separated from the promises of the Church. . . . If anyone could escape who was outside the Ark of Noah, so also may he escape who shall be outside the bounds of the Church." To this one universal Church, he said, all must belong who hoped to be saved.

But if the church in Rome was to provide effective leadership, it had to have authority in order to deal constructively with all the other assemblies. As Irenaeus had pointed out, uniformity in the matter of doctrine was essential. There were many contradictory theological views rife at that time. To assure uniformity it was vital that the leading church have the power to demand it, the alternative being excommunication.

In several of his letters Paul describes in detail what type of man a bishop should be: blameless, patient, vigilant, serious, and interested in teaching. Bishops were thus within the Church structure from the very beginning. Although at first they were mere overseers or superintendents, their duties gradually became

more extensive, and by the year 160 A.D. the first synod of bishops was called. Such prelates became representatives of all the assemblies within their respective districts in the various councils of the Church. One of their basic purposes was preservation of this very uniformity, which soon gave the whole body of Christian believers the name Catholic, in that the Church was consistent throughout in all matters of belief, worship and government.

Although there were many difficulties inherent in founding a new order, and persecution continued, the Christian Church became established in a remarkably short time. Its position was threatened during the second and third centuries by a competitive religion that swept into the West from Persia—Mithraism. Mithra, or Mithras, was the god of light, heat and fertility, and thus the giver of all good things. Since he was popularly represented as the sun god and was in many respects like Apollo, he had a strong appeal for the pagan people of the Roman world. Worship of Mithra was especially strong in the army, and, since it did not conflict with emperor worship, it made many converts and became the most formidable rival of Christianity.

There were also other competitive religions and some rebellious influences within the Church itself. The chief opposition to the Church continued to be emperor worship, which was instituted in an attempt to consolidate the empire still further through a universal faith. Such a compulsory cult also was effective in keeping all citizens subservient to the state.

The relations between the state and the young Church varied widely from 180 A.D. on. Periods of persecution were interspersed with peaceful times, such as the one in the middle of the third century which lasted for forty years, when Christianity expanded rapidly. However, the period that followed proved to be a most difficult one.

In 284 A.D. Diocletian mounted the throne, taking on the manners of an oriental potentate. He wore state robes of silk and gold, and shoes decorated with pearls and semiprecious stones.

The empire was weakened by internal dissension and by the invasion of its northern borders by barbarian hordes which swarmed into Britain, Gaul, northern Italy, the Balkans and Asia Minor. In order to cope with these widespread dangers, Diocletian divided the empire in half, appointing a fellow emperor, or Augustus, to rule jointly with him. Later, each Augustus chose a Caesar to assist him. Thus the empire was split into four sections, with Diocletian retaining for himself not only the eastern part but also keeping in his own name a certain amount of authority over the other three parts.

Diocletian's plan brought order out of near chaos, but did not eliminate all the threats to the empire. He began to encounter opposition from what had formerly seemed a quite unlikely quarter: Christianity. Being a devout pagan, he began to regard the Christians with suspicion, and then with dread; this sect was increasing in numbers and growing unmistakably in influence.

By 303 A.D. Diocletian had determined to undertake the complete suppression of Christianity, and in rapid succession published three edicts to that end, following with a fourth the next year. Together they presented a far-reaching plan of complete extinction. All buildings in which Christians held worship were to be demolished, their lands sold, and the proceeds turned over to the state. All Christian writings of any nature were to be delivered forthwith to local magistrates, who were to burn them in public. All known Christians were to be placed beyond the pale of the law. Complaints could be entered against them, but they were denied legal redress for any injuries they might suffer. And all were commanded to offer sacrifices to the four supreme rulers. Emperor worship now had a pantheon of its own.

Diocletian made his own headquarters at the city of Nicomedia (modern Izmit) at the eastern extremity of the Propontis. It is said that the first Christian martyr under his decrees came from his own capital and won that distinction by tearing down the initial copy of the emperor's edict when it was posted for public viewing. As a punishment he was roasted over a slow fire until dead. But his religious fervor was so great that in spite of the agonies he suffered he smiled to the very end.

His death was a prelude to that of hundreds upon hundreds of others who were convinced that the preservation of their faith was worth the supreme sacrifice. Exactly how many perished is not known. The historian Gibbon, using only documented cases, states that the number was two thousand; other historians believe the figure must have been much higher. By their uncompromising zeal, these early Christians began to prove that they could be as spirited as their Jewish brethren when their freedom of worship was tampered with. Their courage was such that public opinion turned in their favor and magistrates in many cities were forced to temper their handling of the matter. Could it be that Christ was actually about to overcome Caesar?

Diocletian retired from the throne after a twenty-year reign, and Maximian, his associate Augustus, abdicated. As a result, the empire was thrown into civil war for several years. Galerius and Constantius, the two Caesars of the four-man rule, assumed the title of Augusti. Constantius, who had become the Caesar of Gaul and Britain in 293 A.D., died in Britain in 306 A.D. His army at once seized the role which Diocletian had sought to deny it, and enthroned their late leader's son as emperor of the West. He was destined to be known as Constantine the Great, and in all probability deserved the designation linked to his name.

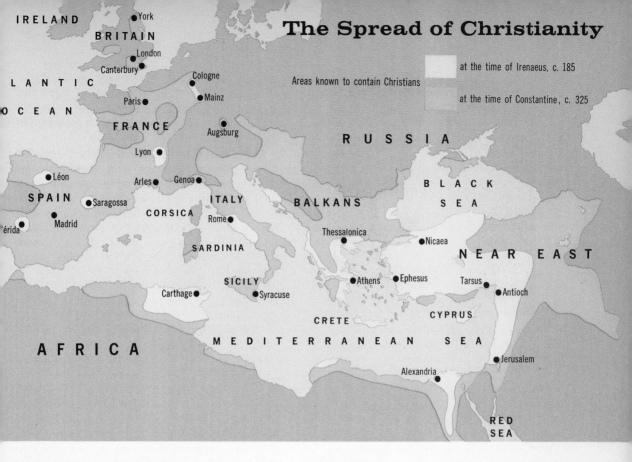

Areas known to contain Christians

at the time of Irenaeus, c. 185

at the time of Constantine, c. 325

However, a number of years would intervene before Constantine was firmly entrenched as ruler of the Roman Empire.

Finally in full power as emperor of the West, Constantine realized that the empire needed a unifying force. By 312 A.D. it became evident that the Christian Church might provide this medium. A large proportion of the different nationalities of the vast population of the empire was Christian. Although Constantine was a pagan, he adopted the Christian cross as his emblem and issued a decree promising toleration and clemency to the members of the faith, providing they did nothing "contrary to discipline." In the next year, 313 A.D., he published another decree making their freedom complete and giving Christianity an equal status with any and all other religions within the empire.

Constantine probably knew little about the beliefs and practices of Christianity. Most scholars believe that, as a thoroughgoing Roman, he was actuated by purely political motives. He needed the Church, and the Church in turn could do very well with his protection and patronage. Under his favor it surged ahead rapidly.

By 319 A.D. Constantine had granted the young Church another favor: the clergy were exempted from public obligations, leaving them free for the primary purposes of their calling. An even greater concession was granted in that same year, one which had strong appeal for the laity. All forms of heathen sacrifice were totally forbidden. Paganism was being stamped out, and Christianity was coming definitely into ascendancy.

Two years later, in 321 A.D., Constantine enacted another significant law by which all work was forbidden on the Christian Sunday. To fortify it financially, the Church was permitted to inherit legacies, and so became the recipient of many fine gifts from the estates of departed members. To hasten the expansion of its physical plant, Constantine made extensive gifts to the clergy and otherwise aided in building fine church structures in the larger cities.

These attentions to the Church had been carried on while the question of who should finally rule as sole emperor was being settled. It was not until 324 A.D. that Constantine disposed of his last remaining rival, Licinius, and became undisputed master of both the

The emperor Constantine, who turned to Christianity for a unifying faith for the Roman Empire

western and eastern parts of the Roman Empire. It was perhaps fortunate that his victory came when it did, for the Church was just then racked from within by the mighty controversy known as the Arian heresy. This debate over the nature of Christ was seriously threatening the stability and unity of the faith.

To adjust the matter Constantine convened a general council of the Church to meet in June, 325 A.D., at the small city of Nicaea (present-day Iznik) in Bithynia. Invitations went out to dioceses and churches throughout the empire, and transportation for leading prelates, along with their maintenance during the sessions, was provided at state expense.

There were some three hundred twenty bishops present, plus a numerous body of presbyters (priests), deacons and members of the laity. Yet the attendance was almost entirely from the East, since the schism precipitated by Arius had not yet agitated Europe and North Africa. Still the turbulence of its discussions pointed up one manifest need—a single declaration of faith that would be binding on all members of the universal Church. Before it was achieved there were stormy sessions, but out of the heat and heroics of the two months of deliberations was forged the celebrated Nicene Creed.

Christianity had indeed become the state religion, and Christ, in a measure, had conquered Caesar. Then, as though to make this welding of Church and state more certain, Constantine was baptized upon his deathbed in 337 A.D.

The Church for a time flourished as never before, but all was not as it should be, for the problem of the intimate association of civil and ecclesiastical affairs, which had concerned and hampered the Hebrews centuries before, now reappeared. The Church of Christ, which had struggled, survived and grown despite many hardships in its earliest days, was now at a point where its efforts must be focused on preserving the purity of its primitive beginnings. There were still uncertain days ahead.

The records from the Council of Nicaea, as well as those from an earlier meeting of bishops held in 314 A.D. at Arles in southeastern Gaul, give an indication of the extent of the Christian Church in the fourth century. In each case a list of the bishops in attendance has been preserved, and it is interesting to find that the conclave at Arles drew three prelates from as far away as Britain — Eborius of York, Restitutus of London, and Adelfius, presumably from Lincoln.

Beyond these factual records, there is also a wealth of tradition which would indicate that the Church had spread well beyond the limits of the Roman Empire. Such expansion would have been to the East, and it is very probable that Christians of this early time lived as far away as Bactria and India. Churches also existed from a very early time in Mesopotamia and Babylonia. The country of Armenia in the mountains of what is now eastern Turkey has the distinction of being the first land to have adopted Christianity as its "official" religion — in 303 A.D., more than two decades before Constantine.

In the Great Commission which closes the Gospel of Mark, Christ ordained a mighty missionary effort, asking His disciples to go into all the world and preach the good news of the Gospel to everyone. And during the three hundred years following His death on the Cross His instructions were carried out faithfully, with fine spirit and purpose, and often in the face of great obstacles and merciless persecution. That wondrous work was to continue unabated down through all the centuries, as He had ordained.

Time Chart of Bible History

The Time Chart of Bible History on the four pages that follow gives the reader a graphic picture of our early civilization, kings and kingdoms, princes and lands, as well as outstanding historical events.

Here the reader can see when empires were born, how long they flourished, and when decay set in and caused their cultural streams to join more powerful rivers of history.

Using the Time Chart the reader can see at a glance the state of the world at any given period: its history and its national development. At the time of the Exodus Rameses II was pharaoh of Egypt, Babylon had yielded to the Assyrians, the Hittites ruled a powerful empire and Greece was still a hundred years away from its war with Troy.

These rivers of life depicted on the Time Chart cover the full span of Bible history, all the centuries of man from the Stone Age to the year 150 A.D., after which Judaism dispersed throughout the ancient world and Christianity spread through the Roman Empire.

TIME CHART OF BIBLE HISTORY

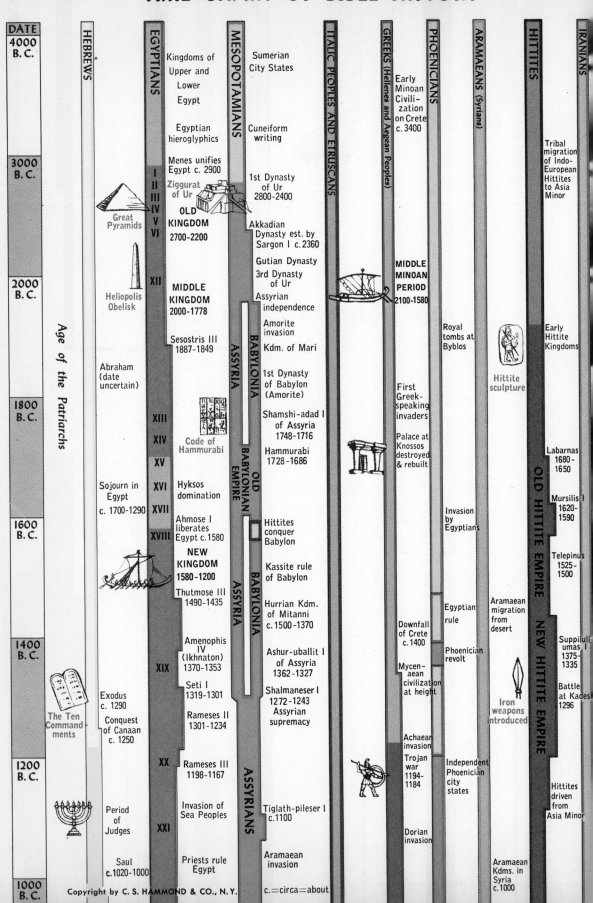

DATE	HEBREWS	EGYPTIANS	MESOPOTAMIANS	ITALIC PEOPLES AND ETRUSCANS	GREEKS (Hellenes and Aegean Peoples)	PHOENICIANS	ARAMAEANS (Syrians)	HITTITES	IRANIANS
4000 B.C.			Sumerian City States		Early Minoan Civilization on Crete c. 3400				
		Kingdoms of Upper and Lower Egypt							
		Egyptian hieroglyphics	Cuneiform writing						
3000 B.C.		Menes unifies Egypt c. 2900	1st Dynasty of Ur 2800-2400						Tribal migration of Indo-European Hittites to Asia Minor
		I II III IV V VI Great Pyramids OLD KINGDOM 2700-2200	Ziggurat of Ur						
			Akkadian Dynasty est. by Sargon I c. 2360						
			Gutian Dynasty						
2000 B.C.		XII Heliopolis Obelisk MIDDLE KINGDOM 2000-1778	3rd Dynasty of Ur		MIDDLE MINOAN PERIOD 2100-1580				
			Assyrian independence					Early Hittite Kingdoms	
		Sesostris III 1887-1849	Amorite invasion			Royal tombs at Byblos	Hittite sculpture		
	Abraham (date uncertain)		Kdm. of Mari						
1800 B.C.	Age of the Patriarchs		1st Dynasty of Babylon (Amorite)		First Greek-speaking invaders				
		XIII XIV Code of Hammurabi	Shamshi-adad I of Assyria 1748-1716		Palace at Knossos destroyed & rebuilt			Labarnas 1680-1650	
		XV	Hammurabi 1728-1686						
	Sojourn in Egypt c. 1700-1290	XVI Hyksos domination XVII	OLD BABYLONIAN EMPIRE					Mursilis I 1620-1590	
1600 B.C.		XVIII Ahmose I liberates Egypt c.1580	Hittites conquer Babylon						
		NEW KINGDOM 1580-1200	Kassite rule of Babylon					Telepinus 1525-1500	
		Thutmose III 1490-1435	Hurrian Kdm. of Mitanni c. 1500-1370			Egyptian rule	Aramaean migration from desert		
1400 B.C.		Amenophis IV (Ikhnaton) 1370-1353	Ashur-uballit I of Assyria 1362-1327		Downfall of Crete c. 1400	Phoenician revolt		Suppiluliumas I 1375-1335	
	Exodus c. 1290	XIX Seti I 1319-1301	Shalmaneser I 1272-1243 Assyrian supremacy		Mycenaean civilization at height		Iron weapons introduced	Battle at Kades 1296	
	The Ten Commandments Conquest of Canaan c. 1250	Rameses II 1301-1234							
1200 B.C.		XX Rameses III 1198-1167			Achaean invasion Trojan war 1194-1184	Independent Phoenician city states			
	Period of Judges	Invasion of Sea Peoples XXI	Tiglath-pileser I c.1100		Dorian invasion			Hittites driven from Asia Minor	
1000 B.C.	Saul c.1020-1000	Priests rule Egypt	Aramaean invasion				Aramaean Kdms. in Syria c. 1000		

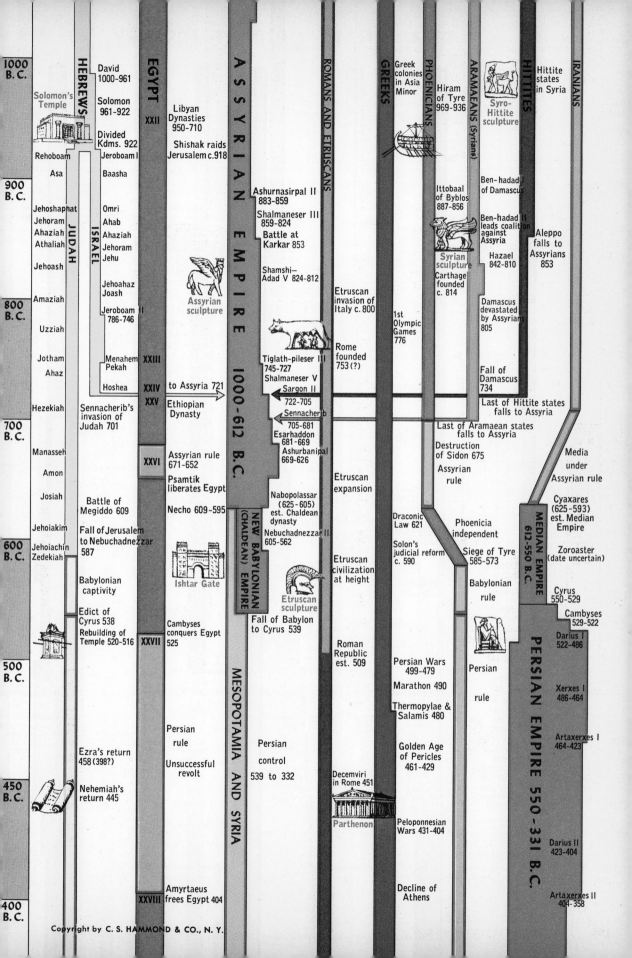

Timeline chart (1000 B.C. – 400 B.C.)

Time scale (left margin): 1000 B.C. | 900 B.C. | 800 B.C. | 700 B.C. | 600 B.C. | 500 B.C. | 450 B.C. | 400 B.C.

HEBREWS
Solomon's Temple
David 1000–961
Solomon 961–922
Divided Kdms. 922

JUDAH
Rehoboam
Asa
Jehoshaphat
Jehoram
Ahaziah
Athaliah
Jehoash
Amaziah
Uzziah
Jotham
Ahaz
Hezekiah — Sennacherib's invasion of Judah 701
Manasseh
Amon
Josiah — Battle of Megiddo 609
Jehoiakim — Fall of Jerusalem to Nebuchadnezzar 587
Jehoiachin
Zedekiah
Babylonian captivity
Edict of Cyrus 538
Rebuilding of Temple 520–516
Ezra's return 458 (398?)
Nehemiah's return 445

ISRAEL
Jeroboam I
Baasha
Omri
Ahab
Ahaziah
Jehoram
Jehu
Jehoahaz
Joash
Jeroboam II 786–746
Menahem
Pekah
Hoshea — to Assyria 721

EGYPT
XXII
Libyan Dynasties 950–710
Shishak raids Jerusalem c. 918
XXIII
XXIV
XXV — Ethiopian Dynasty
XXVI — Assyrian rule 671–652
Psamtik liberates Egypt
Necho 609–595
XXVII — Cambyses conquers Egypt 525
Persian rule
Unsuccessful revolt
XXVIII — Amyrtaeus frees Egypt 404
Ishtar Gate

ASSYRIAN EMPIRE 1000–612 B.C.
Ashurnasirpal II 883–859
Shalmaneser III 859–824
Battle at Karkar 853
Shamshi–Adad V 824–812
Tiglath-pileser III 745–727
Shalmaneser V
Sargon II 722–705
Sennacherib 705–681
Esarhaddon 681–669
Ashurbanipal 669–626
Assyrian sculpture

NEW BABYLONIAN (CHALDEAN) EMPIRE
Nabopolassar (625–605) est. Chaldean dynasty
Nebuchadnezzar II 605–562
Fall of Babylon to Cyrus 539

MESOPOTAMIA AND SYRIA
Persian control 539 to 332

ROMANS AND ETRUSCANS
Etruscan invasion of Italy c. 800
Rome founded 753 (?)
Etruscan expansion
Etruscan civilization at height
Etruscan sculpture
Roman Republic est. 509
Decemviri in Rome 451
Parthenon

GREEKS
Greek colonies in Asia Minor
1st Olympic Games 776
Draconic Law 621
Solon's judicial reform c. 590
Persian Wars 499–479
Marathon 490
Thermopylae & Salamis 480
Golden Age of Pericles 461–429
Peloponnesian Wars 431–404
Decline of Athens

PHOENICIANS
Hiram of Tyre 969–936
Ittobaal of Byblos 887–856
Syrian sculpture
Carthage founded c. 814
Destruction of Sidon 675
Assyrian rule
Phoenicia independent
Siege of Tyre 585–573
Babylonian rule
Persian rule

ARAMAEANS (Syrians)
Syro-Hittite sculpture
Ben-hadad I of Damascus
Ben-hadad II leads coalition against Assyria
Hazael 842–810
Damascus devastated by Assyrians 805
Fall of Damascus 734
Last of Aramaean states falls to Assyria

HITTITES
Hittite states in Syria
Aleppo falls to Assyrians 853
Last of Hittite states falls to Assyria

IRANIANS
Media under Assyrian rule
Cyaxares (625–593) est. Median Empire
Zoroaster (date uncertain)
MEDIAN EMPIRE 612–550 B.C.
Cyrus 550–529
Cambyses 529–522
Darius I 522–486
Xerxes I 486–464
Artaxerxes I 464–423
Darius II 423–404
Artaxerxes II 404–358
PERSIAN EMPIRE 550–331 B.C.

Copyright by C. S. HAMMOND & CO., N. Y.

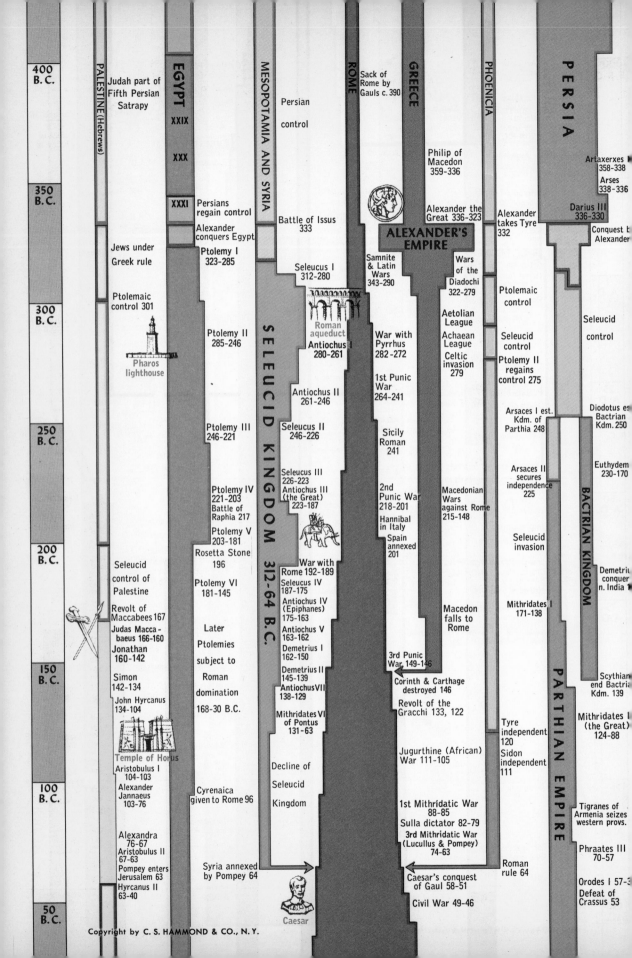

PALESTINE (Hebrews)

Judah part of Fifth Persian Satrapy

Jews under Greek rule

Ptolemaic control 301

Seleucid control of Palestine

Revolt of Maccabees 167

Judas Maccabaeus 166-160

Jonathan 160-142

Simon 142-134

John Hyrcanus 134-104

Aristobulus I 104-103

Alexander Janneaus 103-76

Alexandra 76-67
Aristobulus II 67-63
Pompey enters Jerusalem 63
Hyrcanus II 63-40

EGYPT

XXIX
XXX
XXXI

Persians regain control

Alexander conquers Egypt

Ptolemy I 323-285

Ptolemy II 285-246

Pharos lighthouse

Ptolemy III 246-221

Ptolemy IV 221-203 Battle of Raphia 217

Ptolemy V 203-181

Rosetta Stone 196

Ptolemy VI 181-145

Later Ptolemies subject to Roman domination 168-30 B.C.

Cyrenaica given to Rome 96

MESOPOTAMIA AND SYRIA

Persian control

Battle of Issus 333

Seleucus I 312-280

SELEUCID KINGDOM 312-64 B.C.

Antiochus I 280-261

Antiochus II 261-246

Seleucus II 246-226

Seleucus III 226-223
Antiochus III (the Great) 223-187

War with Rome 192-189
Seleucus IV 187-175
Antiochus IV (Epiphanes) 175-163
Antiochus V 163-162
Demetrius I 162-150
Demetrius II 145-139
Antiochus VII 138-129
Mithridates VI of Pontus 131-63

Decline of Seleucid Kingdom

Syria annexed by Pompey 64

ROME

Sack of Rome by Gauls c. 390

Roman aqueduct

Samnite & Latin Wars 343-290

War with Pyrrhus 282-272

1st Punic War 264-241

Sicily Roman 241

2nd Punic War 218-201
Hannibal in Italy
Spain annexed 201

3rd Punic War 149-146

Corinth & Carthage destroyed 146
Revolt of the Gracchi 133, 122

Jugurthine (African) War 111-105

1st Mithridatic War 88-85
Sulla dictator 82-79
3rd Mithridatic War (Lucullus & Pompey) 74-63
Caesar's conquest of Gaul 58-51
Civil War 49-46

Caesar

GREECE

Philip of Macedon 359-336

Alexander the Great 336-323

ALEXANDER'S EMPIRE

Wars of the Diadochi 322-279

Aetolian League
Achaean League
Celtic invasion 279

Macedonian Wars against Rome 215-148

Macedon falls to Rome

PHOENICIA

Alexander takes Tyre 332

Ptolemaic control

Seleucid control

Ptolemy II regains control 275

Tyre independent 120
Sidon independent 111

Roman rule 64

PERSIA

Artaxerxes 358-338
Arses 338-336
Darius III 336-330

Conquest by Alexander

Seleucid control

Arsaces I est. Kdm. of Parthia 248

Diodotus es Bactrian Kdm. 250

Arsaces II secures independence 225

Euthydem 230-170

BACTRIAN KINGDOM

Seleucid invasion

Demetriu conquer n. India

Mithridates I 171-138

PARTHIAN EMPIRE

Scythian end Bactrian Kdm. 139

Mithridates I (the Great) 124-88

Tigranes of Armenia seizes western provs.

Phraates III 70-57

Orodes I 57-3
Defeat of Crassus 53

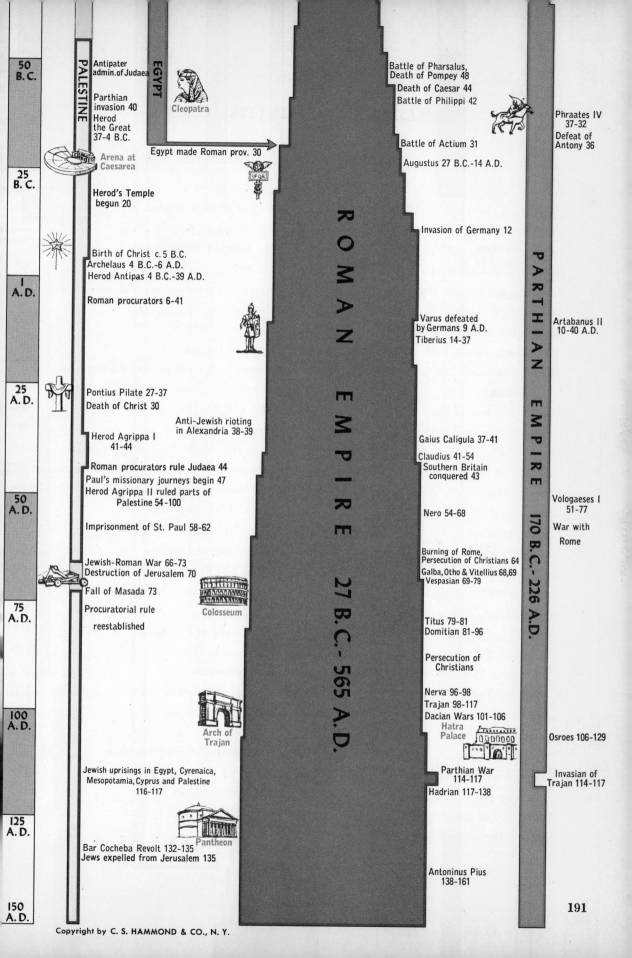

Left scale: 50 B.C. | 25 B.C. | 1 A.D. | 25 A.D. | 50 A.D. | 75 A.D. | 100 A.D. | 125 A.D. | 150 A.D.

PALESTINE

Antipater admin. of Judaea

Parthian invasion 40
Herod the Great 37-4 B.C.

Arena at Caesarea

Herod's Temple begun 20

Birth of Christ c. 5 B.C.
Archelaus 4 B.C.-6 A.D.
Herod Antipas 4 B.C.-39 A.D.

Roman procurators 6-41

Pontius Pilate 27-37
Death of Christ 30

Herod Agrippa I 41-44

Roman procurators rule Judaea 44
Paul's missionary journeys begin 47
Herod Agrippa II ruled parts of Palestine 54-100

Imprisonment of St. Paul 58-62

Jewish-Roman War 66-73
Destruction of Jerusalem 70

Fall of Masada 73

Procuratorial rule reestablished

Jewish uprisings in Egypt, Cyrenaica, Mesopotamia, Cyprus and Palestine 116-117

Bar Cocheba Revolt 132-135
Jews expelled from Jerusalem 135

EGYPT

Cleopatra

Egypt made Roman prov. 30

Anti-Jewish rioting in Alexandria 38-39

Colosseum

Arch of Trajan

Pantheon

ROMAN EMPIRE 27 B.C. - 565 A.D.

Battle of Pharsalus, Death of Pompey 48
Death of Caesar 44
Battle of Philippi 42

Battle of Actium 31

Augustus 27 B.C.-14 A.D.

Invasion of Germany 12

Varus defeated by Germans 9 A.D.
Tiberius 14-37

Gaius Caligula 37-41

Claudius 41-54
Southern Britain conquered 43

Nero 54-68

Burning of Rome, Persecution of Christians 64
Galba, Otho & Vitellius 68,69
Vespasian 69-79

Titus 79-81
Domitian 81-96

Persecution of Christians

Nerva 96-98
Trajan 98-117
Dacian Wars 101-106

Parthian War 114-117

Hadrian 117-138

Antoninus Pius 138-161

PARTHIAN EMPIRE 170 B.C. - 226 A.D.

Phraates IV 37-32
Defeat of Antony 36

Artabanus II 10-40 A.D.

Vologaeses I 51-77

War with Rome

Hatra Palace

Osroes 106-129

Invasian of Trajan 114-117

191

List of Illustrations

Picture Credits

Mikaël Audrain, copyright Arthaud: pages 11, 12, 13, 22, 34, 37, 47, 50, 55, 89, 95, 107, 109, 112, 115, 128-9, 138. Dr. S. H. Horn: pages 7 (right), 31, 51, 64 (top and right), 74. University Museum, Philadelphia: page 19 (bull's head). Metropolitan Museum of Art: pages 19 (necklace), 88, 108, 123, 151, Don L. Gray: pages 20, 23, 30, 67, 139. British Museum: pages 25, 81, 87 (bottom). American Schools of Oriental Research: page 35. Davies, *Ancient Egyptian Wall Paintings:* page 36. Bible et Terre Sainte: page 39. Frank J. Darmstaedter, Jewish Museum, N. Y.: pages 41, 116. Oriental Institute, University of Chicago: pages 58, 69, 71 (photo), 77, 87 (top), 103, 156. Jordan Tourist Attaché: page 59. Palestine Exploration Fund Annual: page 65. Giraudon: pages 70, 97. Turin Museum: page 83. H. J. Campbell: page 94 (photo). New York Public Library: page 102. Royal Greek Embassy, Washington, D. C.: page 104. Brown Brothers, N. Y.: page 121. American Numismatic Society: page 125. The Bettmann Archives, N. Y.: pages 126, 159, 167, 170, 186. Matson Photo Service: pages 131, 139 (bottom), 144, 146. D. E. Mansell: page 143. Robert Emmett Bright, Rapho-Guillumette: page 153. Bonfils: page 155. Ernest J. Dupuy: pages 160, 162. E. L. Sukenik, Hebrew University: page 169 (top). Philip Gendreau, N. Y.: page 169 (bottom). Israel Government Tourist Office: page 175. Hans Hannau, Rapho-Guillumette: page 179. Joe Barnell: page 180. Rapho-Guillumette: page 181. Alinari: page 183. Photos on pages 19 (necklace), 25, 70, 87, 97, 131, 139, 146, 183 courtesy Art Reference Bureau. Photos on pages 17, 20, 23, 30, 31, 51, 64 (top and right), 67, 74, 94, 139 (top), 143 courtesy Andrews University. Paintings by Neil Boyle: pages 16, 17, 26-7, 44, 45, 56, 66-7, 78-9, 90-1, 94, 101, 108, 110-1, 124, 134, 136-7, 140-1, 147, 157, 176-7. Painting by John Ballantine: page 62.

List of Maps

The maps in this volume are as accurate in detail as the most recent scholarship can make them. Nearly every place name found in the Bible is located on the maps, except for those which have never been identified. The names are those of the time of the map, and change with the changing fortunes of the region; thus ancient Beth-shan becomes Scythopolis in Hellenistic times, and Philistine Ashdod is called Azotus in Roman times. When place names change, both names are carried on the map of the time at

Map Index

This index is an alphabetical listing of all cities, towns, countries, regions and physical features found on the reference maps in this volume. Each place name is followed by the page numbers, in order, of the maps on which the name appears, along with the key or grid reference (a letter-number combination) for finding the place on the map. The key reference precedes the numbers of the pages to which it applies. For example, Adullam appears at key reference C5 on the maps on pages 32, 40, 43, 49, 61 and 72; at B5 on page 85; and again at C5 on pages 99 and 114.

which the change occurred, and are cross-referenced in the index. A few modern names appear on maps of ancient times, for the sake of clarity.

In the text biblical references are given for both the King James and Douay translations. The spellings of biblical names in the text and on the maps are those of the Authorized, or King James, version. The indexes that follow include the spellings found in the King James and Douay versions of the Bible, so that the book may be used with either.

196

197

198

203

Subject Index

206